The Capture of New Orleans, 1862

The Capture of
NEW ORLEANS
1862

Chester G. Hearn

LOUISIANA STATE UNIVERSITY PRESS   Baton Rouge and London

Copyright © 1995 by Louisiana State University Press
All rights reserved
Manufactured in the United States of America

Designer: Glynnis Phoebe
Typeface: Cochin
Typesetter: Moran Printing, Inc.
Printer and binder: Thomson-Shore, Inc.

First Printing
04 03 02 01 00 99 98 97 96 95   5 4 3 2 1

Library of Congress Cataloging-in-Publication Data
Hearn, Chester G.
     The capture of New Orleans, 1862 / Chester G. Hearn.
        p.   cm.
     Includes bibliographical references (p.   ) and index.
     ISBN 0-8071-1945-8 (alk. paper)
        1. New Orleans (La.)—History—Capture, 1862.   I. Title.
E472.88.H43 1995
973.7'31—dc20   94-39214
                                                       CIP

The paper in this book meets the guidelines for permanence and durability of the Committee on
Production guidelines for Book Longevity of the Council on Library Resources. ⊗

To Wendy, My Beloved Daughter,
In Love and Remembrance

Contents

ILLUSTRATIONS

MAPS

The Capture of New Orleans, 1862

INTRODUCTION

To understand how New Orleans, the South's largest and greatest city, could be lost to the Union navy as early in the Civil War as it was involves much more than knowing about the passage of two fortifications by Flag Officer David Glasgow Farragut's fleet on the morning of April 24, 1862. The question goes to the heart of government, both Union and Confederate, and the foundation upon which strategic decisions are made. The answer has to do with the way governments select leaders, military and naval, and with the proper employment of resources, human, financial, and natural. If good and bad luck can be eliminated from the equation, the only measurement standard that remains, and the one that must apply, is performance.

The decisions of Jefferson Davis, Stephen R. Mallory, and three different Confederate secretaries of war were as much to blame for the fall of New Orleans as Davy Farragut's warships. The blame, however, fell upon Major General Mansfield Lovell, and to a lesser degree upon Secretary Mallory. Both survived somewhat biased investigations, but Lovell's career as a soldier ended the day he pulled his troops out of the Crescent City and handed it back to the mayor to surrender.

In 1860, New Orleans was a gloriously wealthy city, wedded to the South more by geography and cotton than by its inhabitants. A large foreign population had taken root there and settled into careers as shippers and traders. The enormous commerce of the area had attracted families from the North who brought manufacturing, mechanical, and mercantile skills, and capital to invest. Unlike many southern cities, this one was experiencing a decline in slavery. When secession came under discussion, there were those who fought to establish a "free city." They wanted to accept protection from the Confederate government but not to be caught in the middle of a war.

Governor Thomas Overton Moore had his own agenda. Louisiana belonged to the South and he would brook no free cities, certainly not a city as important as New Orleans. He carefully orchestrated the secession convention to make certain nothing like that happened. Delegates representing the interests of a meager 5 percent of the public voted Louisiana out of the Union.

After celebrating the victory, Moore turned his attention to protecting what the new Confederate States of America had won: the state of Louisiana. President Davis responded by sending Moore seventy-year-old Major General David E. Twiggs, a man so infirm he could barely get from his hotel to his office at City Hall. Naval Secretary Mallory did slightly better. He sent Commodore Lawrence Rousseau, in his late sixties, to buy or build a navy from scratch. Each had different directives, and neither had the stamina or sufficient cooperation from the other to get much done.

Of the two officers, Rousseau accomplished more during his brief tenure. He bought and started to refit a half dozen ships, but when President Davis offered letters of marque and reprisal to the general public, investors interested in turning a quick profit at the expense of Union shipping purchased every available steamer suitable for privateering. Rousseau was left with the tubs of the waterfront. If the Confederate navy wanted gunboats, they were going to have to build them. But what would they build, and where?

The first priority of General Twiggs concerned the defense of New Orleans, beginning with many needed improvements at Forts Jackson and St. Philip, seventy river miles below the Crescent City. The old forts were armed mostly with small smoothbore cannon from twenty to forty years old. The embrasures, parapets, and surrounding earthworks all required extensive repair. Water batteries, new bombproofs, and sturdier magazines had to be built, along with quarters for the men. For six months, Twiggs talked to his lieutenants but accomplished nothing.

In October, 1861, General Mansfield Lovell, formerly deputy streets commissioner of New York City, replaced Twiggs and found the department in total disarray. Why President Davis chose Lovell was something of a mystery, especially to General Pierre G. T. Beauregard, the Crescent City's favorite Creole, and Major General Braxton Bragg, who had his home nearby but held an inconspicuous command at Pensacola. The only explanation was Lovell's availability and the doubt, at least in Davis' mind, that New Orleans was really threatened.

About then, Mallory replaced Rousseau with sixty-two-year-old Commodore George N. Hollins, an independent-thinking sea dog from Maryland who had been in the navy for forty-seven years and still enjoyed a good fight. Although Hollins and Lovell had different instructions, they worked together and shared resources. When Lovell had received his orders for New Orleans, he asked the president for overall command responsibility, which would have included Hollins' flotilla, but Davis decided against that. The two departments had to work together, he said, and for a while they did.

Before Beauregard left for a command in Virginia, he gave Twiggs detailed recommendations for the defense of the city. Neither the general nor his second-in-command, Colonel Paul Octave Hébert, seemed actuated by any sense of urgency. Lovell did. He sent crews downriver to improve the forts. They built a strong barrier across the river, replaced old cannons with heavier-caliber rifled guns, and improved water batteries on both sides of the river. Lovell reorganized the command with skilled officers and trained gunners. Around New Orleans and across the river at Algiers he set other crews to digging entrenchments and building emplacements for the stock of old guns the War Department sent to him from Norfolk.

With help from Governor Moore, Lovell recruited, armed, and trained over thirty thousand volunteers specifically for the defense of the lower Mississippi. As the new regiments developed into fighting units, the War Department siphoned them off for duty in Virginia and Tennessee—and then asked for more. When Farragut's fleet appeared off the levee at the foot of Canal Street, Lovell had about three thousand militia in New Orleans. Many have asked how Lovell could have let this happen. The reasons were many, but the way the War Department played musical chairs with Lovell's regiments and the command confusion Naval Secretary Mallory's actions caused were part of the story.

Three ironclads, *Manassas, Louisiana,* and *Mississippi,* were being built in New Orleans shipyards at roughly the same time, although *Manassas* was finished shortly after the other two were started. *Manassas,* built for profit with private capital, was probably the first ironclad privateer in naval history. The other two vessels were under construction for Mallory by different independent contractors, but neither Hollins nor his predecessor had any control over the projects. *Louisiana* and *Mississippi* made not an iota of difference when the time came for the defense of New Orleans, but both robbed the area of the resources needed to build, refit, and arm gunboats for the security of the river. There was an insensitivity or lack of awareness in Richmond of the difficulties in New Orleans. Was Mallory not informed of these difficulties, or had he not bothered to ask?

The insensitivity to conditions on the lower Mississippi was evident in Mallory's ordering of Hollins' "mosquito fleet" upriver to defend Island No. 10. Sending the fleet to Island No. 10 may have been sound strategy at the time, but leaving it there without a senior naval commander in charge at New Orleans was a costly oversight. One consequence led to another. When Farragut's fleet entered the lower outlets and congregated at Head of Passes, Lovell begged Hollins to return to New Orleans. Hollins left his vessels upriver, came down to evaluate the situation personally with Lovell, and wired Mallory for permission to assist the general. Mallory, who had agonized for months over Hollins' independent behavior, relieved him on the pretext that he had improperly left his command. Although Farragut was in the river and both Lovell and Hollins knew why, Davis and the War Department still held to the impression that any attack upon New Orleans would come from upriver, not down where Farragut was. Both Davis and War Secretary Judah P. Benjamin held to their conviction that Farragut's wooden warships would never get by the forts, although Union ocean-going warships had already passed fortifications and captured Port Royal.

Mallory replaced Hollins with Commander John K. Mitchell on February 1, 1862. Mitchell had been in the vicinity of New Orleans for about two months "assisting the commodore in the discharge" of his duties. Mitchell did not know the river and had very few ships at his disposal, because all the better vessels were upriver. To complicate matters further, Mallory dispatched Commander William C. Whittle to New Orleans as naval commandant. Either by accident or intention, Whittle interpreted his responsibilities as command of the naval station, exclusive of vessels under Mitchell's command. As for *Louisiana* and *Mississippi*, neither commander assumed a shred of responsibility for their completion. Did Mallory intend to divide the command at New Orleans, or had he simply failed to communicate his wishes in detail?

On top of everything else, Secretary of War Benjamin succeeded in obtaining $1.3 million to purchase and refit ten steamers for General Lovell, at a time when Mallory was imploring Congress for funds to support his building programs. Benjamin felt justified in giving Lovell ships because of the absence of a navy at New Orleans. But arming and refitting the so-called River Defense Fleet only magnified the problems of capacity in the New Orleans shipyards. Lovell's later attempts to turn the River Defense Fleet over to the navy were rejected by both Mitchell and the fleet's riverboat captains.

Hollins had tried his best to cooperate with Lovell and was removed. Neither Mitchell nor Whittle went out of his way to help Lovell or, for that matter, each other. The source of the command problem was not in New Orleans but back in Richmond. All these problems bore on the capture of New Orleans. But what most ensured it was Farragut.

The Union navy had its own share of command confusion, but somehow Farragut remained untouched by it. He went to the lower Mississippi to pass the forts and capture New Orleans, and his focus never wavered. He let others politicize and remained indifferent, if not oblivious, to the private skirmishes revolving around his command.

Commander David Dixon Porter, Farragut's foster brother, set out for a piece of glory and quick promotion any way he could get them. His private correspondence to Assistant Naval Secretary Gustavus Vasa Fox criticized Farragut. If the flag officer ever learned of the letters, he kept it to himself. Unlike many manipulators, Porter worked hard and capably for what he wanted.

When Secretary Gideon Welles gave the West Gulf command to Farragut, nobody in the Naval Office was sure that the appointment had gone to a fighting man. Farragut's own peers carped at the selection. But if Welles listened, nothing changed his mind. Unlike Mallory, the northern naval secretary mobilized every resource at his disposal to make it possible for the officer he had selected to succeed. He even conceded the inclusion of Porter's mortar squadron, which may have been useful but was not essential. There were no divided naval commands, no split responsibilities, no unnecessary dilution of resources, and no friction between the navy and the army—at least not where Farragut was concerned.

If the Union War Department, which at the time was controlled more by Major General George B. McClellan than by anyone else, erred in its selection of a military commander, it did so in giving the job to Major General Benjamin F. Butler. McClellan chose Butler for one reason: to bury the political general in the most remote post he could find. Fortunately Butler's troops fought no battles and had to perform only occupation duties. Porter stole enough of Butler's opportunity for national recognition to incur the general's wrath for the balance of their lives.

Distinct differences existed between how the Confederate and Union naval secretaries deployed their resources. Welles sent Farragut to the Gulf with clear, specific instructions and full support. Mallory sent first

Hollins and then Mitchell and Whittle to New Orleans with vague instructions and little support. The Confederate Naval Office's colossal and impossible shipbuilding program seemed to be organized to fail. Mallory did not have his best officers in New Orleans, but more than anything else, nobody was really in command when Hollins departed with his fleet for Island No. 10 in December. For that, Davis and Mallory had nobody to blame but themselves.

Lovell inherited different problems. In a short span of time he had three different bosses. President Davis could never settle on a secretary of war, and when Benjamin moved to the post of secretary of state, his replacement knew little about affairs in New Orleans and expended almost no effort to find out. Lovell may have been remiss to a degree in not keeping the War Department fully informed of his situation, but the general had probably reached the point of believing that nobody in faraway Richmond was listening to his problems, for they had transferred most of his regiments and drained off large stores of arms and ammunition. The War Department did not respond to Lovell's concerns, even after he told them Farragut's vessels had the capability of passing the forts.

To understand the fall of New Orleans requires a study of command, something that can be adequately conducted only through study of all the official and unofficial correspondence exchanged between the principal players in both governments. It also requires attending to the opinions and impressions left by the people who lived through the crisis, alert to the petty jealousies that existed between the participants themselves. News of the loss of New Orleans came to Jefferson Davis and Secretary Mallory as an absolute shock. This short history attempts to explain why.

ONE *The Union Is Dead*

On November 6, 1860, the wharves of New Orleans bulged with the commerce of the great muddy river. Vessels from the seven seas waited by the docks, loading and unloading, and huge piles of merchandise lay heaped along the levee: kegs, boxes, and crates of beef, pork, bacon, butter, and cheese; bundles of hemp, rope, twine, and shingles; sacks of flour, corn, potatoes, rice, and wheat; and household items like glassware, linen, marble, and leather goods. Slaves singing in a deep, mellow cadence bent their backs and shuttled bales of cotton from warehouses to steamers along the levee. Flatboats waited to unload grain from Illinois and Indiana, whiskey from Kentucky and Tennessee, and cotton from Mississippi and Louisiana. Elegant steamboats, sparkling white and gilded, hooted their whistles, filled the air with the noise of their calliopes and squeezed into openings along the levee at the foot of New Canal Street. All along the waterfront and across the river at Algiers, shipbuilders worked six days a week filling orders for a wide range of rivercraft, everything from three-deck paddleboats with spacious salons to small steam-powered tugs.

A few miles north of the city, schooners rubbed against long docks that stretched into Lake Pontchartrain, unloading sugar, clothing, wines, fancy foods, and luxuries from the West Indies, Europe, and the North. Once emptied, they waited for the train from Jefferson City and Carrollton to bring cargoes from warehouses strung along the river, or the loaded wagons from Canal Street that rumbled by the Metairie Racecourse as they freighted goods between the city and the docks.

The principal export of New Orleans was cotton, and the Crescent City continued to expand as the conduit of southern wealth. In 1860, port receipts exceeded $185 million, and cotton accounted for 60 percent of this total. The city handled 2,000,000 bales of cotton that year, whereas the Confederate government, after it came into existence, never held title to more than 400,000 bales of the South's white gold.[1]

New Orleans had grown to greatness. No other southern city compared in wealth or population, and the town was probably the South's most un-southern city. New Orleans had grown great on Louisiana's slave economy and the expansive plantations that filled the city's wharves with over two million bales of cotton each year. Its publicists and newspapers stoutly and vocally favored the slave system — as fervently as any group in the South. They went out of their way to trumpet the slave theme, leaving the impression that New Orleanians would cling as devoutly as any people in the South to the institution of slavery. But the composition of New Orleans differed strikingly from other southern cities. More foreigners lived in the Crescent City than in any other town of the South, and they neither owned slaves nor believed in the slave system. They quietly opposed the system, mostly on economic grounds, and preferred to live their lives in complete separation from the black race. In the decade before the Civil War, the slave population decreased by five thousand, with replacement by mostly Irish immigrants. The foreign element became a silent minority, but many of them had strong commercial ties to the Northeast and interests abroad.

Another group of influential outsiders comprised businessmen, merchants, craftsmen, and workmen who had moved from the North and established homes in and around New Orleans. They had little use for the slave system and maintained close relationships with their friends and associates in the North. But even in alliance with those of foreign origins, they were too few to stem the rushing tide of secession.[2]

On this day, November 6, 1860, the citizens of New Orleans, and all of Louisiana, had a special duty to discharge, at least those who could. They left their farms and businesses long enough to go to the polls and cast their vote. The torchlight parades with hundreds of pine knots aflame, the colorful displays of fireworks, and the dances, grand balls, and golden oratory were over. Political campaigns had run their course, and now there was nothing left but the ballot. Despite the city's commercial ties with the North, the majority of Orleanians did not want Abraham Lincoln as pres-

    1. U.S. House of Representatives, *Report on the Internal Commerce of the United States by William P. Switzler, Chief of Bureau Statistics, Treasury Department. House Executive Document No. 6, Part II.* 50th Cong., 1st sess. (1888), 209–225; Harold Sinclair, *The Port of New Orleans* (Garden City, 1942), 223.
    2. Sinclair, *Port of New Orleans,* 216–17.

ident. A short time later, they learned that their vote had been split: John C. Breckinridge, the secession candidate from Kentucky, had received 22,681 votes; John Bell, of Tennessee, 20,204; and Stephen A. Douglas, the Democrat from Illinois, 7,625. Abraham Lincoln, the dreaded "black Republican," had not been included on Louisiana's ballot.[3]

Especially interesting was the voter turnout. Of a free population of 376,280, only 50,510 Louisianians had gone to the polls. Without Lincoln on the ballot, did the others just stay away? Louisiana's apologists said that the total vote was unimportant, that the proportions conclusively indicated the state's sentiments. But did they?

When word of the national returns electing Lincoln reached New Orleans, the debate over secession sparked editorial warfare. The editor of the *Daily Crescent*, one of the more rabid disunionists, wrote, "The day of compromise is gone. . . . The soul of the Union is dead, and now let's bury the body." John Maginnis, editor of the *True Delta*, disagreed and counseled that "Lincoln cannot, however disposed himself, . . . do aught against the rights of any section of the Union. . . . Why then under such circumstances, should Louisiana countenance designs against the Union?"[4]

But editors of moderate newspapers like the *True Delta* and the New Orleans *Bee*, which became less conservative as time passed, could neither impede the momentum of secession nor deter the public from preparing for war. Even before the elections, leading citizens in New Orleans had taken independent action and formed small military groups to protect their homes and property from nonexistent but anticipated aggression. On November 10, four days after Lincoln's election, these ad hoc groups crowded into Armory Hall and organized the Minute Men of New Orleans. Besides pledging their allegiance to Louisiana, they decided to help protect any southern state that chose to secede from the Union. By early December, military companies calling themselves Minute Men had sprung up all over Louisiana.[5]

A new and aggressive governor, Thomas Overton Moore, had taken office on January 23, 1860, and in his inaugural address made it plain that

3. New Orleans *Daily Crescent*, December 4, 1860; Jefferson Davis Bragg, *Louisiana in the Confederacy* (Baton Rouge, 1941), 19; John D. Winters, *The Civil War in Louisiana* (Baton Rouge, 1963), 6–7.

4. New Orleans *Daily Crescent*, December 11, 1860; New Orleans *True Delta*, November 15, 1860.

5. New Orleans *Daily Crescent*, November 12, 26, 1860; Baton Rouge *Daily Advocate*, November 19, 23, 1860; Lilla McLure and J. Howe (eds.), *History of Shreveport and Shreveport Builders* (2 vols.; Shreveport, 1937, 1951), II, 8; Winters, *Civil War in Louisiana*, 7.

"at the north, a widespread sympathy with felons has deepened the distrust in the permanent federal government, and awakened sentiments favorable to a separation of the states." The unnamed "felons" were the hated northern abolitionists who had supported and glorified John Brown's raid on the United States Armory at Harpers Ferry on October 16–18, 1859.[6] Now on the heels of Lincoln's election, Moore was deluged with petitions and appeals for action, and in isolated instances moderation. Somewhat baffled by the profusion of demands, he in early December called the legislature into a special session.

On December 10, the planter-governor, himself a prosperous slaveholder, opened the meeting by suggesting to lawmakers that Louisiana's future should be decided before Lincoln took office. "I do not think it comports with the honor and self-respect of Louisiana as a slaveholding state to live under the government of a Black Republican president." After preaching "states' rights" and "southern rights" to a receptive audience, Moore enumerated the South's many grievances against the federal government and stressed the importance of defending the state if the legislature should later act to secede. He also asked for the immediate creation of a special military board to purchase arms and munitions and distribute them to volunteer military organizations.[7]

Three days later, the legislature authorized the governor to hold an election of delegates for the purpose of deciding Louisiana's future. With secession considered inevitable, debate focused on whether Louisiana should act independently or together with other southern states. Delegates for the convention were to be elected by January 7, 1861. In setting the date, legislators ignored the state constitution, which required that the question of a convention be submitted to popular referendum.

Before adjourning, the legislators gave Moore authority to establish a military board directly under himself and authorized a half million dollars to arm and equip companies either already formed or judged necessary. Every parish was to have at least one company, either infantry or cavalry, with no fewer than thirty-two men. That was a far cry from mobilizing an army, or even a single brigade, but the beat of drums and the smell of gunpowder began to pervade the atmosphere.[8]

6. New Orleans *True Delta*, January 24, 1860.

7. New Orleans *Daily Crescent*, December 11, 1860; Winters, *Civil War in Louisiana*, 8. Governor Moore's speech is in *Documents of the Second Session of the Fifth Legislature of the State of Louisiana, 1861* (Baton Rouge, 1861) 2–3.

8. New Orleans *True Delta*, December 15, 1860; Bragg, *Louisiana in the Confederacy*, 22–27; Roger Wallace Shugg, *Origins of Class Struggle in Louisiana* (Baton Rouge, 1939), 162.

Before delegates could be elected, New Orleans learned that South Carolina had seceded on December 20. Jubilation spread through the streets, the Pelican flag floated defiantly from windows and rooftops, and hundreds of guns sounded outside public buildings as a band marched over Rampart Street and down Canal Street playing martial airs.

Moore, perhaps carried away by his own enthusiasm, did not wait for the convention to meet in Baton Rouge on January 23. On January 8, almost a year after stigmatizing John Brown as a fanatical "felon," he ordered the Louisiana militia to seize not only the Federal arsenal at Baton Rouge, but also Forts Jackson and St. Philip, which guarded the Mississippi approaches to New Orleans, Fort Pike, at the eastern entrance to Lake Pontchartrain, and the army barracks below the city. He held the action necessary "to prevent a collision between Federal troops and the people of the State," declaring that the forts might otherwise be deployed to suppress the "will of the people."[9]

On January 10, Louisiana senators Judah P. Benjamin and John Slidell sent messages to New Orleans warning Daniel W. Adams at the Military Board that "secret attempts continue to be made to garrison Southern ports. We think there is special reason to fear surprise from the Gulf squadron." Another message to the governor read, "The danger is not from St. Louis, but from the sea."[10] A year later, with the Confederate government comfortably ensconced in Richmond, the War Office held staunchly to the opposite belief—that the threat to New Orleans was upriver, not from the sea—though the secretary of war was none other than Benjamin, the former senator.

On the afternoon of January 10, a detachment of Louisiana militia under the command of Major Paul E. Theard stepped aboard the steamer *Yankee* and chugged seventy miles downriver to capture Forts Jackson and St. Philip. Moore, suspecting Federal reinforcements were on the way, ordered Theard to "hold the forts, and defend them against any and all attacks." With a force of 17 officers, 4 musicians, and 150 men, Theard reached Fort St. Philip at 8 P.M. and surprised Henry Dart, the keeper of the fort, with a demand for surrender. Dart, whose military resources consisted of himself and about a dozen slaves, replied that "he had no objection in the world."

---

9. *The War of the Rebellion: A Compilation of Official Records of the Union and Confederate Armies* (130 vols.; Washington, D.C., 1880–1901), Ser. 1, Vol. I, 489, 491, 493–96; hereinafter cited as *ORA*. Unless otherwise indicated, all citations are to Series 1.

10. *Ibid.*, I, 496.

Flushed with success, Theard left a small detachment at Fort St. Philip and proceeded across the river to Fort Jackson, where Ordnance Sergeant H. Smith relinquished the keys to the fort under protest "to superior numbers." Since it was then dark and quite chilly, Smith invited the men into the fort and made them "feel as comfortable as possible." For the next week they shared each other's hospitality, with fine dinners, choice wines, and good fellowship mingled with a few notes from Theard's four musicians.[11]

Fort Pike, the back door to New Orleans guarding the north inlet into Lake Pontchartrain, surrendered a short time later to another small force of spirited volunteers. Two weeks later, Sergeant D. Wilber reported that he had surrendered Fort Macomb, off the south inlet, to Lieutenant R. C. Capers, of the 1st Regiment Louisiana Infantry. Neither fort was garrisoned, and the ordnance sergeants who occupied them had grown accustomed to romping casually along the shore and diving for oysters. They had no special orders from Washington to defend the forts and probably looked forward to the trip home.[12]

When Moore sent Colonel Braxton Bragg, backed by three companies of militia, to demand the surrender of the United States arsenal at Baton Rouge, Major Joseph A. Haskin, a Mexican War veteran, flatly refused. Haskin did not need orders from Washington to tell him who owned the Federal property under his command. "The safety of the State of Louisiana," wrote Moore, "demands that I take possession of all government property within her limits. You are, therefore, summoned hereby, to deliver up the barracks, arsenal, and public property now under your command. With the large force at my disposal this demand will be enforced. Any attempt at defense on your part will be a rash sacrifice of life."[13]

Haskin had only a small force of regulars, but he replied, "I've lost one arm in the defense of my flag and I will lose the other, or even my life if necessary, before I surrender to that lot of ragamuffins on the Boulevard."[14]

The militia, agitated by Haskin's surly response, wanted to attack immediately, but the sight of two cannon rolled into position at the entrances and manned by determined cannoneers dampened their enthusiasm. Militia scattered along Third Street ducked for cover and returned to camp to sulk in their tents. What started out as a frolic had turned sour. There was

11. *Ibid.*, I, 491, Moore to Militia, January 10, and Smith to Cooper, January 11, 1861; New Orleans *Picayune*, January 11, 1861.

12. *ORA*, I, 492, Wilber to Cooper, January 31, 1861.

13. *Ibid.*, 489–490, Haskin to Cooper, January 11, and Moore to Haskin, January 10, 1861.

14. Milledge L. Bonham, Jr., "Louisiana's Seizure of the Federal Arsenal at Baton Rouge, January, 1861," *The Historical Society of East and West Baton Rouge Proceedings*, II (1917–18), 47–55.

the possibility of somebody getting killed. Moore attempted to negotiate with the feisty old veteran, but Haskin stubbornly refused to surrender his post, especially to a force of undisciplined militia who cowered behind buildings and lampposts. Finally, Moore sent to New Orleans for the Washington Artillery. When the Creole Guards and the Pelican Rifles heard that the governor had asked for reinforcements, they indignantly marched to his mansion, stacked arms, and resigned. Half the remaining companies left town without bothering to inform the governor. Only two companies remained: the Delta Rifles and the Baton Rouge Fencibles.[15]

On the morning of January 10, the Washington Artillery, accompanied by two New Orleans rifle companies and the remnants of Bragg's force, formed in the city and began their march up Third Street. Haskin waited with about sixty artillerymen, prepared to resist attack. Another small force under Lieutenant John W. Todd waited at the Federal Arsenal just east of Third Street. By late afternoon, Haskin, outgunned and surrounded, acknowledged that resistance would only result in bloodshed and surrendered to Governor Moore. State troops ambled into the arsenal and began counting the spoils: fifty thousand stands of small arms, four howitzers, twenty pieces of heavy ordnance, one battery of 6-pounders, another of 12-pounders, and three hundred barrels of gunpowder. Governor Moore, delighted with the haul, envisioned the beginning of his new state arsenal. Major Haskin vacated the Federal buildings on January 12. Parading through Baton Rouge to the tune of "The Girl I Left Behind Me," his small force marched to the steamboat landing. The Washington Artillery returned down the river to New Orleans, reporting that "Sergeant Buck Miller fell down a cellar when performing a 'backward dress,' and two privates, who were overcome by the excitement, were brought under arrest." The first armed engagement in Louisiana was settled without bloodshed, but secession was under way two weeks before the delegates met to discuss the matter. Moore had taken the initiative. All that remained for the delegates was to make secession official.[16]

While the state troops were entering the arsenal in Baton Rouge, Captain Charles M. Bradford took possession of the marine hospital in New Orleans and made plain to Frank M. Hatch, the superintendent, that all 216 patients and invalids had to be removed to make room for state troops being mustered into service. Hatch, who was also the collector of customs,

15. *Ibid.*; Napier Bartlett, *A Soldier's Story of the War: Including the Marches and Battles of the Washington Artillery and Other Louisiana Troops* (New Orleans, 1874), 11–12.

16. Bartlett, *A Soldier's Story*, 11–12; Baton Rouge *Daily Advocate*, January 11, 1861.

complained to John Dix, secretary of the treasury. Dix, who had no power to intervene, could only call Bradford's action "revolting to the civilization of the age." The northern press printed stories about the sick being cast out onto the street, but in reality the infirm were gently transferred to Charity Hospital.[17]

After *Lewis Cass*, a revenue cutter lying at New Orleans for repairs, was seized on the order of Governor Moore, Secretary Dix suspected that the five-gun cutter *Robert McClelland*, operating in the lower Mississippi, would be the next of Louisiana's acquisitions. On January 19, he ordered W. Hemphill Jones to proceed to New Orleans in order to prevent the vessel from falling into the hands of the state. Meantime, Hatch, the customs collector, had the cutter's captain, Robert K. Hudgkins, bring the vessel to New Orleans, and the cutter arrived about the same time as Jones. When Hudgkins proved unwilling to recognize Jones's authority, a wire went to Dix for further instructions. Dix telegraphed Lieutenant Charles H. B. Caldwell to arrest Hudgkins and assume command of the cutter. If Hudgkins interfered, Caldwell was to treat him as a mutineer, and "if any one attempted to haul down the American flag, shoot him on the spot." Dix's order, although filled with spirit and patriotism, was not enough to galvanize Caldwell into making war on the New Orleans militia. For about two weeks no flag flew from the mast of the cutter, but militia had possession of the vessel, and Louisiana could claim a state navy of one ship.[18]

Major William Tecumseh Sherman, superintendent of the Louisiana Seminary, denounced Governor Moore's seizure of government property as a "declaration of war." He notified state authorities that he would quit his post if Louisiana seceded from the Union. Colonel Bragg, Moore's military aide, expressed regret over Sherman's decision, but admitting that he too was pessimistic about the future, he almost fatalistically predicted that "bloodshed" and armed conflict would soon break out between the North and the South.[19]

17. William H. Rooney, "The First 'Incident' of Secession: Seizure of the New Orleans Marine Hospital," *Louisiana Historical Quarterly*, XXXIV, No. 2 (April, 1951), 135–42; New Orleans *Commercial Bulletin*, January 12, 1861.

18. *ORA*, XV, 499, Statement of David Ritchie to James M. Bell. See also J. Thomas Scharf, *History of the Confederate States Navy from Its Organization to the Surrender of Its Last Vessel* (New York, 1887), 24. Scharf claims that J. G. Brushwood captained *McClelland*, but this author prefers to cite the *Official Records*.

19. M. A. DeWolfe Howe (ed.), *Home Letters of General Sherman* (New York, 1909), 187.

All over the parishes of Louisiana, civic leaders anticipated the outcome of the secession convention. With speeches and money they encouraged the formation of more military companies. New Orleans became a center of feverish preparations. Policemen deserted their posts to enlist, and firemen organized their twenty-four engine companies into the Fire Brigade, readying themselves to fight with a musket in one hand and a hose in the other. Alexandria raised a company of cavalry, and in the northwestern corner of the state, Shreveport raised the Caddo Greys and Bossier Parish the Red River Volunteers. Most of the arms, artillery, and ammunition came from the Federal arsenal seized at Baton Rouge.[20]

When the delegates assembled in Baton Rouge on January 23 to determine the future of Louisiana, little was left to discuss. With only slight opposition, 123 delegates drafted an ordinance of secession along lines orchestrated by the governor. Moore explained why he felt the actions he had taken over the previous weeks were necessary. Compromise with the North was no longer possible, he said, and he warned that Louisiana must not be coerced into submission by force of arms. In his bid for secession, he received support from Senators Benjamin and Slidell and from two of Louisiana's congressmen, Thomas G. Davidson and John M. Landrum, who sent a joint letter from Washington to the delegation. Two former governors from other southern states, John A. Winston of Alabama and John L. Manning of South Carolina, spoke to the convention and encouraged prompt approval. Manning offered a copy of his own state's ordinance of secession as a guide in framing Louisiana's resolutions.

A few delegates spoke against secession and tried to stall the vote. James G. Taliaferro, who came from the small farming parish of Catahoula, called the convention treasonist and denied that Louisiana had the constitutional right to leave the Union. In an impassioned plea, he envisaged economic chaos and the end of southern prosperity, stemming from runaway inflation and staggering taxation. He could see no way to prevent the rise of anarchy and destruction. Joseph A. Rozier, of New Orleans, asked the delegation first to seek an amendment to the Constitution on behalf of the South, thereby preserving the Union. He predicted that Europe would refuse to recognize a southern government and economic ruin would follow. Another New Orleans dissenter, Charles Bienvenu, asked that any ordinance

20. New Orleans *Daily Crescent*, January 14, 1861; Thomas O'Conner, *History of the Fire Department of New Orleans from the Earliest Days to the Present Time* (New Orleans, 1895), 140, 153–66; Bragg, *Louisiana in the Confederacy*, 51.

of secession be submitted to popular referendum, but his proposal was defeated by a large majority. Nobody listened. Moore had already set the stage for the inevitable.[21]

On January 26, after all efforts to stall secession failed, Louisiana voted itself out of the Union by 113 to 17. Alexandre Mouton, president of the convention, cast the last vote, returned to his chair, and proclaimed, "I now decree the connection between the state of Louisiana and the Federal Union dissolved, and that she is a free, sovereign, and independent power." As if by cue, Governor Moore entered the chamber, preceded by the state flag and followed by resounding cheers. He lauded the convention for its action and promised great but difficult days ahead. He did not, however, foretell how difficult they would become.[22]

Political chicanery had played a decisive role in the secession vote. When delegates to the convention were selected by popular vote, those favorable to the Union won 17,296 votes, and secession candidates 20,448. Why then did the delegates vote 103 to 17 for secession? They were obviously persuaded by their peers to repudiate those who had sent them to the convention. All told, 20,448 votes were cast for secession candidates in a free population of 376,280. Thus, 5 percent of the voting population took New Orleans and Louisiana out of the Union and into four years of civil war.[23]

When news of secession reached New Orleans, bells rang, guns boomed at the foot of Canal Street, people took to the streets shouting and waving, and from the windows of private homes and the tops of public buildings the Pelican flag fluttered proudly. For people who had harbored resentment over the election of Lincoln, it was the perfect opportunity to let off steam, and the bars and saloons enjoyed a brisk business. Ablaze with lights and filled with music, the drawing rooms and salons of the elegant St. Charles and St. Louis hotels drew huge crowds. Richly gowned southern beauties attended nightly balls and exposed heavily jeweled bosoms at gala soirees. It was the time of Mardi Gras and of celebration, not of war. Almost in a gasp of relief, the New Orleans *Picayune* captured the excite-

21. *Official Journal of the Proceedings of the Convention of the State of Louisiana, 1861* (New Orleans, 1861), 5–20; *See also ORA*, LIII, 614–15; Roger Wallace Shugg, "A Suppressed Cooperationist Protest Against Secession," *Louisiana Historical Quarterly*, XIX, No. 1 (January, 1936), 199; Bragg, *Louisiana and the Confederacy*, 30, 51; New Orleans *Daily Crescent*, January 24, 26, 28, 1861; Willie M. Caskey, *Secession and Restoration of Louisiana* (Baton Rouge, 1938), 29; Winters, *Civil War in Louisiana*, 12.

22. *Official Journal of the Louisiana Convention*, 17–18; New Orleans *Crescent*, January 28, 1861.

23. Sinclair, *Port of New Orleans*, 220–21.

ment and sentiment of the city: "The deed has been done. 'We breathe deeper and freer' for it. The Union is dead; and with it all the hopes and all the fears which divided and agitated our people."[24]

But the Union was not dead—at least, not in the mind of Abraham Lincoln. The country had to wait another six weeks for his inauguration; in the meantime, the South had little to fear from President James Buchanan.

24. New Orleans *Picayune*, January 27, 1861; Dufour, *Night the War Was Lost*, 23–25.

Two *Notions of War*

On January 29, when the regular session of the state legislature met at Baton Rouge, the convention delegates moved to New Orleans and set up shop in City Hall. Six were chosen to attend a meeting at Montgomery, Alabama, on February 4, where representatives from other secession states were to gather and discuss the creation of a confederacy of southern states dedicated to the protection and preservation of states' rights. After several days of debate at City Hall, the six delegates left for Montgomery with no clear instructions, and the convention turned to other business.[1]

On February 2, Richard Taylor, chairman of the convention's military and naval affairs committee, presented an ordinance providing for a standing military force within the state. Taylor, a wealthy planter from St. Charles Parish and son of former president Zachary Taylor, reported Louisiana "utterly defenseless" and pointed to the sorry condition of Forts Jackson and St. Philip, which needed to be repaired "immediately." Taylor's ordinance passed with little debate and provided for one regiment of artillery and one regiment of infantry, each with eight companies. The entire force, including officers and men, was to consist of about eighteen hundred regulars under the command of a major general.[2]

For the new Louisiana army, Moore picked Colonel Braxton Bragg, who had led the force of volunteers against the Baton Rouge arsenal. Forty-three-year-old Bragg had graduated fifth in the West Point class of 1837, served with distinction in the Mexican War, and risen to the rank of lieutenant colonel in the regular army. After a dispute with Secretary

1. Lane Carter Kendall, "The Interregnum in Louisiana in 1861," *Louisiana Historical Quarterly,* XVI (1933), 644–47; *Official Journal of the Louisiana Convention,* January 29, 1861, pp. 24–48.
2. Bragg, *Louisiana in the Confederacy,* 54.

of War Jefferson Davis, he resigned from the army and in 1856 settled as a planter on Bayou Lafourche, about fifty miles west of New Orleans. Bragg was to prove a capable organizer and strategist, but as time passed his querulous and stubborn personality made him unpopular with friends, military peers, and former supporters. He wore a perpetual frown between heavy black eyebrows, and his piercing dark eyes radiated a grouchy, unfriendly, and obstinate disposition.[3]

Moore appointed as Bragg's direct subordinates Major George Deas, adjutant general; Lieutenant Colonel Abraham C. Myers, quartermaster general; and Major Pierre G. T. Beauregard, colonel of engineers in command of the artillery regiment. Myers had on January 28 turned over a Federal supply depot to state troops. The public cheered the appointments, and the New Orleans *Picayune* proclaimed, "These are the elite of the army of the United States. No four men in the whole rank and file of that gallant service have higher standing for skill, courage and conduct in their noble profession." But Beauregard, who had just resigned as superintendent of West Point to return to Louisiana, believed that he, not Bragg, deserved the top military post. Unlike Bragg, who had come from North Carolina, Beauregard had been born in Louisiana and since 1850 occupied the post of engineering officer in charge of the defenses of the state. Although Bragg outranked the Creole in the old army, Beauregard nonetheless refused to play second fiddle to the irascible Bragg and politely rejected the governor's appointment.[4]

At forty-two, Beauregard had all the polish, manners, and social graces that Bragg lacked. He had spoken French before he learned to speak English, and read in his native tongue all the classics on warfare. At the age of twenty he had graduated from West Point, second in a class of forty-five. In the Mexican War, he served under General Winfield Scott, receiving two wounds and two brevets for gallantry. After the war he supervised the building of coastal defenses, and between 1858 and 1860 was chief engineer in charge of draining New Orleans and directing the construction of the city's new federal customhouse. Moore replaced Beauregard with Paul Octave Hébert, another West Pointer who had worked on river defenses in the early forties. Beauregard, in a gesture of humility and perhaps contempt, enlisted as a private in the Orleans Guards, all blue-blooded Creoles.[5]

3. Patricia L. Faust (ed.), *Historical Times Illustrated: Encyclopedia of the Civil War* (New York, 1986), 75; hereinafter cited as *HTI*.

4. New Orleans *Picayune*, February 4, 11, 12, 1861.

5. Faust (ed.), *HTI*, 51–52, 355–56; Dufour, *Night the War Was Lost*, 28–29.

Beauregard had no intention of remaining a private. He had connections in Montgomery, and friends lobbied on his behalf for a brigadier general's commission in the Confederate army. When it came, Beauregard reappeared before members of the Military Board in New Orleans and urged them to "look to our most vulnerable point, the Mississippi River." He believed that given the condition of Forts Jackson and St. Philip, any steamer could pass them in "broad daylight." Even if the forts were brought to a proper state of defense, Beauregard warned, they could not "during a dark or stormy night" prevent the passage of warships without the "assistance of a properly constructed raft, or strong wire-rope across the river." He stressed the importance of being able to repel an attack for at least a half hour, long enough for cross fire from the forts to pulverize the vessels leading the attack.[6]

He submitted a written recommendation that prompt and special attention be given to constructing a floating boom at each of the forts, and he included plans for two booms to be used together or separately. One plan called for a floating barrier of long twelve-inch-thick timbers tightly bound together in sections of four, with heavy chains connecting each section. Half of the boom would stretch from Fort Jackson to midriver, where it would be joined by a similar section from Fort St. Philip. A strong wire rope operated from Fort Jackson would enable friendly vessels to pass and would relieve strain when debris backed up at the barrier.

A second plan called for a boom of five barges strung by chain between the two forts. At night, the barrier could be watched by patrol boats and illuminated by well-concealed Drummond lights. He suggested that John Roy, the former assistant architect at the customhouse, be put in charge of the project. "No expenses ought to be spared to put those two works in a most efficient state of defense," he warned, "for fifty thousand or a hundred thousand dollars spent thus might, a few weeks hence, save millions of dollars to the State and the city of New Orleans."[7]

He recommended shipping all heavy guns located anywhere in Louisiana to Forts Jackson and St. Philip, to be "mounted at once" on the riverfronts. Beauregard seemed to be aware that Union warships were much heavier than the frigates and the ships of the line built a few decades earlier. Many had been refitted with chain armor to withstand cannon fire from guns of the type mounted in the forts and in shore batteries. He urged that as newer and heavier guns be emplaced, "they be tried forthwith by dou-

6. *ORA*, I, 500–501, Beauregard to Military Board, February 13, 1861.
7. *Ibid.*

ble charges of shot and powder," and that trees along the river be removed so that the guns could be sighted in on enemy vessels coming upriver, with a view to damaging them before they reached the forts.[8] After leaving his thoughts with the Military Board, Beauregard departed for his new post at Charleston, South Carolina, where a crusty major in the Union army refused to evacuate Fort Sumter.

When Roy followed up by calling on Hébert, the colonel showed a passive interest in the young architect's floating pontoon boom but suggested that he look about for available lumber. Returning the next day to report, Roy found the colonel distracted, as if he had forgotten the matter. Roy restressed the importance of the project, but Hébert had other priorities and sent him to the customhouse to make gun carriages. Despite Beauregard's warnings, military authorities in New Orleans lagged in recognizing that the safety of the city depended on the two forts seventy miles downriver. For almost a year, Beauregard's suggestions languished.[9]

While the Military Board contemplated its role, the convention continued to order the seizure of Federal assets. In New Orleans, nearly $500,000 in gold and silver were removed from the United States Mint, and another $147,519.66 scooped up at the customhouse and transferred to the treasury at Montgomery. These were small sums in comparison with the wealth of the city. In 1860, a report by the United States secretary of the treasury showed that the city's thirteen banks had capital totaling over $24 million, with deposits of $20 million and specie in the vaults of over $12 million. In the most prosperous city of the South, hard money was everywhere, but little of it flowed into Governor Moore's war chest.[10]

The convention sent copies of the Ordinance of Secession to Washington, where Benjamin and Slidell had it read to the Senate. Fired by a new patriotism, the two senators made emotional farewell addresses. Slidell warned the Senate that interference would bring about a boycott of northern products. Southern ships would soon ply the seas, he said, and trade with foreign countries would prevent the North from blockading southern ports. Slidell cautioned that any attempt to blockade the South would

8. *Ibid.*; Alfred Roman, *The Military Operations of General Beauregard in the War Between the States 1861 to 1865: Including a Brief Personal Sketch and a Narrative of His Services in the War with Mexico 1846–8* (2 vols.; New York, 1884), I, 422–23; T. Harry Williams, *P. G. T. Beauregard: Napoleon in Gray* (Baton Rouge, 1954), 45–50.

9. John Roy Memorandum Book, February 11, 14, 15, 16, 19, 1861, Howard-Tilton Library, Tulane University, New Orleans.

10. *Executive Documents Printed by Order of the 36th Congress, 1859–1860, Series 49* (Washington, D.C., 1860), 163–68; Bragg, *Louisiana in the Confederacy*, 37–40.

mean war, which the South was prepared to meet with "efficient weapons."
After rattling the chambers of the Senate with threats, Benjamin and Slidell
packed their bags and, along with the members of the House from Louisiana,
started home.[11]

Many in the Crescent City still hoped for a peaceful solution, especially
those whose convention delegates had turned out unreliable or who would
have liked to vote for Lincoln in the election of November, 1860. But the
military tempo continued to increase. By mid-February, eight new companies had formed in New Orleans, and the Military Board had distrib-
uted arms and ammunition to 1,765 men throughout the state. Each new
unit adopted its own style of uniform, none more gaudy than the tasseled
caps, tight-fitting red jackets, and full blue pantaloons of the Louisiana
Zouaves. Mostly Frenchmen and Italians, the Zouave membership included veterans of the Italian, Crimean, and African wars, as well as thieves
and murderers recruited from the jails of New Orleans. Crowds gathered
each evening to stare at the unforgettable riffraff with their scarred faces
and dirty, unwashed uniforms as they snapped through their drills with
impeccable precision.[12]

The popularity of the little company of Louisiana Zouaves led it to mush-
room into three regiments, the original Zouaves, the Avegno Zouaves, and
the Tigers, sometimes called Bob Wheat's Zouaves, all outfitted in bril-
liantly colored kepis, short coats, and flaring pantaloons. A theater group
calling itself the traveling Zouaves appeared on stage in New Orleans and
drew huge crowds. But when bullets began to fly, the fancy uniforms came
off. Union riflemen trained their sights on the brightly colored targets, and
the Zouaves shed their prized garments for simple butternut.[13]

While New Orleans girded for war, delegates from Louisiana, Mississippi,
Alabama, Georgia, Florida, and South Carolina—and later, Texas—checked
into the Exchange Hotel in Montgomery, Alabama, and on February 4 began drafting the provisional constitution of the Confederate States of America. Patriotic enthusiasm ran high. Delegates soon assumed the legislative
function of government and within six weeks produced a constitution,
elected Jefferson F. Davis president and Alexander H. Stephens vice-pres-
ident, and established a financial basis to support the new nation. The men

11. Caskey, *Secession and Restoration*, 34–35; Winters, *Civil War in Louisiana*, 14–15.

12. "Report of Military Board," *Documents of the Second Session of the Fifth Legislature of the State of Louisiana, 1861* (New Orleans, 1861), 4–7; Eliza McHatton-Ripley, *From Flag to Flag* (New York, 1889), 10–13.

13. New Orleans *Daily Crescent*, February 25, 26, 28, 1861; Ella Lonn, *Foreigners in the Confederacy* (Chapel Hill, 1940), 101–102; Winters, *Civil War in Louisiana*, 16–17.

engaged in this difficult work were drawn from the South's most experienced political talent. They were well-educated, experienced legislators mainly from the propertied class. Ironically, the fire-eating radical secessionist leaders sank into the background as the government took shape, and that made it easier for Arkansas, North Carolina, Tennessee, and Virginia to align themselves with the secessionist government.[14]

To protect and defend the new nation, the delegates, now the first Confederate Congress, passed an act on February 21 establishing the navy department. Seven days later they provided for a provisional army. Military units were forming in every southern state, with a soldier's term of service set at twelve months. Little, however, had been done toward developing a navy. Each state had collected a few ships through seizures of revenue cutters and tugboats, but prior to Davis' appointment of Stephen R. Mallory as naval secretary on February 21, no effort had been made to unify this ragged collection of miscellaneous vessels.[15]

Forty-eight-year-old Mallory had lived most of his life near the water in Key West, where he had read law and in 1840 been admitted to the bar. He became a customs inspector and a judge and served briefly in the Second Seminole War. In 1851, he won election to the Senate, where he continued until Florida seceded on January 10, 1861. During his ten years in Washington he served on the Committee of Naval Affairs and in 1853 became its powerful chairman, pushing relentlessly for a larger and stronger navy. He carefully prepared his speeches, which demonstrated impressive knowledge, but he was not a gifted orator and his words lacked the luster needed to win enthusiastic support. In 1855, rather than building the navy, he created the Naval Retiring Board, which placed a large number of senior naval officers on half pay and put them on a dreaded reserve list. That drew sharp criticism, especially from those affected. Many old navy men came to distrust him and disapproved of his selection as Confederate naval chief.

Distrust of Mallory extended beyond navy men. Unlike many moderate secessionists, Mallory opposed disunion altogether. His biographer, Joseph T. Durkin, writes that prior to the war, Mallory had shown "undue timidity in defense of Southern rights. He was . . . a Unionist whose Unionism overshadowed his devotion to the Southern land of his birth; he was lacking in vigor and courage at the moment when the Southern cause was most in need of those qualities in her sons."[16]

14. Faust (ed.), *HTI*, "Confederate Congress," 157–158.
15. Scharf, *Confederate Navy*, 27–28.
16. Faust (ed.), *HTI*, 470–71; Joseph T. Durkin, *Stephen R. Mallory: Confederate Navy Chief*

Still, Davis had served in the Senate with the man, knew him as a loyal, capable administrator, believed him to be hardworking and innovative, and probably knew of no southerner who better understood naval organization and policy. There were many senior officers with long careers in the navy. They could command squadrons and fight their ships, but could they create a navy? Davis asked for Mallory and got him.

When the Confederate government was formed, Davis, who considered himself a military man, wanted a representative from each state in his cabinet. He filled the war secretary's post last. At the time, the only state not represented in the cabinet was Alabama. Delegates from the state recommended Leroy Pope Walker, a capable forty-three-year-old lawyer who had helped lead the southern-rights forces in his state. After Lincoln's election he had worked diligently for secession. Walker would have been a better choice for attorney general, but since that post had been filled by Louisiana's Judah P. Benjamin, he became the Secretary of War. He had no military experience and no known credentials as an administrator. Unlike Mallory, Walker was quarrelsome, opinionated, and somewhat sickly, and he disliked detail work. Davis tolerated his combination of faults for about six months.[17] Fortunately, the governors of all the states had already authorized the formation of militia units, thereby sparing Walker the task of total mobilization. By Governor Moore's decrees, a military capability already existed in Louisiana.

On February 14, even before Mallory accepted the post of naval secretary, the Confederate Congress passed a resolution authorizing Charles M. Conrad, chairman of the Committee on Naval Affairs, to initiate a search within the United States navy for officers whose sympathies lay with the South. Congress empowered Conrad to guarantee them retention of their rank if they joined the Confederate navy. Almost immediately old southerners like Captains Lawrence Rousseau, Duncan N. Ingraham, and Victor M. Randolph, and Commander Raphael Semmes, resigned their commissions to answer the call. Davis was inaugurated on February 18, and three days later he sent Semmes to the United States and Caleb Huse to England to purchase arms and munitions.[18]

About the time Mallory arrived in Montgomery, a letter containing a copy of Beauregard's report landed on the secretary's desk. It reiterated

(Chapel Hill: 1954), 11–156 *passim*, with quote from p. 113; Scharf, *Confederate Navy*, 28–30. The actual year of Mallory's birth is uncertain; he was born in Trinidad.

17. Faust (ed.), *HTI*, 797.

18. Scharf, *Confederate Navy*, 27–28, 89.

the suggestions Beauregard had made to Louisiana's Military Board and warned that the lower Mississippi was the South's "most vulnerable point." Beauregard suggested the use of mines, saying that experiments "ought to be made in the city to blow up by use of galvanic batteries any hostile vessels that might come to anchor opposite the city. Not a stone should be left unturned. . . . We should be thoroughly prepared 'for the ides of March.'"[19]

In March, 1861, Mallory's navy consisted of twelve small ships but two hundred officers from the rank of commodore down to chief gunner. The disparity in numbers between men and ships demanded correction. It was natural for Mallory to be more interested in building ships than expanding fortifications, which he considered the job of the army. When Congress, on March 15, the ides, appropriated funds for ten gunboats, which were to be ship-rigged propeller-driven steamers of a thousand tons capable of carrying at least one 10-inch and four 8-inch guns, Mallory could find no place to build them, and Semmes, then in the North, was unable to buy any.[20]

Mallory faced daunting obstacles. The skilled labor, materials, and special shipbuilding facilities needed to complete one gunboat could not be found in any single location in the Confederacy. Earlier, one steam sloop of war had been built, launched, and outfitted at the Pensacola Navy Yard, but with difficulty. Virginia had not yet seceded, and did not do so until April 17, 1861, leaving the well-equipped Gosport Navy Yard, at Norfolk, in Union control until April 21. Next to Gosport, the best shipyards in the South were in the vicinity of New Orleans, where many forms of river-craft, from steamboats to launches, had been built and repaired for many years. Mallory believed New Orleans was well protected from attack, and he sent a commission under Rousseau's leadership to the Crescent City to organize a shipbuilding effort. He hoped to build his ten gunboats there. The vessels were to be of light draft and great speed, criteria no honest ship-builder could guarantee.[21]

After the commission completed its disappointing survey of facilities, Rousseau reported they had located three vessels that could be purchased

19. Beauregard to the Editors of the [New Orleans] *Daily Delta*, February 15, 1861, in *Official Records of the Union and Confederate Navies in the War of the Rebellion* (30 vols.; Washington, D.C., 1894–1927), Ser. 2, Vol. II, 42–43, hereinafter cited as *ORN*. Unless otherwise indicated, all citations are to Series 1.

20. Durkin, *Mallory*, 146; Scharf, *Confederate Navy*, 263.

21. Scharf, *Confederate Navy*, 263.

and refitted as gunboats. Mallory bought the 520-ton steam sloop *Habana* and placed her under the command of Semmes, who outfitted her as CSS *Sumter*, the first Confederate cruiser. She carried one 8-inch pivot gun, four 32-pounders in broadside, and a crew of 109 men. Lieutenant Thomas B. Huger took command of the 830-ton steam sloop *Marquis de la Habana* and refitted her for commerce raiding. Armed with one 9-inch pivot gun and six 32-pounders in broadside, she was renamed *McRae*. Huger never got to sea because of *McRae*'s chronic engine problems. The third steamer, *Jackson*, was a large tug refitted and armed for service on the river. From the hundreds of hulks laid up in the river, these three were all Rousseau could recommend to the Committee on Naval Affairs.[22]

Another vessel, the fast New York mail steamer *Bienville*, was targeted for seizure by two members of the Louisiana Military Board, accompanied and encouraged by the ship's agent in New Orleans. Of all the vessels tied at the wharf, none came closer to meeting Mallory's specifications for speed and light draft. When the Military Board inspected the vessel, her commander, James D. Bulloch, a Georgian, had gone to the city to post a letter to Attorney General Benjamin offering his services to the Confederate navy. He proposed to go to Montgomery as soon as he settled personal affairs in New York, where he lived with his family. On posting the letter he learned that hostilities had erupted in Charleston harbor, and he returned to his ship. At the time, the swift *Bienville* had a full passenger list of businessmen and families anxious to go north before war broke out in earnest. The Military Board told Bulloch that *Bienville* had to be sold to the navy, and they asked him to name a price, assuring him that Governor Moore would meet it. Bulloch refused. He had "no authority to sell the ship" and "could not fix a price," and he would consider no "arrangements for transferring her to the Confederate States."[23]

The Military Board left in a huff, warning that if Bulloch spurned their offer, they would take the ship by force. They promised to return as soon as they received Governor Moore's decision.

Bulloch, a bright, thirty-eight-year-old former naval officer, had in 1853 been detailed by the government to go into the mail service to acquire experience on steam vessels. Working with New York partners, he supervised the construction of several fast mail steamers and obtained a lucrative command. He developed exceptional business skills, and neither the

22. *Ibid.*, 263–64; *ORN*, Ser. 2, II, 76, Mallory's Report, July 18, 1861.

23. James Dunwoody Bulloch, *The Secret Service of the Confederate States in Europe, or How the Cruisers Were Equipped* (2 vols.; New York, 1884), I, 31–35.

Military Board nor the governor could intimidate him. As a man who had just offered his services to the South, he said, "It was inexpressively painful to contemplate the possibility that I might be forced into a collision with the Government." Before any attempt could be made to seize the vessel, Bulloch elected to escape. He shifted the mooring line so it could be slipped from on board and ordered the engineer to keep pressure in the boilers.[24]

Governor Moore referred the matter to Montgomery. President Davis wired back, "Do not detain the *Bienville*; we do not wish to interfere in any way with private property." The Military Board returned late that night to ask once more that Bulloch name his price, but when he was unbending, they told him he was free to sail in the morning. The Confederate government almost lost one of its most gifted administrators. Bulloch went to Great Britain as a Confederate purchasing agent, and during the war supervised production of three high-seas commerce raiders and numerous blockade runners. He came within a few weeks of providing Mallory with a fleet of armored corvettes.[25]

Rousseau, who had been in the navy since 1809 and was considered by most standards to be an old man, reminded the Committee on Naval Affairs that Beauregard's warnings should not be ignored—that guns, carriages, and heavy armament should be moved immediately to Forts Jackson and St. Philip and that new earthworks should be dug and fortified at suitable points along the river. But in Mallory's report of July 18 to Davis, there was no mention of river fortifications. Since forts did not fall within his purview, he did not bother to mention them. He spent his days searching for steamers, needed for duty in the river and the Gulf.[26]

Military and naval preparations proceeded swiftly in Louisiana, although the state convention did not ratify, by a vote of 101 to 7, the permanent Constitution of the Confederacy until March 21, 1861. Louisiana transferred to the Confederate government full use of all fortifications, military supplies, revenue cutters, and former possessions of the United States seized by the state. Prior to ratification, Secretary of War Walker had asked Governor Moore for seventeen hundred men to be used with other southern troops to garrison forts seized by other states. Louisiana's legislature went a step further. It authorized the governor to transfer both troops and military supplies to the central government, and permitted

24. *Ibid.*; Faust (ed.), *HTI*, 89–90.

25. *ORA*, LIII, 668, Moore to Walker and Davis, April 13, 1861.

26. *ORN*, Ser. 2, II, 41–42, 76, Rousseau *et al.* to Conrad, February 21, and Mallory's Report, July 19, 1861.

Louisiana citizens to volunteer for Confederate service. After Major Walde-mar Hyllested left New Orleans with four companies of Zouaves to de-fend Pensacola, Moore discovered he had left New Orleans temporarily un-protected and vulnerable to Union attack.[27]

Realizing the danger, the governor ordered that no additional troops could be spared from the state and rushed Captain Johnson K. Duncan's artillery company downriver to garrison Forts Jackson and St. Philip. But the Confederate army's appetite for troops continued to grow. Lin-coln had turned away the Confederate peace commission's attempt to com-promise national differences, and in Charleston harbor Beauregard had heavy guns pivoted to fire upon Fort Sumter if the Union garrison did not withdraw. Davis felt obliged to protect the South from northern aggres-sion, and on April 8 asked Moore for an additional three thousand troops.[28]

The governor choked on the request, and New Orleans grumbled over the departure of more of its sons. Moore received information that Union warships had left New York, and he warned Walker they were headed for New Orleans. "The forts can be passed," he wrote. "We are disorganized, and have no general officer to command and direct. I doubt the policy of drain-ing this place of troops to be sent to Pensacola. They are needed here." Walker replied curtly that President Davis "is entirely satisfied that the fleet is not intended for any demonstration on New Orleans. . . . Either send troops at once to Pensacola or call out volunteers . . . to fill the req-uisition."[29]

Despite a flood of local protests, the Orleans Cadets and the 1st Louisiana Regulars, commanded by Colonel Adley H. Gladden, embarked for Florida. A week later they were followed by the Louisiana Battalion, comprising the Caddo Greys, Crescent Rifles, Louisiana Guards, and Grivot Guards. With bands playing and people cheering, the troops left in high spirits, in-fused with optimism. They would teach the Yankees a harsh lesson. Mat-ters would be settled in "sixty days." Governor Moore saw them off and called for new volunteers to fill his depleted ranks.[30]

    27. *ORA*, LIII, 668, Moore to Walker, Mar. 28, 1861; Bragg, *Louisiana in the Confederacy*, 43–46; *Documents of the Second Session of the Fifth Legislature of the State of Louisiana, 1861*, 113; *Official Journal of the Louisiana Convention*, March 21, 25, 26, 1861; Van D. Odom, "The Political Career of Thomas Overton Moore, Secession Governor of Louisiana," *Louisiana Historical Quarterly*, XXVI (October, 1943), 1005–1006.

    28. *ORA*, Ser. 4, I, 213, Hooper to Moore, April 9, 1861.

    29. *ORA*, LIII, 669–70, Moore to Walker, April 10, and Walker to Moore, April 11, 1861.

    30. Odom, "Political Career of Moore," 1006; "Historical Militia Data on Louisiana Militia," April 1–20, 1861, p. 35, in Louisiana and Lower Mississippi Historical Collections, Louisiana State University, Baton Rouge; New Orleans *Bee*, March 29, April 18, 19, 20, 1861.

Enlistments went slowly until the morning of April 12, when Beauregard opened his guns on Fort Sumter. For a day and a half, shot and shell tore bricks off the old bastion in Charleston harbor. Finally, on April 14, Major Robert J. Anderson gave up all hope of reinforcements or supplies and surrendered. On April 15, President Lincoln reacted to the attack by calling for seventy-five thousand volunteers. The following day, Jefferson Davis asked the Confederate states to furnish thirty-two thousand infantry, and Governor Moore received an order to supply another five thousand men.[31]

Irregular companies from hunting and political clubs and from civic organizations, and planters and old men, almost entirely armed with their own weapons, banded together to protect their homes and began drilling in earnest. Some units hired drillmasters to turn raw volunteers into stalwart soldiers. But when Moore tried to muster them into the Confederate army for service outside of the state, they resigned from their units and joined the state militia. Men who chose to serve in the Confederate army marched to Camp Walker, the old Metairie Racecourse at New Orleans, pitched their tents on marshy soil, and waited for an officer to arrive and muster them in. Surrounded by swamps choked with rank vegetation growing along ditches that carried away the sewage of New Orleans, the new citizen-soldiers found conditions cruelly unlike those at home. Daily drill, guard duty, and new military duties were attended by a constant swarm of mosquitoes that attacked day and night. Heavy rains turned the camp into a quagmire, and heavily loaded wagon teams left the track a soupy, black, larva-infested morass. Within a week, three thousand men piled into camp, shuffled through the mud, and fell sick. Moore's patience was running short. He wrote War Secretary Walker on April 22, "If you do not authorize the mustering of the companies under your call they will disband. They are restless and Louisiana cannot support them in camp. . . . Answer without delay."[32]

Four days later, Moore sent an officer to the Baton Rouge arsenal with requisitions for weapons to arm his volunteers, but Captain John C. Booth refused to fill them. When the officer returned to the governor's mansion empty-handed, Moore exploded. After all, it was his men who had captured the arsenal. Off went another angry letter to Walker: "I want enough [rifles] to arm all volunteers called for and some for the city, and must have them. Telegraph officer to let me have them, with the proper supply

31. *ORA*, Ser. 4, I, 219–20, Walker to Moore, April 16, 1861.

32. *ORA*, LIII, 675, Moore to Walker, April 22, 1861.

of cartridges. Otherwise I cannot send men off unarmed." Walker complied, assuring the governor there was "no need of any excitement. Whatever the arsenal contains is for the defense of the country."[33]

Militia Brigadier General Elisha L. Tracy, in nominal charge of Camp Walker, splattered about in the mud each day, raving about poor sanitation, the scarcity of supplies, a lack of arms, and the physical inadequacy of the camp for the undisciplined troops, who grew in number each day. A veteran of the Mexican War, this feisty little man had never seen such chaos in a military camp. To handle the overflow of recruits, Camp Lewis, a few miles from New Orleans, was prepared for occupation, but conditions there were not much better. Finally, on May 13, Tracy received orders to move his men to Camp Moore, a fresh, clean, carefully prepared campsite in the piny woods of upland St. Helena Parish, about seventy-eight miles north of New Orleans, but Moore retained Colonel Louis Hébert and the 3rd Regiment Louisiana Volunteers at Camp Walker to keep the city protected from the unexpected. Within a few months, Louisiana had a force in the field of 23,577 men.[34]

By May 31, when Major General David E. Twiggs arrived to take command of Department No. 1, consisting of Louisiana and the southern portions of Mississippi and Alabama, the troops were already in motion to serve in brigades being formed elsewhere. The Washington Artillery had left for Virginia, sent off by salvos from old 32-pounders, the blare of brass bands, and cheering crowds. The 13th Louisiana passed through New Orleans on its way to Tennessee, looking natty in brilliant red caps and baggy trousers as it marched up the gangplank. When the steamboat pulled into the current and headed upriver, people waved from the levee, bells tolled, and steam whistles hooted until the vessel slipped out of sight. One by one, regiments left the state, each more than 1,000 strong, off to fight a war that had not yet started but could no longer be avoided.

Twiggs, the ranking general in the South at the time, settled into comfortable quarters in New Orleans and gathered a staff of cronies. The people of New Orleans would have preferred to have General Beauregard, their native son, in command, or even General Bragg, who knew less about the river than Beauregard but more about everything else than Twiggs. But

33. *Ibid.*, 675–76, Moore to Walker, Walker to Moore, April 26, 1861.

34. *ORA*, Ser. 4, I, 752, Grivot to Moore, November 22, 1861; *ORA*, LIII, 679–80, Grivot Order No. 330, May 12, 1861; William Watson, *Life in the Confederate Army: Being the Observations and Experiences of an Alien in the South During the American Civil War* (New York, 1888), 127, 141–42; Winters, *Civil War in Louisiana*, 22.

the only general officer Walker could spare was Twiggs, a man seventy-one years old, physically infirm, and often unable to leave his quarters. He was too old for the demands of his command. For a while he met his enlistment quotas by enjoying a little momentum from the governor's efforts. By summer, Louisiana had placed eight thousand men in active service outside the state, four thousand were being trained at Camp Moore, five thousand men were encamped around New Orleans, and new companies were still forming.[35]

But Forts Jackson and St. Philip and the lower Mississippi defenses needed attention, and time was starting to run out.

35. *ORA*, LIII, 739, Roman to Davis, September 15, 1861; New Orleans *Bee*, May 26, 1861; William Miller Owen, *In Camp and Battle with the Washington Artillery of New Orleans* (Boston, 1885), 10–12; Bartlett, *A Soldier's Story*, 116–21; Faust (ed.), *HTI*, 767.

THREE *Mr. Lincoln's "Impudent" Blockade*

On April 17, 1861, the day following President Davis' call for thirty-two thousand infantry, the Confederate president issued a proclamation "inviting all those who may desire, by service in private armed vessels on the high seas, to aid this Government in resisting so wanton and wicked an aggression, to make application for . . . letters of marque and reprisal to be issued under the seal of the Confederate States." The act, issued on May 21, enabled a private citizen to arm a vessel, attack Union commerce, and upon a valuation made by a board of appointed naval officers, collect 20 percent of the value of every enemy vessel captured or destroyed. Since the government had no money for the purpose, payments were to be in the form of 8 percent interest-bearing bonds of the Confederate States.[1]

On April 19, annoyed by Davis' call for privateers, Lincoln countered with a proclamation establishing a blockade of southern ports: "An act of insurrection against the Government of the United States has broken out . . . and the laws of the United States for the collection of revenue cannot be effectively executed therein. Now, therefore, I, Abraham Lincoln . . . , deem it advisable to set on foot a blockade. . . . For this purpose a competent force will be posted so as to prevent entrance and exit." The ports under blockade were those in South Carolina, Georgia, Florida, Alabama, Mississippi, Louisiana, and Texas. Lincoln warned that any privateer molesting "a vessel of the United States, or the persons or cargo aboard of her," would be subject to punishment for "piracy." A week later, Virginia se-

---

1. *ORN*, V, 796–97, Davis Proclamation, April 17, 1861; *ORA*, Ser. 4, I, 264, Davis Report to Congress, April 29, 1861; *ORN*, Ser. 2, II, 61–63, Congressional Enactment, May 14, 21, 1861.

ceded, followed by North Carolina on May 20, and Lincoln added them to the list.[2]

Davis considered the proclamation an astonishing document. The North had only forty-two vessels available and in commission to blockade more than thirty-five hundred miles of coastline. Another twenty-seven vessels were available but not in commission, and beyond that, twenty-one vessels were not serviceable, including nine ships of the line and three frigates. All told, the ships on the United States' list came to just ninety. Davis believed that the announcement of a "mere paper blockade" violated international law, and considered it incredible "that it could have been issued by authority." He expressed outrage over Lincoln's threat to punish privateers as pirates, since privateering had been an important and effective naval strategy against British commercial shipping during the Revolution and the War of 1812.[3]

Davis received some support for his criticism of Lincoln's blockade from an unexpected source, Gideon Welles, Lincoln's own secretary of the navy. In a cabinet meeting on April 14, 1861, Welles argued that the government was engaged in putting down an insurrection, not a foreign war, inasmuch as the coastline to be blockaded was not foreign territory but an integral part of the Union. He warned Lincoln that if a blockade were proclaimed, foreign powers would extend belligerent rights to the Confederacy. He tacitly recognized that, with only about fifty ships available, he could not interdict Confederate commerce. Britain and France would flout the blockade, and the United States would be able to do little to stop them without risk of drawing both powers into an expanded naval conflict.

Welles suggested that a better policy would be to proclaim southern ports "closed." Under municipal law, the Union navy would be empowered to seize any vessel attempting to enter a closed port and could prosecute violators as smugglers. Although Welles had boned up on international law to make his point, he may have overstated his case. He convinced most of the cabinet that the United States would look ridiculous in the eyes of the world if it announced a blockade of its own ports. Lincoln and Secretary of State William Seward agreed with Welles that Great Britain and France would in all likelihood grant belligerent status to the Confederacy, but un-

2. *ORN*, IV, 156–57, 340, Lincoln's Proclamation, April 19, 27, 1861.
3. James R. Soley, *The Blockade and the Cruisers* (New York, 1883), App. A, 241–43; *ORA*, Ser. 4, I, 264, Davis to Congress, April 29, 1861.

like Welles, they believed European powers would remain watchfully neutral. With the policy of blockade formalized, Welles had no choice but to deploy his ships and begin to build his navy.[4]

The fifty-eight-year-old Welles had spent much of his life as a Hartford newspaper editor, a Democrat, and a postmaster. He had held minor political offices, including a short stint as head of the Naval Bureau of Provisions and Clothing during the Mexican War. In 1854, he became a Republican and worked for Lincoln's election. Although untrained in naval matters, Lincoln recognized Welles's administrative abilities and considered him capable of evaluating and molding public opinion. By temperament, Welles was a combination of stubborn righteousness and hard-bitten practicality, mixed with devotion to duty and a penchant for thrift. He was slender but with a large face and a heavy cleft chin that he covered with a white flowing beard. He wore spectacles, something his photographs seldom revealed, which gave him an elderly appearance, but he was well known for his energy, both mental and physical. Known as Father Neptune, he gave balance to the cabinet. Lincoln did not always agree with him, but he always listened.[5]

Nonetheless, Lincoln recognized Welles's deficiency in naval experience and provided him with a capable assistant, thirty-nine-year-old Gustavus Vasa Fox. Fox had spent nearly twenty years in the navy before resigning to become an agent for Bay State Mills. Early in 1861, his powerful brother-in-law, Montgomery Blair, invited him to the White House to consult on the Fort Sumter crisis. Fox proposed to resupply the fort by sending steam-powered vessels past Charleston's harbor batteries at night, but President Buchanan vetoed the plan. When Lincoln took office he liked Fox's ideas and sent him to Charleston to seek a solution to the mounting tensions.

At 3 A.M. on Friday, April 12, Fox arrived at his rendezvous off Charleston harbor and waited for daylight. At 4:30, Beauregard opened his bombardment upon Fort Sumter from all sides. Fox watched in dismay from his position ten miles off the harbor as shells arced across the still-dark western skies and plummeted toward the fort. At six o'clock, Fox went aboard

---

4. "The Interdiction of Commerce and the Insurgent States," in Gideon Welles Papers, Library of Congress; Welles to Lincoln, August 5, 1861, in Abraham Lincoln Papers, Library of Congress; Stuart L. Bernath, *Squall Across the Atlantic: American Civil War Prize Cases and Diplomacy* (Berkeley and Los Angeles, 1970), 18–21; New York *Times*, April 20, 1861; John Niven, *Gideon Welles: Lincoln's Secretary of the Navy* (New York, 1973), 355–57.

5. Niven, *Welles*, 3–4, 303–23; Faust (ed.), *HTI*, 813; Richard S. West, Jr., *Mr. Lincoln's Navy* (New York and London, 1957), 15–16.

USS *Pawnee* and told Captain Stephen C. Rowan that in spite of the shelling, he was going to land provisions. He asked for naval support, but Rowan refused to risk his vessel on the whim of a civilian. Early the next morning, *Pocahontas* arrived—just in time to witness Major Robert J. Anderson's surrender. Fox went into the harbor under a flag of truce and had the ignominious task of transporting the major and his men back to New York. Though Fox's peace-keeping effort failed, Lincoln had warmed to the man, recognized his talent, and offered him the post of assistant secretary of the navy. At first, Welles felt Fox had been thrust upon him, which was true, and he resented Lincoln's interference, but little time passed before the secretary admitted that his assistant was indispensable.[6]

Welles, a good listener who studied a situation before taking action, found Fox the opposite. No two people could have been more different. Welles was soft voiced, thoughtful, and abstemious; Fox was flamboyant, outgoing, impatient, often brusque, and excessive in his enjoyment of rich food and good wine. Father Neptune brought to a social gathering the solemnity of a Puritan prayer meeting. Fox gave it vibrancy and color. Where Welles laid his cards on the table, Fox played his close to the vest. The relationship worked because Welles knew the president wanted it to work.

While Welles and Fox adjusted to each other's idiosyncrasies and puzzled over implementing the blockade, newspapers in London printed Lincoln's proclamation and then Davis' call for privateers. For a while, Prime Minister Lord Palmerston and Foreign Minister Lord John Russell, both of them participants at the highest levels of government for more than thirty years, wondered what the talk of war meant for Great Britain. For the moment, textile mills in the Midlands had warehouses full of raw cotton. So what if Charleston, Savannah, Mobile, and New Orleans were sealed off from commerce, and both imports and exports stopped? But almost before official word reached London from Washington, British vessels were being stopped by Union warships and warned away from southern ports.

On May 6, Lord Russell told the House of Commons that, after consultation with law officers, he believed both the Confederate and United States governments had to be treated as belligerents, and on May 14, Great Britain issued a proclamation of neutrality that acknowledged the exis-

---

6. Robert M. Thompson and Richard Wainwright (eds.), *Confidential Correspondence of Gustavus Vasa Fox, Assistant Secretary of the Navy, 1861–1865* (2 vols.; New York, 1920), I, 32–33; Faust (ed.), *HTI*, 283. Montgomery Blair became Lincoln's postmaster general.

tence of a civil war and, as Welles had warned, granted both entities belligerent rights. Other maritime powers, including France, the Netherlands, Spain, and Brazil, followed in short order with similar announcements.[7]

Although the conceding of belligerent rights fell short of full recognition, the Confederate government was justified in celebrating its progress on the diplomatic front. Among other things, its privateers had won the status of lawfully commissioned vessels, though they were interdicted from carrying their prizes into the waters of neutral countries or their colonies. Davis considered such interdiction unreasonable, because the South had no navy to protect its ports. Once the coast came under blockade, as far off in the future as that might be, privateers would be unable to return home with prizes and eventually would be stopped from getting to sea.

In the meantime, the Confederate naval secretary was joined in a mobilization race with his Union counterpart. Mallory had to keep important ports open for trade and commerce raiding, and Welles had to build a navy capable of closing over thirty-five hundred miles of coastline, including 180 harbors and navigable inlets. In the spring of 1861, each seemed asked to do the impossible.

On April 21, Mallory received good news and Welles bad. Virginians had captured the Gosport Naval Yard, at Norfolk. Union efforts to destroy the yard had been hasty. The Federals left behind ships, shops, a dry dock, and huge stocks of heavy naval ordnance in repairable condition. There were enough guns to fortify coastal defenses all the way from Virginia to Forts Jackson and St. Philip and up the Mississippi River to Memphis and beyond. The capture of Gosport Navy Yard took pressure off New Orleans as the Confederacy's principal shipbuilding site.

While Welles studied ways to blockade the four outlets of the Mississippi, some of the more enterprising shipyards in New Orleans turned their attention to fitting out privateers. Owners of vessels that could have been converted for river defense besieged the Confederate capital with applications for letters of marque and reprisal. Investors entered into partnerships to buy fast steamers and cash in on the profits from privateering. In the search for vessels, the Committee on Naval Affairs found itself in direct competition with wealthy Orleanian entrepreneurs who were swamping the best shipyards with work.

When the steamer *Calhoun*, a converted 509-ton towboat, captured the bark *Ocean Eagle*, out of Rockland, Maine, with 3,144 casks of lime valued

7. Allan Nevins, *The War for the Union* (2 vols.; New York, 1960), II, ch. 10; Warren F. Spencer, *The Confederate Navy in Europe* (University, Ala., 1983), 10; Scharf, *Confederate Navy*, 55–56.

at twenty-four thousand dollars, New Orleans greeted the prize crew with cheers. The *Calhoun* stayed at sea and captured two more enemy merchant ships in the Gulf, the 699-ton ship *Milan*, on her way from London to New Orleans with fifteen hundred sacks of salt, and the 92-ton schooner *Ella*, traveling from Tampico to Pensacola with a cargo of fruit.

Almost immediately, three more privateers went to sea: the 273-ton *Music*, the 454-ton *V. H. Ivy*, and the 655-ton *William H. Webb*, all lightly armed steamers with crews ranging from fifty to a hundred men. The little *Music* scored but one prize, *John H. Jarvis*, which she found lying at anchor opposite the telegraph station on Pass à l'Outre. With several armed privateersmen, Captain Stephen C. McLelland stepped on board, flourished his letters of marque, and took possession of the ship and 2,980 sacks of salt "in the name of Jefferson Davis." *Webb* stalked and captured three Massachusetts whalers ninety miles off the passes. *Ivy* did even better, capturing four large, valuable merchant ships in the Gulf, one being the 387-ton *Enoch Train*, which speculators immediately bought and converted into another privateer. Within a week, New Orleans privateers hauled in eleven prizes worth about $120,000.[8]

Despite euphoria in New Orleans, privateering ended almost as abruptly as it had started. British consul William A. Mure received word that a blockade of the passes would begin about May 25 and advised local authorities in New Orleans that neutral vessels there must leave in fifteen days or risk capture. Nobody gave the information much thought until the afternoon of May 27, when the 2,070-ton *Brooklyn*, armed with twenty-two 9-inch guns, dropped anchor off Pass à l'Outre and her commander, Charles H. Poor, dispatched a boat to Fort Jackson to inform Major Johnson K. Duncan, the commander there, that the Mississippi was officially under blockade. Three days later Poor captured the bark *H. E. Spearing* as she sailed innocently toward the pass and seized her cargo of Brazilian coffee, worth $120,000. With a single prize, the United States navy had matched the value of all vessels and cargoes captured by New Orleans privateers.

While stationed off Pass à l'Outre, Poor observed that vessels had great difficulty getting over the bar. At one point forty merchantmen, among

8. *ORN*, Ser. 2, I, 350–51, 382–83, Register of Commissions, and Stevenson to Hunter; New Orleans *Daily Delta*, May 17, 20, 23, 28, 1861; New Orleans *Daily Crescent*, May 18, 1861; Frank Lawrence Owsley, *King Cotton Diplomacy* (Chicago, 1931), 32, 36, 43–47, 90–91, 146–47. For the cruise of the New Orleans privateers, see William M. Robinson, Jr., *The Confederate Privateers* (New Haven, 1928), 35–47.

them several American ships, had run aground on the constantly shifting mud. Poor, in a meeting with Confederate officials, agreed not to interfere with river tugs pulling the stranded traders out to sea. By June 15, most of the vessels were over the bar, and the tugs disappeared upriver. What Poor had learned about the bar was to be invaluable, however, to another Union commander almost a year later.

Brooklyn, with her sixteen-foot draft, did not even try to cross the bar, although Poor's lookouts could observe the smoke of several tempting targets waiting two or three miles upriver. For two months one heavily laden English ship remained fast in the mud, and Poor did not wish to join her. Three other passes remained unguarded, two to the south and the other to the west. Nobody in the Union navy yet knew whether those outlets had channels deep enough to allow heavy warships to cross into the river.[9]

Another commander who was later to play an important role in the unfolding drama on the Mississippi was forty-seven-year-old Lieutenant David Dixon Porter, skipper of the 2,415-ton *Powhatan,* a fast but aged side-wheeler carrying one 11-inch and ten 9-inch Dahlgren smoothbores and five 12-pounders. On May 29, on his way to blockade Southwest Pass, Porter overhauled the schooner *Mary Clinton,* bound to her home port of New Orleans from Charleston. He discovered that the schooner had been warned off the southern coast a few days earlier by USS *Niagara.* Porter placed a crew on the vessel and sent the ship and her cargo of foodstuffs to New York for adjudication. There would be prize money for him and the crew, one of the rewards of war even when it is against your brethren.[10]

Porter came from a family steeped in naval tradition. His famous father, Commodore David Porter, had distinguished himself in the War of 1812 as the young navy's greatest commerce raider. David Dixon Porter went to sea with his father at the age of ten, mastered the profession, and chafed for action, but advancement came slowly in the peacetime navy. He was of medium height and small boned but wiry and energetic. His hair, like his eyes, was dark brown, and for most of his naval career he wore a medium black beard, sometimes short, often long and scruffy. He was ambitious, outspoken, and politically astute, and in some ways quite like his friend Fox, the assistant secretary of the navy. Just prior to the war, Porter had planned to leave the navy and use his talents in the lucrative Pacific

9. *ORN,* Ser. 2, I, 60, Statistical Data of U.S. Ships; *ORN,* IV, 187–88, 190–91, 193–94, Poor to Welles, May 29, 30, and Porter to Welles, June 1, 1861.

10. *ORN,* IV, 188–89, 208, Porter to Welles, May 30, 1861, and Log of *Powhatan; ORN,* Ser. 2, I, 183, Statistical Data of U.S. Ships.

packet trade. The secession crisis changed his mind, and on April 1, 1861, he eagerly took command of *Powhatan*. He was to see much of the Mississippi Valley during the four-year war.[11]

Porter and Poor had similar problems in trying to guard thirty-five miles of water day and night, often with fires banked to conserve coal and with crew allotments sized for peacetime operations. Every captured prize further depleted the crew, and every chase burned up coal. Porter had been at sea for fifty-four days without recoaling and would soon, he wrote, "only be able to lie at the bar like a sailing ship." From his position off Southwest Pass, he ventured westward as far as Atchafalaya Bay, where he observed shallow-draft blockade runners bringing cargoes into the town of Berwick, from which they were shipped by train to New Orleans. Small schooners hugged the shore, slipped through Caminada Pass, and ran cargoes into Barataria. The traffic was constant, but too far inshore to stop.

On the opposite side of the Delta and north of Pass à l'Outre, Poor observed schooners and light steamers moving along the coast from Mississippi Sound and passing inside Ship Island into Lake Pontchartrain. He and Porter both wrote Welles asking for at least two armed vessels at each of the Mississippi's four outlets, and shallow-draft gunboats to stop the coastal trade that continued to flourish within a crescent 120 miles long.[12]

The sudden arrival of *Powhatan* at Southwest Pass, the only other deep channel, surprised New Orleans, and especially the shippers who were still loading cotton on neutral vessels waiting their turn along the city's levee. No one had expected a second Union warship that soon. For many shippers, business had continued to flow through the other passes. On May 30, Porter gave Confederate authorities at Pilottown the customary fifteen-day period of grace to allow vessels of foreign register to depart for their home ports. When word reached New Orleans, skippers tripped their mooring lines and made a frantic rush for the Gulf of Mexico. So hurried were their departures that dozens of vessels plowed into the muddy bars off Southwest Pass and remained stuck for weeks. The congestion became so bad that Porter could not differentiate between a Confederate privateer hiding among the stranded vessels, waiting to escape to sea, and a legitimate neutral legally leaving port. Within three hundred yards of *Powhatan* lay a forest of tall-masted vessels stuck side by side and so askew

11. Faust (ed.), *HTI*, 594.
12. *ORN*, IV, 187–89, 193–94, Poor to Welles, May 29, and Porter to Welles, May 30, June 1, 1861.

their riggings had become entangled. To make matters worse, incoming ships carrying immigrants ran aground as they tried to thread their way through the mired vessels, forcing Porter to supply food from his own scant larder.

When Pilottown officials asked permission to lend their tugs to the attempt to free the neutrals from the bar, Porter agreed, provided that the same assistance went to vessels registered to the United States. In a few weeks both passes cleared, but Porter learned later that some Confederate tugs, after hauling northern vessels across the bar, recaptured them and towed them back to New Orleans as prizes.[13]

Porter stopped several vessels heading to sea with cargoes of cotton. They were manned by southern captains and crews, but their owners had secured British registry from the local consul. Wondering whether to take them as prizes, he wrote Welles asking for instructions. The naval secretary referred the question to Salmon P. Chase, the secretary of the treasury, who eventually decided that the navy might take vessels of British registry only in the rare instance that collusion could be proved in admiralty court. By then, all the vessels were off the bar and gone.[14]

Between Pass à l'Outre and Southwest Pass, enough water remained open for shallow-draft Confederate steamers to ease through the two smaller passes. For a while privateers continued to operate, but without the assurance of being able to bring their prizes into port and collect their prize money. New Orleans began to feel the pinch but not the squeeze. That would come later.

General David E. Twiggs, commanding Department No. 1, learned that Union sympathizers and Delta farmers were furnishing "Black Republican blockading vessels" with fresh fruit, fish, vegetables, meat, and local newspapers. He directed that all boats passing downriver beyond Fort Jackson or by Fort Pike, which guarded the Rigolets entrance to the Mississippi Sound, were to be stopped and searched. Newspapers were to be thrown overboard and excess food confiscated. Any person observed communicating with the enemy was to be arrested and prosecuted.[15]

In New Orleans, Thomas K. Wharton scratched in his diary, "The blockade at the mouth of the River has been commenced by the War Steamer *Brooklyn!* We must take her." Still, nobody in authority seemed to grasp

---

13. *ORN,* XVI, 528–29, Poor to Welles, June 7, 1861; Richard S. West, Jr., *The Second Admiral: A Life of David Dixon Porter, 1813–1891* (New York, 1937), 91.

14. *ORN,* XVI, 570, Welles to Mervine, July 3, 1861; *ORN,* V, 759–61, Chase to Welles, June 27, 1861.

15. Winters, *Civil War in Louisiana,* 47.

that necessity or voice any degree of urgency about eliminating the threat. Was it possible to capture the *Brooklyn?* Wharton thought so. But on the lower Mississippi innovative thinking and fast action still lay dormant.[16]

Raphael Semmes also felt the pinch. He had spent the previous six weeks attempting to convert the packet steamer *Habana* into the first Confederate cruiser. "My patience is sorely tried by the mechanics," he wrote. "The water-tanks for the *Sumter* are not yet completed. . . . Carriages for the 32-pounders are promised by Saturday next, and also the copper tanks for the magazines. Our ammunition and small arms arrived yesterday from Baton Rouge. Besides *the Brooklyn,* we learn today that the *Niagara,* and *Minnesota,* two of the enemy's fastest and heaviest steamships, have arrived to . . . lie in wait for some ships expected to arrive, laden with arms and ammunition for the Confederacy." Semmes pressed hard to get to sea while he still could.[17]

When Welles sent two more of the navy's heaviest ships to blockade the remaining passes of the Mississippi, he was employing his resources wisely. One of the world's busiest ports, New Orleans was second only to New York in the volume of commerce. River trade had reached a peak in 1860, and thirty-three different steamship lines shuttled goods and passengers to and from the city. Between river traffic and ocean trade, goods worth nearly $500 million passed through New Orleans in 1860. After the blockade was established, annual receipts dropped to $51,510,990.[18]

The little 520-ton *Sumter,* with her seven guns, was no match for any of the Union vessels, and the arrival of the 52-gun, 3,307-ton *Minnesota* and the 32-gun 4,582-ton *Niagara* reduced her chances of escape. All four Federal vessels stationed themselves just off the bars, elevated their long Toms to eighteen degrees, and let fly a fifteen-second shell every time a lookout spotted smoke near the mouth of an outlet. As each day passed, Semmes grew more impatient, confiding to his journal, "We are losing a great deal of precious time. The enemy's flag is being flaunted in our faces, at all our ports by his ships of war, and his vessels of commerce are passing and repassing on the ocean, in defiance, or in contempt of our power, and as yet, we have not struck a blow."[19]

16. Thomas Kelah Wharton Diary, May 27, 1861, Manuscript Division, New York Public Library.

17. *ORN,* I, 691–92, Journal of *Sumter;* Raphael Semmes, *Memoirs of Service Afloat During the War Between the States* (Baltimore, 1869), 103.

18. Henry Rightor (ed.), *Standard History of New Orleans, Louisiana* (Chicago, 1890), 566–71; Winters, *Civil War in Louisiana,* 46.

19. Semmes, *Service Afloat,* 104.

Every morning that Semmes sent the former privateer *Ivy* down South-west Pass to check on the presence of *Powhatan*, Porter watched the smoke and itched for an opportunity to relieve the boredom of blockade duty. *Ivy* developed a pattern. In the evening she hovered a mile or two upriver from the telegraph station at Pilottown to keep an eye on the pass. Semmes expected Porter or Poor to send boats up one or the other pass and try to board *Sumter*—and that was exactly what Porter had in mind.

On the night of June 27, Lieutenant Watson Smith shoved off from *Powhatan* with thirty-five men and rowed toward shore. The party kept close to the dark alluvial bank and landed in the shadows a short distance from the Confederate telegraph station at Pilottown. They struck the station from all sides, captured the telegraph operator, and cut the wires. Then, according to Porter's orders, the men hid their boat and waited for *Ivy*'s morning run. But *Ivy* did not come, not that day or any of the next three, for when the telegraph station failed to respond, Semmes suspected what had happened.

Three days passed before a Confederate mail steamer crept downriver, cautiously tying up opposite the telegraph station. Smith loaded sixteen men into the bottom of an old boat, hoisted sail, and started across the river. As he tacked to come abeam and board, the skipper of the mail steamer, having taken one horrified look at the approaching boatload of sailors, cut his lines and fled upriver under full steam. "My intention," wrote Porter, "was to seize the *Ivy*, put 200 men in her at once, carry the *Sumter* by boarding, and proceed to New Orleans under the disguise of the se-cession flag, and burn the *Star of the West*. The only thing that prevented this was the want of one more minute of time, for the boarding was almost accomplished." [20]

After waiting nearly two weeks at Head of Passes for a chance to es-cape, Semmes finally got *Sumter* to sea on June 30, when *Brooklyn* left her post to chase a sail. Even with an eight-mile head start, all sail set, and the boilers close to bursting, he barely escaped capture. When Poor spotted *Sumter* crossing the bar, he wheeled *Brooklyn* around for a long-stern chase. Only by maneuvering to cheat *Brooklyn* out of wind did Semmes make good his escape. The first Confederate raider was loose at sea. [21]

20. *ORN*, XVI, 571–72, Porter to Mervine, July 4, 1861. *Star of the West* was a large steamer captured by the Confederates at Indianola, Texas, and taken to New Orleans. Porter believed it was being armed with two 68-pounders and four 32-pounders and would cause trouble (*ibid.*, 563). The Confederate navy renamed it CSS *St. Philip*.

21. *ORN*, I, 694, Journal of *Sumter*; Semmes, *Service Afloat*, 117–18; David Dixon Porter, *The Naval History of the Civil War* (New York, 1886), 605–606.

Poor apologized for not overhauling *Sumter,* explaining that he observed the vessel standing down the river while he was preparing to board a suspicious bark several miles away. After three and a half hours, he broke off the chase when he spotted another sail heading for Pass à l'Outre. Poor was lucky. The war was still young, and he did not get the reprimand he deserved. A naval officer never breaks off a chase as long as the enemy is in sight, since a change in wind or a mechanical breakdown can quickly alter the fortunes of the fleeing ship. *Sumter* cruised for six months, captured seventeen vessels, burned seven, bonded two, and caused Secretary Welles and his navy countless hours of pursuit, frustration, and embarrassment.[22]

Semmes, who knew both Porter and Poor from the old navy, made the right decision in choosing to be chased by *Brooklyn.* Porter was tenacious. He would have dogged Semmes until all his coal was burned or his engines failed. *Powhatan* was faster than *Brooklyn,* but for some reason Semmes believed the opposite. Still, both Union vessels were faster than *Sumter.* Semmes simply outsailed *Brooklyn.*

Porter, always quick to condemn a fellow officer, wrote, "Commander Poor was by no means a staunch loyalist, and actions since the escape of the 'Sumpter' have given no proof of energy or zeal in the cause of the Union. He has never, to my knowledge, been under fire nor has he sought in any instance, to place himself where he could do the government the least service."

Porter disliked blockade duty, especially when living conditions off Southwest Pass worsened. As summer wore on, afternoon winds blew swarms of mosquitoes out of the marshes to wing their way to the ship. Evening rainsqualls, accompanied by howling winds and violent thunderstorms, temporarily beat down the mosquitoes and drove away the heat but left the passes in a dense fog, blotting out everything from sight. Lookouts hugged the tops, scanning across the milky film for the telltale signs of smoke or for the crosstree of a runner snaking its way to sea.

Here, on miserable blockade duty, a dejected Porter saw no opportunity for promotion. He had been a lieutenant since 1841, and his advancement to commander was years overdue. When a letter from his friend Fox arrived promising an increase in grade to the first naval officer who captured a fort, Porter wondered how he would ever get off blockade duty and earn that extra stripe. Somehow, he needed to position himself better for promotion. He would take the first offer thrown his way.[23]

22. *ORN,* I, 34, Poor to Mervine, June 30, 1861; Scharf, *Confederate Navy,* 817.

23. *ORN,* XVI, 643–44, Pope to Welles, August 22, 1861; Thompson and Wainwright (eds.), *Fox Correspondence,* II, 73–79.

Gideon Welles, U.S. Secretary of the Navy.
Courtesy National Archives

Gustavus Vasa Fox, U.S. Assistant Secretary of the Navy.
Courtesy National Archives

Admiral David Glasgow Farragut, U.S. Navy.
Courtesy U.S. Naval Photo Center

Rear Admiral David D. Porter, U.S. Navy, *ca.* 1863.
Courtesy Naval Historical Center

Major General Benjamin F. Butler, U.S. Army.
From *Battles and Leaders of the Civil War*

Rear Admiral Theodorus Bailey, U.S. Navy.
From *Battles and Leaders of the Civil War*

Rear Admiral Charles S. Boggs, U.S. Navy, commander of the *Varuna*.
Courtesy U.S. Military History Institute

Rear Admiral Thomas T. Craven, U.S. Navy, commander of the *Brooklyn*.
From *Battles and Leaders of the Civil War*

Commander James Alden, U.S. Navy. Courtesy U.S. Military History Institute

Judah P. Benjamin, Confederate Secretary of War.
Courtesy U.S. Military History Institute

Stephen R. Mallory, Confederate Secretary of the Navy.
Courtesy National Archives

Captain Raphael Semmes, Confederate Navy, commander of C.S.S. *Sumter*.
Courtesy U.S. Navy

Commander John K. Mitchell, Confederate Navy.
Courtesy U.S. Navy

Captain George Hollins, Confederate Navy.
Courtesy U.S. Navy

Lieutenant Thomas B. Huger, Confederate Navy, commander of *McRae*.
Courtesy U.S. Navy

Captain Beverley Kennon, Louisiana State Navy.
From *Battles and Leaders of the Civil War*

Major General David E. Twiggs, C.S.A.
Courtesy U.S. Army Military History Institute

General Pierre G. T. Beauregard, C.S.A. From *Battles and Leaders of the Civil War*

Major General Mansfield Lovell, C.S.A. From *Battles and Leaders of the Civil War*

Brigadier General Johnson K. Duncan, C.S.A.,
commander of Forts Jackson and St. Philip.
Courtesy U.S. Navy

Opportunity came when *Powhatan* recaptured one of Raphael Semmes's prizes, *Abby Bradford*, as the Confederate prize crew attempted to slip into Barataria. Porter interrogated each of Semmes's sailors, pieced their statements together, and reached surprisingly accurate conclusions. He convinced Flag Officer William Mervine that if given the chance, he could catch the "pirate." Porter loaded up with coal and tracked Semmes through the Caribbean, along the northern coast of Brazil to São Luis, Maranhão, and back up through the West Indies without ever seeing the wily Confederate commander. Porter, however, had not hurt his career. Welles detached him from the blockade and summoned him to Washington to discuss a strategy that could have a telling effect on New Orleans. But the visit to Washington still lay in the future, and the destiny of New Orleans had not yet been committed to the drawing board.[24]

On the upper watershed of the Mississippi, far from the passes, the United States mapped a plan to disrupt the free navigation of the river. On May 8, as the first Union warships were being dispatched to the mouth of the Mississippi, the squeeze on commerce started with the head of customs at Louisville, Kentucky, receiving orders to intercept all shipments of arms, ammunition, and provisions destined for points beyond, in the secession states.[25]

On May 10, the Confederate Congress reacted, passing a bill to sever all trade with the United States. It expected northern mills to be ruined for want of cotton. No cotton would be going to Great Britain or France, either. Europe had purchased its cotton through northern brokers, and the South hoped that what was on hand in Britain and France would soon run out. With those countries' enormous knitting industries at a standstill, it was believed that they would intercede in the war and dismantle the Union blockade to save their industry. To add substance to that forlorn hope, the Confederate Congress on May 20 passed a second act, which prohibited the exportation of cotton from any but southern and Mexican seaports, thereby creating a quasi embargo.

In July, 1861, cotton brokers in New Orleans asked growers to hold their cotton until the blockade was crushed, and early in the fall Governor Moore refused to allow more cotton to enter the city. Growers wanted

24. David Dixon Porter, "Private Journal of Occurrences During the Great War of the Rebellion, 1860–1865," Manuscript Division, Library of Congress, 109, 114, 116–21, 125–28; *ORN*, I, 65, 68–69, 78–80, 91–95, 103, 104, Porter to Welles, August 13, 19, September 24, October 10, and Porter to Mervine, October, 1861; West, *Second Admiral*, 103–11.

25. Scharf, *Confederate Navy*, 240; Alfred T. Mahan, *The Gulf and Inland Waters* (New York, 1883), 3–4.

their money and grumbled, but thinking the war could not last, and perhaps contemplating even greater profits in exchange for their patience, they held their crop. Large shipments stored in warehouses by the levee were withdrawn and moved back to plantations. On the whole, though, the cotton embargo harmed the South more than the North. The crop of 1860 had been unusually large, and both Great Britain and France had ample supplies of the raw product on hand.[26]

Through the summer of 1861, New Orleans began to feel the pinch of the blockade. People who held specie refused to part with it, and paper money flooded the market. Coffee rose to $1.25 a pound, and people began to drink cocoa as well as coffee substitutes made from dried and pulverized sweet potatoes. Red meat became scarce, but for a while chicken, fish, and shellfish remained plentiful. Shipments of grain dribbled in from the Midwest on fewer and fewer flatboats, and prices for flour soared. Thousands of laborers, out of work because of the growing trade paralysis, faced starvation, and those with savings could not afford necessities like soap, starch, fats, and candles. As the relief lines lengthened at the free market for the poor, young men and old enlisted in the army, knowing they would be fed and paid by the government, at least until the war decided their future.[27]

In mid-August, the *Picayune* credited the blockade with one hygienic benefit: "The health of the city was never in better condition at this season of the year. . . . Is the blockade of our ports the cause of the absence of yellow fever?" Wharton noted in his diary, "The impudent 'Lincoln Blockade' is acting in our favor by keeping out yellow fever." In trying times, people counted small blessings.[28]

New Orleanians felt the squeeze on their accustomed freedom, as well as on their wallets and stomachs, and with each passing month they wondered when something would be done to drive off the Union blockade. They looked to the Confederate navy and Captain Lawrence Rousseau for answers, but the old sailor seemed overwhelmed and stupefied by the magnitude of the problems. They worried about the safety of the city, knowing that General Twiggs was too infirm to visit the forts and on many

26. Winters, *Civil War in Louisiana*, 45.

27. Clara E. Solomon Diary, 1861–1862, Louisiana and Lower Mississippi Valley Collection, Louisiana State University, 1–132 *passim*; Bragg, *Louisiana in the Confederacy*, 76–77; George W. Cable, "New Orleans Before the Capture," in Robert Underwood Johnson and Clarence Clough Buel (eds.), *Battles and Leaders of the Civil War* (4 vols.; New York, 1887–88), II, 18. Hereinafter cited as *B&L*.

28. New Orleans *Daily Picayune*, August 13, 20, 1861; Wharton Diary, July 28, 1861.

days barely able to hobble into his office at City Hall. They sought military and naval protection and expected it to be arranged by Governor Moore, who deferred the matter to the central government. About military affairs, even the press turned circumspect, publishers wondering what, if anything, was happening behind the scenes. The people of New Orleans rejoiced when Beauregard and Joseph E. Johnston defeated the Union army at Manassas, and probably wished their Creole would come back: Beauregard got things done. But in New Orleans the citizens walked the streets, visited the rotting hulks at the wharves, rooted through the marketplace for bargains, attended church, and prayed that their city and their lives would not be destroyed by apathy.

FOUR   *Emergence of the Mosquito Fleet*

With four Union warships guarding the passes, Confederate privateering came to a standstill on the lower Mississippi. New Orleans businessmen who had invested large sums of money to convert steamships into privateers began looking for ways to recover their money. Shipping was no longer a safe alternative, except for flatboats running upriver to towns like Shreveport, Helena, Alexandria, Vicksburg, and Memphis. Small coasting vessels still sailed out of Lake Pontchartrain, passing through Mississippi Sound to enter Mobile Bay or make a midnight lunge for the shores of Cuba. From Barataria Bay, schooners followed the Texas coast all the way down to Brownsville and Matamoras. If chased, they ducked into inlets too shallow for Union vessels to follow. Trade remained vigorous, but on a scale too small to whet the appetites of big investors. The problem was the Union blockade.

While Naval Secretary Stephen B. Mallory and the ancient Captain Lawrence Rousseau considered their options, businessmen like John A. Stevenson (sometimes spelled Stephenson), a commission merchant, began to take matters into their own hands. On May 12, 1861, Stevenson opened subscription books at the Merchant's Exchange to raise $100,000, intending to buy and convert the steamer *Enoch Train*, captured by *Ivy*, into a seagoing privateer. He raised the money about the time *Brooklyn* appeared off Pass à l'Outre, and a few days before *Powhatan* reached Southwest Pass.

The presence of Union blockaders caused Stevenson to reconsider his plans. Even a strengthened and armed *Enoch Train* was no match for a Union warship, but there might be still greater rewards for Stevenson and his investors if the steamer could sink a few blockaders. Destroying just one warship like *Brooklyn,* valued at $500,000, would not only aid the Confederacy but return a tidy profit. That would mean modifying *Enoch Train* into a vessel capable of taking on the Union navy's best.

Stevenson, who was also the secretary of the New Orleans Pilots Benevolent Society, went to Montgomery to discuss his plans with Mallory. Two light-draft Union vessels had been reported in Northeast Pass (Balize) by General David E. Twiggs. Somebody had to clear them out, and Stevenson wanted approval—and pay—to do it. With encouragement from Mallory and Rousseau, Stevenson returned to New Orleans and set to converting *Enoch Train* into a sturdy, swift ironclad ram.[1]

Enoch Train had been built in Boston in 1855 by J. O. Curtis as a packet and passenger ship. To convert the vessel to an ironclad, Stevenson had to strip the ship and and remove all vestiges of her former lines. The length was expanded from 128 feet to 143 feet, beam from 26 feet to 33 feet, and depth from 12 feet 6 inches to 17 feet. Then Stevenson rebuilt the ship with massive seventeen-inch-thick beams, making a solid bow of twenty feet, fastened securely. Over this mass of heavy lumber workmen layered a covering of iron plates, riveted together and fitted to make the exposed portion of the vessel shotproof. The only entrance was through a trapdoor aft. Above the water the ship's lines resembled an elongated eggshell, shaped so a shot striking any point would carom off. Her back was formed of twelve-inch oak, covered with one and one-half-inch bar iron. Unlike many renditions of her appearance, the vessel had two stacks, not one, and both were designed to telescope down in time of action. Unfortunately, Stevenson located the pilothouse in the stern, partially obscuring the helmsman's vision. The engines, built by Harrison Loring of Boston, were quite powerful, but when the rebuilt *Enoch Train* was cut loose for the first time, she could barely stem the current.

As a precaution against boarding, the engine was provided with pumps for ejecting steam and scalding water from the boiler, but if used, this apparatus would reduce further the engine's efficiency during a fight. The ship's main weapon was an underwater iron ram designed by the owners to bash in the sides of Welles's wooden-hulled warships. She carried a single stationary 32-pounder carronade covered by a spring-back shutter in the bow, but the gun was a luxury and probably a nuisance to the crew.

1. *ORN,* Ser. 2, I, 48, Statistical Data for USS *Brooklyn*; *ORN,* XVI, 821, Twiggs to Walker, June 10, 1861; William Morrison Robinson, Jr., *The Confederate Privateers* (New Haven, 1928), 154–55; John S. Kendall, *History of New Orleans* (3 vols.; Chicago, 1922), I, 246.

The vessel would have been improved by removing the gun and moving the pilothouse forward.[2]

While work progressed on the ram at Algiers, Stevenson made every effort to keep the project secret. He succeeded for a while, but on July 11 the *National Intelligencer* reported that in New Orleans a powerful tugboat was being covered with railroad iron and would soon attack the blockaders at the mouth of the Mississippi. A week later a launch from *Powhatan* captured a pleasure party who claimed they had left New Orleans "to prevent being persuaded to enter the Army." Porter questioned them and on July 19 wrote Flag Officer Mervine: "The blockade here has put a stop . . . to fitting out privateers, of which there were twelve getting ready. One steamer only is fitting out, a poor concern without speed, and her boilers are just being tried. There is no danger to be apprehended from the boat with the iron horn. She will likely never be finished, and if she is she won't come down here."[3]

Porter, of course, was guessing. At this phase of the war there were no ironclads: the battle between *Monitor* and *Virginia (Merrimack)* was still eight months away. When Porter wrote his report on July 19, the "boat with the iron horn" had not been named, although the people of New Orleans referred to it as "the Turtle." The owners found an appropriate name when word of the Confederate victory at Manassas reached New Orleans. And when the ram *Manassas* came down the river three months later to attack the Union fleet, Porter was not there to see her. He was deep in the Caribbean searching for Raphael Semmes and the elusive little *Sumter*.[4]

In the annals of shipbuilding, *Manassas* was unique, but whether she was any good remained to be seen. Captain George N. Hollins, who had come to New Orleans to replace Rousseau on July 31, 1861, did not think so, but Hollins had no jurisdiction over *Manassas*; the ironclad was still a privateer owned by Stevenson and his investors.

By reputation, George Hollins was well known in New Orleans. A native of Maryland, he had joined the navy in 1814 as a fifteen-year-old midshipman and fought with Stephen Decatur against the British in the War of 1812. He earned a reputation as a fighter, and even at the age of sixty-two, he still looked combative and exuded more energy than most of the younger officers around him. At the time Fort Sumter surrendered, Hollins was in

2. Scharf, *Confederate Navy*, 264–65; *ORN*, Ser. 2, I, 259, Statistical Data for CSS *Manassas*; Dufour, *Night the War Was Lost*, 71–72.

3. *ORN*, XVI, 601–602, Porter to Mervine, July 19, 1861.

4. For Porter's report of the *Sumter* chase, see *ORN*, I, 103–109, Porter to Welles, October 10, 1861.

command of USS *Susquehanna* on station in Naples, Italy. Naval Secretary Welles needed the vessel for blockade duty and recalled her, but he also had misgivings about Hollins' fidelity to the North. When Hollins returned to the United States, he resigned his commission, and on June 8, 1861, Welles responded by dismissing him from the service. On June 20 Hollins became a captain in the Confederate navy and promptly demonstrated his aggressiveness. He needed a ship to command and nine days later organized a raid to capture *St. Nicholas,* a Union side-wheeler moored in the lower Potomac. Once on board, Hollins raised steam and captured three more prizes in Chesapeake Bay.

Hollins, who was active and self-starting, had little patience for red tape and ignored whatever he considered to be a wasteful administrative matter. He hated paperwork and barely tolerated bureaucracy, but he seldom lost time because of either. This characteristic eventually irritated Mallory, his boss, but at this stage of the war Hollins' fighting spirit attracted the naval secretary's notice. Mallory needed a man like Hollins who could get things done in New Orleans, and on July 31 he promoted Hollins to commodore and sent him to the Crescent City. His instructions were simple: build a navy and remove the blockade.[5]

Hollins preferred getting and giving simple, clear, crisp instructions leading to a specific action, but building a navy was easier said than done. The untested *Manassas,* whatever value she represented to Hollins' navy, remained under the ownership of Stevenson's consortium. This left Hollins with *Livingston,* a side-wheeler purchased by Rousseau and sitting in the shipyard of John Hughes and Company; the 7-gun *McRae,* an 830-ton sloop-rigged steamer; the 2-gun *Ivy,* a 454-ton side-wheel river steamer; and the 2-gun tug *Tuscarora,* another side-wheel river steamer. Of the four vessels, *Livingston* looked the most promising as a gunboat. She was laid on the keel of a ferryboat and more sturdily constructed than other modified gunboats. However, she had a peculiar oblong shape, circular both fore and aft, where three guns each were mounted in a wide arc. *Livingston* could play her guns to the greatest advantage, but like most armed vessels built in the Confederacy, she lacked mobility and motive power.[6]

Commodore Rousseau had also purchased three other vessels and refitted them for river defense. The 500-ton side-wheel steamer *Calhoun* started

---

5. Faust (ed.), *HTI,* 365. See also *Dictionary of American Biography,* IX, 152. *St. Nicholas* was recommissioned as CSS *Rappahannock* but should not be confused with the cruiser purchased in London by Matthew Fontaine Maury. See *ORN,* Ser. 2, I, 264.

6. *ORN,* Ser. 2, I, 256, 258, 259, 270, Statistical Data of Vessels. See also *ibid.,* 471–72, Investigation of the Navy Department; Scharf, *Confederate Navy,* 266.

her career as a privateer, but her five small deck guns were no match for the firepower of the Union navy's big sloops of war. Nonetheless, she was a spacious vessel, and Hollins made her his flagship. The small side-wheel river tug *Jackson* (formerly the steamer *Yankee*) carried two smoothbore 32-pounders in pivot, and the converted revenue cutter *Pickens* carried three guns, an 8-inch columbiad and two virtually useless 24-pounder carronades. Converted river steamers had many things in common: they were all light-draft side-wheelers, well built for commercial usage but too frail to withstand the impact of firing heavy ordnance. A few shots from a 32-pounder could wreak havoc on flimsy makeshift gundecks.[7]

Hollins found two more vessels waiting for him on Lake Pontchartrain, both purchased and commissioned by Rousseau. The small screw steamer *Florida* carried a battery of four guns, and her consort, the side-wheel river steamer *Pamlico*, carried two. Hollins ordered construction of two additional gunboats for duty on the lakes. In early August he tallied up his fleet. Excluding *Livingston*, which was still in the Hughes shipyard, and the ram *Manassas*, still privately owned and under construction, he had eight vessels mounting twenty-seven small guns. The six vessels in the river he aptly dubbed the "Mosquito Fleet."[8]

The commodore's counterpart at New Orleans, General Twiggs, had developed his own thoughts on the defense of the city. Both commanders operated from different assumptions, an awkward situation that never changed even after Hollins and Twiggs later left the department. Hollins worried about the Union navy slipping into the Mississippi and attacking the city from downriver, and Twiggs followed the advice flowing from the government in Richmond and focused on the likelihood of an attack from upriver. Twiggs's worries were not unfounded. Union timberclads had been undergoing conversion in Cincinnati since early summer, and in August construction of ironclads began in Carondelet, near St. Louis, and in Mound City.

In New Orleans Twiggs located "six large floating docks of immense strength" that he wished to convert into "floating batteries of tremendous power at a comparatively trifling cost." He planned to have the batteries towed to any point upriver "where the channel is narrow and [could] be made an impassable barrier to the vessels of the enemy." On August 24, 1861, War Secretary Walker, who also viewed the menace to New Orleans as

---

7. Scharf, *Confederate Navy*, 263–64; *ORN*, Ser. 2, I, 250, 257, 263, Statistical Data of Vessels.

8. *ORN*, Ser. 2, I, 252–62. There are wide discrepancies in the number and sizes of guns carried by Hollins' fleet. The author has chosen to follow the *Official Records*.

coming from upriver, approved the project.[9] Nobody considered the potential of what six floating batteries might accomplish if stretched across the channel between Forts Jackson and St. Philip. Twiggs, who was responsible for strengthening both forts, still believed they could repulse wooden warships if attacked from below.

There is little evidence to indicate whether Twiggs and Hollins conferred with each other on defensive strategy. To make matters worse, private enterprise continued to work behind the scenes. Attracted by the Confederate government's promise to pay 20 percent of the value of all enemy gunboats destroyed, innovators and individuals were encouraged to raise money for other *Manassas*-like projects, usually with the approval of the Confederate Naval Office but often without Hollins' full knowledge. The commodore was probably a little surprised when he found a small cigar-shaped vessel, looking much like a steam boiler, sitting in a cradle at the government shipyard on New Basin.

James R. McClintock and Baxter Watson, two practical marine engineers and owners of a small steam-gauge factory at 31 Front Levee, had developed plans for building a vessel capable of submerging and driving a torpedo into the hull of an enemy warship. With help from engineers at the Leeds Foundry, they put their drawings in order and attracted investors. Men like wealthy sugar broker Horace L. Hunley, John K. Scott, Robbin R. Barron, and H. J. Leovy paid their subscriptions and periodically visited the yard to watch large sheets of quarter-inch boiler plate bolted onto an iron frame. As the vessel's lines became clearer, workmen characterized her shape to that of a large fish, twenty feet long, four feet deep, and six feet wide, with every contour streamlined for speed. There was no superstructure or funnel, just a stubby hatch amidship and a tiny propeller fitted to a shaft projecting from the stern. A small pair of iron diving vanes, operated from inside, spread from the stem like the fins of a dolphin. There was no room for a pilothouse, only two groupings of sealed glass windows a foot in diameter mounted forward. The propeller was rotated by two men hunched low inside the hull, turning cranks. When the vessel submerged, candles allowed the helmsman to watch a magnetic compass mounted on the frame. A hand-operated pump next to a sea cock enabled the crankers to empty the water ballast tank.

Neither Hollins nor anyone else from the Confederate navy received invitations to watch the launching of *Pioneer*, as the submersible was called.

9. *ORN*, LIII, 722, 731–32, Twiggs to Walker and Walker to Twiggs, August 9, 24, 1862.

Only the builders and owners were there. Part-owner Scott took the helm and headed into the lake. In a short dive, the magnetic compass wobbled out of control, and Scott, when he surfaced, admitted that when submerged he had no idea where he was. Scott abandoned the compass. He would take his bearings on the target before making his dive, and if necessary, come to porthole depth to make any adjustments.

With a few modifications the novel submarine became watertight, but she had no reserve air supply, and the vessel could only stay under water a few minutes. Months passed before the investors risked another underwater test. With a sealed container of gunpowder capped with a sensitive percussion fuse, *Pioneer* submerged and successfully blew a barge "so high that only a few splinters were heard from." McClintock, Watson, and Hunley eventually took their design to Mobile, and later to Charleston, but *Pioneer* ended up on the bottom of Bayou St. John, where two crankers and a helmsman met death by suffocation. They would not be the last to die testing Confederate submarines.[10]

By September, 1861, every shipyard in New Orleans was either building, converting, or repairing some type of warlike vessel for someone in the Confederacy, but few were intended for the Confederate navy. If Hollins had plans for building more of Secretary Mallory's gunboats, he had no place to do it. Since Hollins' arrival in New Orleans, *Bienville* and *Carondelet*, each with six guns, had been started in the John Hughes yard on Bayou St. John, where *Livingston* was being outfitted. *Manassas* was under construction in Algiers, and the 5-gun steamer *General Polk* and 6-gun side-wheeler *Maurepas* occupied other yards. In the North, Union shipyards were turning out vessels in record numbers, and if there was any doubt, the citizens of New Orleans could read about it in their own *Picayune*.[11]

Without conferring with Hollins on details such as shipyard capacity, iron availability, skilled workmen, sources of lumber, or any other matter, Mallory signed two contracts, one with E. C. Murray to build the ironclad *Louisiana*, and the other with Nelson and Asa F. Tift to build the ironclad *Mississippi*. To start work, the eager contractors faced the problem of erecting new facilities, because all the other yards were occupied. They

10. *ORN*, Ser. 2, I, 399–400, Hatch to Benjamin, April 1, 1862; Robinson, *Confederate Privateers*, 166–72; Milton F. Perry, *Infernal Machines: The Story of Confederate Submarine Warfare* (Baton Rouge, 1965), 94–96. There is evidence of other submarines being attempted in New Orleans during this period.

11. *ORN*, Ser. 2, I, 249, 253, 259, Statistical Data of Vessels; Scharf, *Confederate Navy*, 266–67; New Orleans *Daily Picayune*, September 10, 1861.

chose a four-acre tract in Jefferson City, just north of New Orleans, and began clearing the land. Murray and the Tifts shared the same plot of land but operated separate yards.

E. C. Murray enjoyed a well-deserved local reputation as a practical shipbuilder. In twenty years he had built more than 120 boats, steamers, and sailing vessels, but never an ironclad. The Tift brothers claimed no shipbuilding credentials, but each carried a little political influence and a lot of loyalty. Nelson came from Georgia and Asa from Key West, Florida, where Mallory once lived. Asa Tift, who owned a ship-repair yard, had signed Florida's Ordinance of Secession, and when the Union navy captured his home town and seized his property, he fled to Nelson's estate in Georgia. Together they discussed their alternatives.

When the war drove Asa Tift to Nelson's home, he knew the lifeline of the Confederacy depended upon keeping southern ports open to foreign commerce and friendly diplomats. With few naval architects, mechanics, or shipbuilders available, the Tifts believed that a southern navy must be built by workmen with no more skill than ordinary house carpenters. Warships would have to be made from green pine timber and shielded with iron, and the vessels would have to be built quickly to equalize or surpass the shipbuilding program in the North.

In a workroom on his plantation Nelson started to build a small model of his concept of such a vessel. When he finished, he had a miniature of CSS *Mississippi*, a vessel with flat, straight surfaces, except for the four corners that connected the two ends of the ship with her sides. The model looked much like an odd toy boat built by a youngster with no more than a saw, hammer, and nails, which was exactly what Nelson Tift wanted. There were no curved frames, crooks, and knees, and for that matter, no frame. Nelson Tift envisioned a vessel shaped much like an oversized scow, but built of planks three feet thick covered with three-inch iron plates.[12]

In August, 1861, on their way to Richmond with the model, the Tifts stopped at Savannah and Charleston and obtained endorsements from senior naval officers like Flag Officer Josiah Tattnell. Asa Tift had no trouble scheduling a meeting with his old friend Secretary Mallory, and a board of naval officers convened to study the model and review the plans. They were impressed by the simplicity of the design. Based upon the Tifts' measurements, the vessel scaled out at 260 feet in length with a beam of 58 feet and a depth from the surface of 15 feet. Estimates of the weight of the vessel ranged as high as four thousand tons. The Tifts rated her speed

12. Scharf, *Confederate Navy*, 267–69; Durkin, *Mallory*, 34.

at fourteen knots, although there was no engine builder in the Confederacy who could produce a power plant capable of pushing a giant four-thousand-ton scow at that speed. But the power plant, like the vessel, was innovative and appealing to a visionary like Mallory; two sets of boilers, each forty-two inches in diameter and thirty feet long, provided steam power to three engines, each working independent propellers eleven feet in diameter fastened to wrought-iron shafts.

Mallory liked the concept. Here was an impregnable vessel, capable of repelling any shot fired at her, and armed with twenty big casemated guns, two forward, two aft, and sixteen broadside. Above the gundeck was a cupola where smaller guns and sharpshooters could crouch in safety and pick off enemy boarders. As far as Mallory was concerned, nothing afloat could match the ship's firepower. It was just what the Confederacy needed in New Orleans, and if the naval secretary had any misgivings, the Tifts removed them by offering to superintend the project "without pecuniary compensation from the government for our services." All they asked was that Mallory appoint "such officers (from the navy) as may be found necessary to cooperate with us in the early and economical construction of the vessel."[13]

On September 1, Mallory made his decision. "I have concluded to build a large warship at N. Orleans upon Nelson Tift's plan, & will push it." The following day he wired Commodore Hollins, ordering him to inquire into costs and the length of time required to build the vessel. He sent Hollins rough specifications but no details. The commodore had enough worries trying to pry his mosquito fleet loose from overcrowded shipyards, and turned the telegram over to John Roy at the customhouse, who puzzled over demands for three eleven-foot propellers, driven by three high-pressure engines, powered by sixteen boilers thirty feet long. Dutifully, Roy hurried out requests for bids to the Leeds Foundry and area machine shops, perhaps wondering what he would tell them when they asked for more information.[14]

On September 5, well before John Roy had any information regarding costs or even a glimmer of insight into the viability of the project, Mallory authorized the Tifts to proceed. He asked that the vessel's completion "not be delayed beyond the 15th of December next." He also reminded

13. *ORN*, Ser. 2, I, 269, Statistical Data; *ibid.*, 571, Tifts to Mallory, August 26, 1861; Scharf, *Confederate Navy*, 268–69.

14. Stephen R. Mallory Journal, September 1, 1861, Southern Historical Collection, University of North Carolina, Chapel Hill; Roy Memorandum Book, September 2, 1861.

the Tifts that they were not contractors but agents of the Naval Office, and that all their labors and responsibilities would receive "neither commission or reward." He gave them freedom to modify the vessel to improve its efficiency and to negotiate with contractors bonuses for early deliveries or penalties for late.[15]

The Tifts arrived in New Orleans on September 18 and checked into the St. Charles Hotel. Commodore Hollins met them and turned them over to John Roy. During the next few days the trio, with only rough sketches, traveled from shop to shop signing contracts for engines, boilers, equipment, and framework. Leeds Foundry, the largest, busiest, and most competent engine builder, asked for at least four months time after receipt of detailed drawings and $65,000 to make and install the machinery. This exceeded Mallory's December 15 completion date, so the Tifts awarded the contract to Jackson & Company of the Patterson Iron Works, who agreed to manufacture and install the machinery in ninety days for $45,000 and a $5,000 bonus.[16]

In the meantime, John Roy studied the boiler and horsepower calculations and declared that *Mississippi* required ten times more heating surface than estimated by the naval office's engineer. On October 9, the Tifts advised Mallory that the vessel had to be widened by twenty feet to provide more boiler and furnace space. Because of the error, construction cost would increase an undetermined amount. The Tifts blamed the error on an incompetent naval engineering staff.[17]

To build the hull, Roy conducted the Tifts to John Hughes, owner of the city's best shipyard, who already had plenty of work from Commodore Hollins. After examining the Tifts' specifications, Hughes declined to bid but offered to rent a corner of his yard and the use of his sawmill at a reasonable rate. Contractors Hyde & Mackay, whom Hollins was also keeping busy, agreed to build the hull for $125,000, "but without being bound to time." Harram & Company, also busy, wanted $147,000 and would deliver when time permitted. The shipyards were mostly on the west bank of the Mississippi and the timber and machinery on the east side. Laurant Millaudon (or Millandon), who had graciously lent a four-acre parcel of land at Jefferson City so E. C. Murray could build the hull of *Louisiana,* provided the Tifts with an adjoining plot for *Mississippi.* Millaudon wanted

15. *ORN,* Ser. 2, I, 601, 602, Mallory to N. and A. F. Tift, August 28 and September 5, 1861.

16. *Ibid.,* 572, 573, Jackson & Co. to Mallory, September 25, and N. and A. F. Tift to Mallory, September 28, 1861.

17. *Ibid.,* 575, N. and A. F. Tift to Mallory, October 9, 1861. See also the Tifts' testimony, *ibid.,* 532–33; Roy, Memorandum Book, September 20, 1861.

his property back by February 1, and the Tifts assured him *Mississippi* would be afloat and breaking up the blockade by then.[18]

In addition to the time and expense of setting up their own yard, neither E. C. Murray nor the Tifts had considered the amount of lumber they jointly needed for the two vessels, although both understood that the timber had to be cut from the far side of Lake Pontchartrain, hauled to the New Orleans and Jackson Railroad, then carted to Jefferson City. Murray, in referring to *Mississippi* after the fact, estimated the vessel had taken "no less than 2,000,000 feet of lumber." By comparison, he purchased for his own vessel, *Louisiana*, about 1.7 million feet.[19]

Although Murray signed his contract to build *Louisiana* on September 18, 1861 — about two weeks after the Tifts received theirs for *Mississippi* — he managed to get a good start. Unlike Asa and Nelson Tift, Murray was the primary contractor with twenty years of shipbuilding experience, and although he came from Kentucky, he was more familiar with local resources. For the *Louisiana*, a 264-foot ironclad with a 62-foot beam, he would be paid $196,000. He also had contract incentives: aside from his anticipated profit, he would receive $98 for each day he delivered prior to January 25, or be penalized $98 for each day he was late, although his contract provided for a revocation of the delivery penalty if unavoidable deliveries of materials occurred, and the Navy Department assumed the responsibility for any rise in cost for iron above $60 per ton. Based upon contract dates, Murray had about four more weeks to complete his vessel than the Tifts, and unlike the latter, his motivation sprang from the opportunity to turn a profit. [20]

There is no evidence that either Murray or the Tifts knew of each other's contracts at the time completion dates were discussed with Mallory, nor is there evidence that Mallory attempted to confer with Hollins on the availability of shipyards, machine shops, or resources prior to issuing the contracts. Mallory, who depended upon New Orleans becoming the South's greatest shipbuilding center, had not been there himself and knew little of the situation. By jamming contracts for two huge ironclads into a city with little available capacity, Mallory set a course certain to lead to disappointment. How many workman with the required skills could be hired? Where would 1,500 tons of iron plating come from when the army needed it for cannon? Could the navy usurp the demands of the army for heavy

18. *ORN*, Ser. 2, I, 573, N. and A. F. Tift to Mallory, September 28, 1861.
19. *Ibid.*, 754, 758, Investigation of the Navy Department.
20. *Ibid.*, 434, 757; Dufour, *Night the War Was Lost*, 102–103; Scharf, *Confederate Navy*, 266.

guns to arm the vessels? Who could forge and machine the enormous shafting needed for the machinery? Would there be coal to fire the huge boilers? And who would command these novel vessels when they were ready and train the crews to fight them properly?

These questions, if asked, probably drifted through the Naval Office in a blue haze of optimism, but E. C. Murray knew better. He had talked to John J. McRea of the Naval Office as he left Richmond on September 18 and learned of the Tifts' project. When he reached New Orleans he conferred with Hollins and wasted no time scooping up five hundred tons of railroad iron sequestered by the government from the Vicksburg and Shreveport Railroad in Algiers. The Tifts were not so fortunate. They were forced to go around "to all the principal houses" in New Orleans and buy "all the iron fastenings they had . . . for 3 1/2 to 5 1/2 cents," or roughly $70 to $110 per ton.

The best engine Murray could find was on the river steamer *Ingomar*, so he bought the vessel and engaged the firm of John McLean to remove it. Robert Kirk of the Patterson Foundry agreed to manufacture the two propellers and dual drive trains. On October 15, one day after the Tifts laid the first timbers for *Mississippi*, Murray began work in the neighboring lot on *Louisiana*, and as far as Murray was concerned, the race for resources and time had begun. [21]

In the meantime, on September 27 Joseph Pierce arrived from Richmond as acting naval constructor. Pierce had been seeking employment in the Naval Office since the outbreak of war, but he was not hired until Mallory needed someone to work with the Tifts. Pierce preferred employment at the Gosport Navy Yard, but he took the job when Mallory promised him promotion to naval constructor if he met the schedule. He joined the Tifts to superintend the building of *Mississippi*'s hull and brought with him twenty ship carpenters from Richmond. Before he finished the work, he had employed as many as six hundred workmen. [22]

For a while, activity in the adjoining lots manifested the spirit of competition. As lumber came into the yard, steam-operated sawmills screeched late into the night as green lumber was roughed to shape and foundations laid. But on November 6, progress suddenly stopped when all the ship carpenters in New Orleans struck for a dollar increase to their $3.00 daily wage. For a while, Murray convinced his workers to stay, promising to pay whatever increase resulted from the strike, but the Tifts lost all their men

21. *ORN*, Ser. 2, I, 532, 754, 788, Investigation of Navy Department.
22. *Ibid.*, Pierce testimony, 540–543.

except the twenty who came from Richmond with Pierce. Strikers from the Tift yard, joined by others, threatened to throw Murray's "tools in the river" if his men did not join the strike. Shocked by the delay, Asa Tift asked shipbuilder Hughes if carpenters had ever struck before. Hughes replied that the last strike had taken six weeks to settle. Neither the Tifts nor Murray could tolerate a delay of this length. Pierce crossed the river, attended a meeting of the strikers in Algiers, and on behalf of both Murray and the Tifts, agreed to meet the carpenters' demands.[23] On November 12 work resumed.

To compound the congestion in New Orleans' shipyards, General Twiggs began work on two floating batteries, the 20-gun *New Orleans* and the 18-gun *Memphis*, and Hollins, who was forever trying to strengthen his mosquito fleet, acquired, without Mallory's approval, two 3-gun revenue cutters, *Pickens* and *Morgan*. Mallory grew upset with Hollins' unapproved expenditures and reminded him that red tape could not be ignored regardless of necessity. He mentioned nothing about the money being pumped into the army's floating batteries, but the monstrous *New Orleans* with her two rifled 32-pounders and her eighteen 8- and 9-inch columbiads was attracting more local notice than all the other gunboats being built around the Crescent City.[24]

Hollins, however, needed fast, heavily armed steamers with lots of mobility, and *New Orleans*, for all her guns, was nothing but a floating fort with no motive power of her own. He considered incredible Mallory's persistent belief that the threat to New Orleans would come from upriver. On October 10, four Union vessels had come over the bars and occupied Head of Passes, fifteen miles inside the Delta, and Hollins believed they must be driven out before others joined them. By occupying Head of Passes, the Union navy needed fewer vessels to blockade the main stem of the river, but Head of Passes also represented the logical staging area for a Union fleet to marshal its warships for an ascent of the river. Hollins could not permit the Union to establish an interior base of operations. If the forts fell, New Orleans would follow in a matter of days.

But how could Hollins defeat the steam sloop of war *Richmond* with her 22 guns (mostly 9-inch Dahlgrens) the sailing sloops *Vincennes* (19 guns) and *Preble* (10 guns), and the side-wheel steamer *Water Witch* (4 guns)? A

23. *Ibid.*, Tift testimony, 553; Murray testimony, 756.

24. *Ibid.*, 259, 260, 261, 263, Statistical Data of Vessels; *ibid.*, 799, Investigation of Navy Department; *ibid.*, 514, Mallory to Hollins, November 22, 1862 [1861]; New Orleans *True Delta*, October 19, 26, 1861; Dufour, *Night the War Was Lost*, 105–106.

single broadside from *Richmond* could throw more metal than the combined guns of the mosquito fleet. And how long would it be before more Union warships gathered in the river?[25]

Hollins felt compelled to do something.

But what?

25. *ORN*, Ser. 2, I, 184, 192–93, 232, Statistical Data of Vessels.

FIVE *The Night of the* Turtle

While New Orleans shipyards bulged with construction work, Gideon Welles, in the Washington Naval Office, read with some disdain the dismal reports of Flag Officer William Mervine, commander of the Gulf Blockading Squadron. Since the spring of 1861, Welles had given Mervine the benefit of the doubt, but now, six months later, he could wait no longer. In his diary he wrote: "He proved an utter failure. He is not wanting in patriotism, but in executive and administrative ability; is quite as great on little things as on great ones. He was long on getting out to his station, and accomplished nothing after he got there."[1] Perhaps it was time for someone to pay for the depredations of Raphael Semmes's *Sumter,* and if Mervine did not have the backbone to remove Commander Poor, then the time had come to remove Mervine.

On September 6, 1861, Welles replaced Mervine with Captain William W. McKean. Of all the senior officers in the Gulf, McKean had shown the most initiative. At sixty-one years of age, McKean had spent forty-seven of them in the navy. He had taken command of USS *Niagara* and in April joined Mervine's Gulf Blockading Squadron. When on July 6 he learned *Sumter* had entered the port of Cienfuegos, Cuba, he loaded coal at Fort Pickens and went in chase. He had no more luck in capturing the wily Semmes than Porter two months later, but Welles liked the idea that McKean had made the effort. The Union's sea dogs were up in years, and Welles had to cull out those who had become too accustomed to rocking

1. Gideon Welles, *The Diary of Gideon Welles, Secretary of the Navy Under Lincoln and Johnson* (3 vols.; Boston and New York, 1909–1911), I, 76.

at anchor. On August 7, he gave McKean command of the vessels blockading the mouth of the Mississippi.[2]

Orders for the command change did not reach Mervine and McKean until September 22. After a few days of cogitation, Mervine felt slighted and demanded a court of inquiry to justify his performance. Welles refused, claiming "neither the time nor the service in this crisis can be wasted in courts of enquiry . . . growing out of the substitution of one officer for another for any duty. Mere forms and rank cannot be permitted to control efficient and necessary action in an emergency like this. . . . I must decline ordering a court of enquiry in your case." After replacing Mervine, Welles instructed McKean "to lock up the outlets of the great central valley of the continent so that her products . . . shall not reach the ocean, and so that the craving wants of her population for the products of other lands shall not be supplied while their hands are raised against the [Federal] Government."[3]

When McKean arrived at Southwest Pass, he recognized the complexity of shutting off all enemy traffic into and out of the Mississippi by striving to blockade all four passes. If he could occupy Head of Passes, the point from which the four outlets branched, he could then build fortifications and close off river traffic. But was this possible?

On September 19, the shallow-draft side-wheeler USS *Water Witch*, commanded by Lieutenant Francis Winslow, entered Pass à l'Outre to make a reconnaissance. On board was First Lieutenant Walter McFarland of the U.S. Army Engineers, whose mission was to survey Head of Passes and determine where land batteries could be constructed. As *Water Witch* steamed toward the Head, Winslow spotted Lieutenant Joseph Fry's CSS *Ivy* rapidly ascending Southwest Pass with an armed schooner in tow, and the race was on for the Head. *Ivy* got there first and steamed upriver, firing shot and shell from her stern 24-pounder. Winslow replied with a rifled howitzer, but the shots fell short. *Water Witch* gave up the chase and returned to Head of Passes to enable McFarland to conduct his survey. *Ivy* steamed back downriver to watch, staying carefully out of range. McFarland located two likely sites for land batteries and at 4 P.M. departed on *Water Witch*.[4]

2. Faust (ed.), *HTI*, 462; *ORN*, XVI, 598, 599–600, 614–15, McKean to Mervine, July 31, Mervine to Welles, and Welles to Mervine, August 1, 1861. For the change of command, see Fox to Mervine, Fox to McKean, and Welles to McKean, September 6, 1861, *ibid.*, 660–61.

3. *Ibid.*, 693, 695–96, Mervine to Welles, September 29, and Welles to Mervine, October 2, 1861; *ibid.*; 661, Welles to McKean, September 6, 1861.

4. *Ibid.*, 683, 684, 685, Winslow to Pope, McFarland to McKean, McKean to Welles,

McFarland's exploratory survey was probably the first indication Commodore Hollins received of Union naval activity *in* the river, but he knew there would be more. If the enemy established itself in force at Head of Passes, they could build a strong base of operations for launching an attack on the forts, and ultimately on New Orleans. Hollins could not let that happen, but he wondered whether his lightly armed mosquito fleet — six ships with about twenty guns — could do much harm. For the moment, he waited and watched.

On September 26, informants from Pilottown observed the 22-gun USS *Richmond*, commanded by Captain John Pope, attempting to enter Southwest Pass. In ten feet of water, the ship grounded and had to be pulled off by *Water Witch* and *South Carolina*. On the 29th, *Richmond* found the channel, entered the pass, and anchored opposite Pilottown. The following day, *Water Witch* towed Commander Robert Handy's 19-gun *Vincennes* over the bar and moored her beside *Richmond*. McKean sent orders to Commander Henry French at Ship Island to bring the 10-gun sailing sloop *Preble* to Pass à l'Outre.

On October 5, Lieutenant Fry of CSS *Ivy* reported three of the four vessels at anchor at Head of Passes. Fry moved close enough to shell *Richmond* with his two rifled 24-pounders. *Richmond*'s 9-inch smooth bores could not reach *Ivy*, and this made Captain Pope nervous. Even though Fry's rifles were mere popguns, a well-placed shell could cause a lot of damage, and Pope was not accustomed to being under fire. When *Ivy* returned on October 9, Pope dispatched a hurried note to McKean, grumbling, "We are entirely at the mercy of the enemy. We are liable to be driven from here at any moment, and, situated as we are, our position is untenable. I may be captured at any time by a pitiful little steamer mounting only one [actually two] gun."[5]

Pope, despite his nervousness, failed to send picket boats upriver to warn him if Hollins decided to stage a night attack. After midnight there was no moon, and the first sentinel for the squadron would be the night watch on the small prize schooner *Frolic* anchored a short distance above *Richmond*. Furthermore, Pope had devised no plan to repel a surprise attack, yet he felt threatened by the "pitiful little steamer" *Ivy*.[6]

September 20, 22, 1861.

5. *Ibid.*, 689–90, 692, 697–98, 699–700, 700–702, McKean to Welles, September 28 and October 10, Pope to McKean, September 26 and October 9, and French to McKean, October 5, 1861.

6. *Ibid.*, 714, 703–705, 709–11, Winslow to McKean, October 24, and Pope to McKean, October 13, 17, 1861.

From his flagship off Fort Pickens, 180 miles away, McKean suddenly realized that inside the passes *Vincennes* and *Preble*, two sailing sloops, were dependent on steamers for mobility. "I am placed in a very trying and embarrassing position," he wrote Welles. "The vessels in the river are in jeopardy. The *Water Witch* is needed to aid the sailing vessels, in case it becomes necessary for them to drop down." He instructed Captain Francis B. Ellison of the speedy 9-gun screw steamer *R. R. Cuyler* to join the squadron at Head of Passes as quickly as he could be relieved from his station off Apalachicola. To compound the confusion, First Lieutenant McFarland, who had earlier made surveys of the area and proposed two battery sites, now recanted after acknowledging that the two small isolated works he had recommended would be difficult to defend. McKean believed he would win praise from Welles by occupying Head of Passes, but now he began to wonder if he had tried to do too much.[7]

On his flagship *Calhoun* off New Orleans, Commodore Hollins received steady intelligence on Union activity downriver. Every day the swift little *Ivy* sent him updated reports from the telegraph at Fort St. Philip. Hollins probably wondered why the enemy had brought two armed sailing vessels into the river, but there they were, floating targets inviting attack.

On October 9, Hollins headed downriver with *Calhoun, Jackson, Tuscarora,* and the recently acquired revenue cutter *Pickens. Ivy* and *McRae* were already at Fort Jackson waiting for the rest of the flotilla. Hollins could not match the enemy's firepower with his mosquito fleet, but he believed he could even the odds if he could commandeer *Manassas.*[8]

The iron-armored "Turtle" still belonged to John Stevenson's investors, but Hollins had his eye on her. On the evening of October 11, he steamed downriver with his fleet and found *Manassas* riding at anchor off Fort St. Philip. He sent CSS *McRae* with Lieutenant Alexander F. Warley and a boarding party to the anchored ram with instructions to seize her "politely" on behalf of the Confederate navy. The crew of *Manassas* refused to yield, warning Warley that he "did not have enough men to take her." *McRae* ranged up alongside the ram and lowered a boat. By then, the crew of the ironclad had lined up on the turtleback, swearing "they would kill the

---

7. *Ibid.,* 697, 700–701, McFarland to McKean, October 3, McKean to Welles, October 10, 1861.

8. Based upon a report in the Richmond *Dispatch* dated October 15, 1861, *Calhoun* carried 3 guns; *Ivy,* one rifled 32–pounder; *Jackson,* two 8–inch columbiads; *McRae,* 6 guns; *Tuscarora,* 2 guns; *Pickens,* one 8–inch columbiad and four 24-pounder carronades; and *Manassas,* one 64-pounder. This disagrees with the *Official Navy Records,* but not substantially. *ORN,* XVI, 728.

first man who attempted to board her." James Morris Morgan, a midshipman on *McRae*, left the following account:

> There was a ladder reaching to the water from the top of her armor to the water line. Lieutenant Warley, pistol in hand, ordered me to keep the men in the boat until he gave the order for them to join him. Running up the ladder, his face set in grim determination, he caused a sudden panic among the heroic(?) crew of longshoremen who incontinently took to their heels and like so many prairie dogs disappeared down the hole of a hatchway with Mr. Warley after them. He drove them back on deck . . . some of them jumping overboard and swimming for it. [9]

Warley assembled all remaining hands and read them his authority. Their prize money agreement as privateers was revoked, because "under the Navy Regulations all [Confederate] war vessels in sight at the time of a capture were entitled to share in the prize money." Fourteen privateersmen gathered their baggage and went ashore, followed by part-owner Stevenson, who departed with his hopes of prize money dashed and "with tears in his eyes." If Stevenson carried a handkerchief, he would need it a few months later when he participated in another scheme with equally sad results.

Volunteers from the fleet stepped forward and filled the vacancies on *Manassas*. Later, when Hollins was questioned on his precipitant seizure of the turtle, he replied curtly, "I seized the *Manassas* and paid for her afterwards." This time, nobody asked about red tape, not even Mallory. [10]

With *Manassas* manned by some of Warley's regulars and with his mosquito fleet anchored under the guns at Fort Jackson, Hollins prepared to strike the Union intruders with everything he had: six lightly armed riverboats and the untested ram. When midnight passed on the morning of October 12, Hollins waited for the moon to set. The night was clear with a slight mist rising off the river, just enough to shroud the river in darkness. In another hour, the mist would thicken and perhaps help hide his vessels from watchful pickets—pickets who were not there but should have been—pickets whom he fully expected to encounter somewhere downriver. Before proceeding with the attack, Hollins called his officers together for a

9. James Morris Morgan, *Recollections of a Rebel Reefer* (Boston, 1917), 55.
10. Robinson, *Confederate Privateers*, 157–58; *ORN*, Ser. 2, I, 472, Investigation of Navy Department.

final briefing. Warley would take the lead in the slow-moving *Manassas* and draw the enemy's fire, then when contact was made, he would search for the largest enemy vessel. With a full head of steam, *Manassas* would crush the hull of *Richmond*, or the next best target, then back off, pull free, and go on down the line, battering one after the other.

Hollins' plan was simple. After striking the first enemy vessel, Warley would send up a rocket, signalling the men on *Tuscarora*, *McRae*, and *Ivy* to light three fire rafts and cut them loose. The tugs would pilot the rafts, keeping them abreast of each other a short distance above the ram. Held together by cables, the rafts were to be spread apart. If a cable snagged on an anchor chain or caught on the bow of an enemy ship, the fire rafts would close on both sides of the vessel and set her on fire. Then, with the Union squadron scattering in confusion, the mosquito fleet would descend upon the enemy and destroy every ship in sight.

The commanders of the gunboats returned to their vessels and waited for *Manassas* to ease into the five-knot current. From the deck of *Calhoun* Hollins watched as *McRae*, *Ivy*, and *Tuscarora* tugged the fire rafts into the current, and with *Jackson* and *Pickens* following behind, he ordered his flagship ahead. With all lights extinguished, Hollins could barely see the outline of the vessel ahead of him, and all he could feel was the slow pulsation of *Calhoun*'s paddlewheels as they steadied the vessel in the current. Everything depended upon *Manassas*, the fire rafts, and the three gunboats in the van. They must be careful and not overtake the turtle, and in the darkness and mist Hollins worried about all the things that might go wrong, or how close his vessels could approach before they were detected by the enemy.[11]

Warley had had less than a day to get the feel of *Manassas*, which handled sluggishly, especially in swift water. Moving with the current, the vessel seemed to take forever to respond to the helm, and facing upstream, she could barely stem the current. Warley knew that once he sighted the enemy, he would not be able to maneuver; he would have to strike fast and hard with all the downstream momentum he could muster, then pray he could reverse engines, extract the prow, and build enough speed to reach another target. He worried that the moment he rammed and fired the first signal rocket, the fire rafts would begin their descent. They were as much

11. H. Allen Gosnell, *Guns on the Western Waters: The Story of River Gunboats in the Civil War* (Baton Rouge, 1949), 37–38.

a menace to *Manassas* as they were to the enemy, and Warley had visions of his crew being roasted in their own iron pot.[12]

Under easy steam *Manassas* moved quietly ten miles downriver toward Head of Passes, her engines throbbing softly, the river gurgling over the buried prow. From the four-inch opening in the forward hatch Warley could see nothing behind him and nothing ahead, only the dim white wake curling over the snub-nosed bow. He trusted everything to Acting Master Charles Austin, who knew every inch of the river, and to J. Stevens Mason, a pilot who had stayed with the vessel after she was seized. Below in the cramped engine room Chief Engineer William H. Hardy kept the boilers hot. Not a spark escaped from the stack to warn the enemy, but buckets of "hot-stuff" lay within arm's length of the firebox. The gun crew huddled behind their lone 32-pounder carronade, an ancient relic from wars long past. With only ten shells in the magazine, Hollins ordered them fired only if confronted by an emergency.

As *Manassas* neared the Head, a dark shape loomed ahead. Warley was almost abeam *Preble* before he saw her. He moved to the center of the river to study the odd Union formation, which looked much like an inverted *V*. Off to starboard, a few hundred yards downstream, he spotted *Richmond*.

"Let her out, Hardy," Warley shouted down into the engine room. "Let her out now!"

On Hardy's signal, firemen tossed prepared buckets of tar, tallow, and sulphur into the furnace. Instantly, the steam gauge whirled upward as pressure built in the boilers. A plume of sparks shot from the stack, but detection now made no difference. With the flow of the current the dial in the engine room touched ten knots. The iron monster was moving, slowly gathering speed, and ahead lay *Richmond,* her deck watch too absorbed loading coal from the schooner *Joseph H. Toone* to see the turtle coming or to wonder about the cause of those odd sparks that seemed to glow like a streak of phosphorescence on the surface of the river.[13]

The Union ships lay sleepily at anchor. Despite rumors of an impregnable ironclad somewhere upriver and the worrisome exchange of cannon fire with *Ivy,* Captain Pope had deployed his four vessels haphazardly. The most advanced vessel was *Preble,* a sailing sloop almost helpless in the river. She lay anchored near the eastern bank, followed a few hundred

12. Robinson, *Confederate Privateers,* 158–61.
13. *Ibid.; ORN,* XVI, 730a, Warley to Hollins, n.d.

feet astern by *Water Witch,* an old steamer. On the opposite bank and several hundred yards downriver lay *Richmond,* and behind her *Vincennes,* a sailing vessel anchored close to the head of Southwest Pass.

Commander French, who had been on the deck of *Preble* most of the night, had just climbed into his berth when a midshipman broke into his cabin shouting, "Captain, here is a steamer right alongside of us."

Men were already rushing to quarters as French started for the deck, but as he paused to peer through a port, he saw "an indescribable object not 20 yards distant from our quarter, moving with great velocity toward the bow of the *Richmond.*" The officer of the deck had already hoisted a red signal light on the gaff to warn *Richmond,* and when French reached the quarterdeck, the first of *Preble*'s three broadsides boomed high above the black object in the water and rattled off into the woods. Moments later, guns on *Richmond* opened, but between the darkness and the smoke, gunners blasted at every imaginary shadow floating across their sights. Only the occasional plume of sparks marked the position of the ram.

After *Manassas* passed *Preble,* French noticed rockets arching skyward and supposed they came from the ram. Moments later he saw three bright lights upriver. At first he thought they were enemy gunboats, but they grew brighter and brighter. "Fire rafts!" he shouted. The crew rushed to weigh anchor, but the capstan broke. Men rigged tackles, but the work seemed to take forever. From French's perspective, all three rafts were headed straight for him. The wind was light, but he issued orders to get under-way. He hoped that by steering into the current, he could work his vessel to the opposite side of the river. French wanted a tow, but at this stage of the attack, *Richmond* was in a state of chaos. When the flaming rafts approached to within 150 yards, French ordered his cable cut. He left the anchor behind, hoisted sail, and headed for Southwest Pass. As French drifted past *Richmond,* he hollered, "I can hear your orders; what are they?" Pope answered back, "Proceed down the Pass."[14]

Pope had his own problems, but for several critical moments he could not determine what they were. He observed the red light from *Preble*'s gaff, heard a broadside fired at something in the water, and before his men could cut loose the coaling schooner, a dark object resembling a huge whale struck *Richmond* "abreast of the port fore channels, tearing the schooner from her fasts," and setting it adrift downriver. Three planks had been crushed about two feet below the waterline, leaving a seam about five

14. *ORN,* XVI, 712–13, French to McKean, October 22, 1861.

inches wide through which water poured. Pope, jarred nearly off his feet, scrambled about the quarterdeck shouting orders for a damage report.[15]

Warley backed off and prepared to deliver a blow to *Preble*, which was still struggling to hoist her anchor, but Chief Engineer Hardy reported that the shock of the first collision had dismounted one of the engines. With only the other running, there was not enough power to ram another vessel and barely enough to stem the current. At this point Warley probably vented his anger at the installers, because directly off his starboard lay the fully exposed beam of *Preble*. If French then observed *Manassas* steaming back up the river and firing her signal rockets, the ram could not have been traveling at ten knots.

Warley's orders were to fire three rockets immediately after ramming *Richmond*, but like most unrehearsed exercises, well-conceived plans suffer unexpected disruptions. When a nervous midshipman cracked the after-hatch on the turtle and prepared to send up the first rocket, he burned his hand in lighting it, dropped the stick, and sent the rocket streaking down into the hold. The crew, believing a shell had penetrated the deck, ran for cover, tumbling into corners and crevices. When the missile finally fizzled out, they enjoyed a good laugh on themselves. The midshipman eventually got all three rockets airborne, and the steamers promptly lit and released the fire rafts.

French, still immobilized by *Preble*'s stubborn anchor, noticed *Richmond* steaming upriver in chase of the *Manassas*, firing as she passed. Both *Water Witch* and *Vincennes* had opened fire on every dark object in the water, but at that time the only craft clearly visible were the three fire rafts drifting toward *Preble*. When Pope discovered that he was headed into an inferno, he reversed course and swung back downstream. French could not believe Pope was running from the fight. It was probably at this point he ordered the cable cut. Pope went to the rear of his squadron, taking station at the head of Southwest Pass with one eye upriver and the other down.

Of the scattered shots aimed at the slow-moving *Manassas*, one struck the mailed deck, making a slight dent. Another broke off the flagstaff, and a third severed one of the smokestacks. Warley still had a little power to maneuver, albeit slowly. Another random shot struck the remaining stack and knocked it against the vent of the other. Suddenly, the updraft choked and asphyxiating gases filled the fireroom, rapidly spreading through the vessel. Hardy, gasping for air, grabbed an axe and rushed up the com-

15. *Ibid.*, 703–704, Pope to McKean, October 13, 1861.

panionway to cut away the guys of the fallen funnel. Warley tried to stop him, but Hardy brushed him off and struggled to the deck. At first he could not get a foothold on the arched and slippery plates, but Austin gained a foothold behind him and gripped his belt. Hardy slashed away until the vent cleared, and then both men ducked through the hatchway as more shot and shell whizzed overhead.[16]

With both smokestacks shot away, *Manassas* lost power. Rather than drift downstream and lodge on a mudbank near the enemy, Warley attempted to ground the vessel, but she was surrounded by so much of her own smoke that he could not see the shoreline. He headed into the current, and when the smoke cleared, he observed all three fire rafts directly ahead, followed indistinctly by three steamers of the mosquito fleet. Helmsman Austin swung the turtle out of the fiery path and headed for shore.

From *Ivy*, Lieutenant Fry spotted *Manassas* directly ahead and offered a line, but Warley eased into the shallows and grounded in the mud. With the turtle out of action and exposed to attack, all Warley could do was to prepare a long fuse to the magazine, hold a match in readiness, and await the outcome.

Fry had assisted in the design of *Manassas* and suspected her limitations. "I believed her calculated to run down a single vessel, not to sustain a cross-fire at a short distance directed at her sides. My delight was unbounded to see her slowly emerge from the smoke. . . . Her progress was so slow I was convinced she was crippled; but her commander declined my offer of assistance."[17]

Leaving *Manassas* on a mudbank, Fry ordered *Ivy* downstream, only to observe *Tuscarora* aground a short distance away. With no Union vessels in sight, Fry probably wondered what had become of the enemy. Puzzled, he turned into Southwest Pass and followed the sound of distant cannon fire, hoping to buy enough time for *Manassas* and *Tuscarora* to work themselves free. Ahead, he could see the three fire rafts sputtering toward the pass, but they had all drifted over to the west bank. Fry steamed on, still looking for the Union squadron, but they had all fled from the fire rafts.

After *Preble* passed *Richmond*, the crew of *Vincennes* raised sail, pulled away from the west bank (where the fire rafts were headed), and followed. This left *Water Witch* alone somewhere upriver. Captain Pope's anxiety to get *Richmond* to safety loomed greater than his concern for Winslow's ship, and he ordered the heavy steamer down the pass to Pilottown.

16. Robinson, *Confederate Privateers*, 160–61.
17. *Ibid.*, 704, Pope to McKean, October 13, 1861; Fry to Hollins, October 14, 1861, in Dufour, *Night the War Was Lost*, 80.

The watch on *Water Witch*, stationed across the river from *Preble*, had also spotted *Manassas* steaming toward *Richmond* and heard a loud crash. Captain Winslow came on deck immediately. He observed all three fire rafts drifting toward his anchorage, ordered the prize schooner *Frolic* cut loose, and with his four small guns hammering away at a dark object in the water, he steamed to the opposite shore and headed upriver to meet the attack. Because of the darkness, Winslow did not observe the others desert him.

At first light, Winslow spotted smoke from the entire mosquito fleet a short distance upriver. To his dismay he observed the Union squadron three to four miles down Southwest Pass and in full retreat. Not prepared to fight the enemy alone, he sheered off and sped away, following far behind the fleeing *Richmond*, but he stopped long enough to take the *Frolic* in tow.

When *Water Witch* caught up with *Richmond* and ranged alongside, Winslow suggested that the squadron return to Head of Passes, but Pope replied, pointing to the *Preble*, "Get the sloop over the bar." Winslow steamed over to *Preble* and dropped off his executive officer, Lieutenant John Lee Davis, who piloted the vessel out of the pass.

In the meantime, *Vincennes* grounded hard on a flat to the left of the channel, and Winslow could not bring his guns to bear. In attempting to meet an attack from upriver, Pope swung *Richmond* around and grounded a short distance from *Vincennes*. At this point, the mosquito fleet came down the pass and began shelling *Water Witch* and *Richmond*. *Vincennes* answered from its 9-inch shell gun mounted on the forecastle and a rifled howitzer on the poop. The only long-range rifled gun on *Water Witch* was a 12-pound howitzer, which the gunner brought to bear on *Ivy*.

Rather than remain in an exposed position where he could fight *Richmond*'s twenty-two guns and provide covering fire for the grounded *Vincennes*, Pope backed off into deeper water, drifted a quarter mile downriver, and grounded again. But this time *Richmond* swung into position to deliver a full broadside, the only problem being that both *Water Witch* and *Vincennes* lay in *Richmond*'s line of fire.[18]

By 8 A.M. Pope had had enough. He signaled to the vessels below the bar "to get underway," which was erroneously reported to Commander Handy on *Vincennes* as "abandon ship." Handy sent a young officer to *Water Witch* for confirmation, and Winslow replied "that no such signal had been made, and that Captain Handy should continue to defend his vessel." A little earlier in the action, Handy had complained to Pope, "We have only two guns that will bear in the direction of the enemy. Shall I re-

18. For Union navy reports concerning the action at Head of Passes, see *ibid.*, XVI, 703–17.

main on board . . . with my crippled ship and worn-out men? . . . Would it not be better to leave the ship? Shall I burn her when I leave her?" Pope promptly replied, "It will be your duty to defend your ship up to the last moment, and not fire her, except . . . to prevent her from falling into the hands of the enemy. . . . You have boats enough to save all your men. I do not approve of your leaving your ship until every effort to defend her from falling into enemy hands is made."[19]

Pope was stunned when at 9:30 A.M. Handy appeared alongside *Richmond* with all of his officers and part of his crew, the remainder having gone on board *Water Witch*. "Commander Handy," Pope wrote, "having wrapped around his waist in broad folds the American flag . . . stated he had abandoned his ship in obedience to [my] signal. Being told no such signal had been made, he insisted he so read it; that Captain Winslow had so read it. The following day Winslow admitted "he saw no such signal."[20]

Handy advised Pope that he had "lighted a slow match at the magazine" and expected the explosion momentarily. Pope fumed as he paced the quarterdeck, waiting for the detonation, and wondered how he would explain this to his superiors. But unknown to Handy, the gunner ordered to light the fuse to the magazine had cut off the burning end and thrown it in the water. After waiting a half hour for the promised explosion, Pope sent Handy back to the *Vincennes* with his crew and directed them to throw overboard some of the fourteen guns in order to lighten the ship until she could be kedged off the bar. About the same time, Hollins' fleet unaccountably ceased fire and withdrew up the river. By the following morning, October 13, both *Richmond* and *Vincennes* floated over the bar and anchored in the Gulf.[21]

When orders came from Hollins to withdraw, Lieutenant Fry became understandably upset. For the first time, *Ivy*'s big 8-inch (132-pounder) rifle had been able "to hull the *Richmond*" with every shot. Late in the action, Fry claimed *Richmond* had shown a white flag. "I was astonished beyond measure at this," he wrote, "and stopped my firing . . . I started to report the circumstances, when the flag was hauled down, the act being *preceded* by the discharge . . . of an eleven-inch gun and her whole broadside. The only explanation of the flag to my mind was that the sloop-of-war [*Vincennes*] being aground with her stern to us, *Richmond* being also

19. *Ibid.*, XVI, 711, 712, 716, Winslow to McKean, October 24, 1861, Handy to Pope and Pope to Handy (n.d.).

20. *Ibid.*, 710, Pope to McKean, October 17, 1861.

21. *Ibid.*, Handy to McKean, October 14, and Pope to McKean, October 17, 1861; Gosnell, *Guns on the Western Waters*, 43.

in the mud, they presumed our other steamers were armed with rifled cannon, and being at our mercy, they meant to make an appeal to us to stay proceedings."

At this point Hollins recalled his gunboats and withdrew up the pass. Fry's clerk had kept score on the shots fired, attributing to *Richmond*, 107; *Water Witch*, 18; *Vincennes*, 16; *Ivy*, 26; *McRae*, 23, and *Tuscarora*, 6. Hollins' lightly armed flagship *Calhoun* took no active part in the fight. Fry stated that some of *Richmond*'s shots passed over *Ivy*. If so, Pope's gunners seemed unaware of the range of their own guns.[22]

In the aftermath of the Union retreat, Pope wrote McKean: "I am sorry to say it, but . . . Handy is not fit to command a ship. He is a laughingstock of all and everyone. I do not know what you can do in the case."[23]

McKean had no trouble deciding what to do with Handy. He detached him without recourse to a court of inquiry and sent him north on the first supply steamer. Later, three members of *Vincennes'* crew gave sworn statements verifying that the flag signal shown by *Richmond*—blue, white, blue— was indeed an order to abandon ship, and when Seaman Nathaniel P. Allen responded from *Vincennes*, the signal was hauled down. Nonetheless, Handy's second appeal for a court of inquiry was also denied. Without a vessel to command, he faded into naval oblivion. The white signal flag might also explain what Fry had mistaken as the surrender of *Richmond*.[24]

Somebody had to pay for the disaster at the passes, and at first Handy's ineptitude in handling his ship drew the sharpest criticism. After McKean reviewed the facts, Captain Pope's performance came under harsh scrutiny. By not re-entering Southwest Pass and making an attempt to recover control of Head of Passes, and by ordering all other vessels in the area to his assistance, he opened the other outlets of the Mississippi and raised his own blockade. If McKean considered cashiering his flag officer, Pope made it easy by applying to be relieved, giving reasons of health. McKean promptly placed Captain Francis B. Ellison in command of *Richmond*.[25]

On the morning of October 13, reports began to drift into New Orleans. The *True Delta* reported that "our gallant little mosquito fleet . . . was a complete success, and perhaps the most brilliant and remarkable naval ex-

22. Fry's account of the fight appears in Jennie Mort Walker, *Life of Captain Joseph Fry: The Cuban Martyr* (Hartford, 1875), 147–50.

23. *ORN*, XVI, 722, Pope to McKean, October 14, 1861.

24. *Ibid.*, 706, McKean to Welles, October 25, 1861; *ibid.*, 719–21. Sworn statements of William Burrows, Nathaniel P. Allen, and Thomas Whoole, October 28, and Handy to McKean, October 20, 28, 1861.

25. *Ibid.*, 748, McKean to Welles, October 24, 1861.

ploit on record." The newspaper went on to report erroneously: "The sloop of war *Preble* is sunk, another vessel captured, and the balance driven ashore. All honor to the heroic Hollins." The paper cannot be entirely blamed for the error—from Fort Jackson Hollins had wired the same story to Richmond.[26]

As late as October 23, the newspapers still did not have the correct story, printing that *Manassas* penetrated "the *Preble* 16 feet, and the force of the Mississippi took her stern around and tore open the planks. The *Preble* then drifted stern on the bar, and there will rest her ribs." The report switched to *Richmond*: "Our fleet opened fire on her. The *Richmond* fired several broadsides briskly. It was all Commodore Hollins desired, for every broadside shook her to such a degree that it buried her deeper in the sand." As southern readers offered words of praise to Hollins and his mosquito fleet, *Preble* pulled into Ship Island for supplies and *Richmond* rocked at her old station off Southwest Pass. Nonetheless, Mallory heaped words of praise upon his newly promoted flag officer, George Hollins, who for most of the action remained well upriver and beyond sight of the actual engagement.[27]

The vessel that started Pope's headlong rush for the safety of the bar, the humpbacked and stackless turtle, limped into New Orleans on October 23 under tow and bumped against the dock for repairs. Warley and the crew received a hero's welcome and two months later a few kind words from Secretary Mallory. *Manassas* did little actual damage but succeeded in scaring the "living daylights" out of Captain Pope. She was the first of the ironclads to attack a Union vessel, and the first to create a fear among Union commanders that eventually grew into a syndrome referred to in naval circles as "ram fever." Aside from her uniqueness, *Manassas* proved to be a poorly designed vessel with no fighting power and little mobility. Nonetheless, she made an impression on Captain Pope, who wrote, "Everyone is in great dread of that infernal ram. I keep a guard boat out up river during the night."[28]

While New Orleans and the Confederate Navy Department celebrated Flag Officer Hollins' great victory, nobody but Lieutenant Fry asked why,

26. *Ibid.*, 727–28, Hollins to Mallory, October 12 [13], 1861; New Orleans *True Delta*, October 13, 1861.

27. *ORN*, XVI, 730, Mallory to Hollins, October 26, 1861; Richmond *Dispatch*, October 23, 1861.

28. Richmond *Dispatch*, October 23, 1861; *ORN*, XVI, 722, 730a, Pope to McKean, October 14, 1861, Hollins to Warley, January 20, 1862.

on the morning of October 12, the mosquito fleet withdrew at a time when both *Vincennes* and *Richmond* had gone aground. At times, the long guns of the mosquito fleet overshot *Richmond* by as much as five hundred yards. According to Hollins' later reports, he may not have had sufficient coal and ammunition to continue the contest, but he certainly had the opportunity to damage both vessels severely and with a little luck, perhaps destroy them both. *Ivy, McRae,* and *Tuscarora* could have remained beyond the range of Union guns and with better marksmanship, fired effectively at their leisure. *Richmond* lay fast on the bar until late in the day, and *Vincennes* remained stuck until the following afternoon. Hollins had the Union squadron at his mercy, and he left it embarrassed and in chaos, but virtually undamaged. [29]

For the Confederate navy, this "victory" turned out to be a lost opportunity. With the exception of a few days when some of the passes were open, the engagement accomplished little but to scare off four Union vessels and force the replacement of two timid Union skippers. The action, or lack of it, sent signals to Gideon Welles. If he intended to breach the Mississippi, he had to send stronger vessels and more competent commanders. The message also included a new threat — Confederate ironclads. A few rumors had already drifted into the Union naval office of ironclads on the stocks of the busy shipyards in New Orleans.

And what had become of the turtle? Would she return more powerful than ever? Pope certainly did not know; he was too busy exiting Southwest Pass and never saw her again. Had he taken his squadron back upstream, he may have found her still lodged on a mudbank. Union Naval Secretary Welles dubbed the whole affair "Pope's Run." Years later, Admiral David D. Porter summed it up: "Put this matter in any light you may, it is the most ridiculous affair that ever took place in the American Navy."[30]

But for now, New Orleans celebrated. Flag Officer Hollins languished on the balcony of the St. Charles Hotel and watched bands play and military units salute as they marched past his headquarters. He had embarrassed the mighty Union navy, but that was all. His was a half-won victory, but it was enough to give the Confederacy, and especially New Orleans, a reason to celebrate.[31]

29. *Ibid.*, 704, 710, Pope to McKean, October 13, 17, 1861; *ORN*, Ser. 2, II, 516, Hollins to Mallory, October 24, 1861.

30. Porter, *Naval History*, 91.

31. New Orleans *True Delta*, October 22, and New Orleans *Daily Picayune*, October 22, 1861.

SIX *Father Neptune Picks a Captain*

On the heels of "Pope's Run," Lieutenant David D. Porter returned to Southwest Pass on *Powhatan* on October 25, 1861. He had been on the trail of *Sumter* and its wily captain, Raphael Semmes, since August 16 and never caught him. Porter was disappointed, because capturing *Sumter* may have meant a big promotion and more prize money. He had waited a long time for the promotion, and during his absence, he had been advanced a grade to commander, his new rank dating from April 22, but now all he had to look forward to was more blockade duty, a duty he despised.

To chase Semmes, Porter had pressed the ship hard, calling for the last ounce of steam as she tumbled through the seas, and the old side-wheeler was falling apart. "Her boilers were unfit for use," he wrote, and "she is rotten throughout . . . 25 feet of her false keel is knocked off, part of her forefront is gone, 500 sheets of copper are off the bottom, and what is left is loose." For the moment, Porter was spared further blockade duty. McKean ordered Porter and his worn side-wheeler to the Brooklyn Navy Yard, where they arrived on November 9. By then, Secretary Welles was in a better mood. Captain Samuel F. DuPont had just scored an important victory at Port Royal, demonstrating that with proper preparation, wooden warships could safely pass heavily embrasured enemy fortifications. Porter quickly observed that if DuPont could do it at Port Royal, perhaps it could be done on the lower Mississippi. But there was a complication: he was only a commander, and a junior one at that, and a commander does not lead a flotilla of warships against heavy fortifications. Besides, the earthworks at Port Royal were sandhills compared to the powerful works at Jackson and St. Philip.[1]

1. *ORN*, XVI, 750, 751, Porter to McKean and McKean to Welles, October 25, 28, 1861; West,

Leaving *Powhatan* in New York, Porter took a train to his home in Georgetown. He had not seen his family for seven months, but he stopped barely long enough to greet his wife and children. An idea sputtering in the back of his mind had taken shape during the sweltering months off Southwest Pass and the days at sea chasing Semmes. Porter had hesitated to discuss it with any of his superiors, but DuPont's victory opened the way. Now, while on leave, he would see his friend Assistant Naval Secretary Fox, who would know what to do and how best to do it. A lowly commander had no business barging in upon the secretary of the navy with a wild plan to capture New Orleans.

Porter found Fox friendly but uncommunicative, and he tried but could not obtain an interview with "Father Neptune." On November 12, he lingered at the Naval Office until he spotted two Republican senators of the Naval Affairs Committee, John P. Hale of New Hampshire and James W. Grimes of Iowa. Both stood chatting outside the entrance to Welles's office. They greeted Porter warmly and asked what business brought him to Washington. When Porter replied "to lay a proposition for the capture of New Orleans before the Secretary of the Navy," the senators listened approvingly and invited him to join them for a meeting with the secretary.[2]

Welles had heard of Porter but not met him, although he might have known the commander's reputation as a somewhat devisive opportunist prone to taking independent action. If members of the Naval Affairs Committee thought Porter had something of value to say, Welles would listen. Besides, the granite-tough, black-bearded commander with the flashing dark eyes appeared to be a naval officer who got things done.[3]

Among the Union's naval officers, probably no one knew the lower Mississippi better than Porter. He had served with the Coastal Survey, resided briefly in New Orleans as a naval recruiting officer during the Mexican War, and afterward captained the mail steamer *Crescent City* on her regular run between New York, Havana, and New Orleans. He knew the river, its outlets, and its bars; he had visited the nearby lakes and bays; and in his regular trips to New Orleans, he may have stopped at the ram-

Second Admiral, 105–12, 114.

    2. David Dixon Porter, *Incidents and Anecdotes of the Civil War* (New York, 1885), 64. The date of the meeting is not clear. Mrs. Gustavus Vasa Fox's diary in the Blair Papers, Library of Congress, places the discussion on November 14.

    3. Welles's distrust of Porter went back to April, 1861, when Secretary of State Seward and President Lincoln issued secret instructions to Porter without the knowledge of the naval secretary. See West, *Second Admiral,* 77–86.

shackle forts above Head of Passes and bought fresh fish for the ship's larder.

Speaking, Porter said, from personal observation, the best way to blockade New Orleans was to capture and occupy it. Citing the example of DuPont's victory at Port Royal, Porter believed that wooden ships could pass Forts Jackson and St. Philip, provided they were preceded by a smothering forty-eight-hour bombardment of 13-inch mortar shells. Mortars had always been considered the army's foremost siege weapon, but Porter proposed a unique use for them, mounting the weapons on modified schooners to eliminate the need for a large cooperating land-based force. At most, all the navy would need to carry out the mission was support from a few thousand soldiers to garrison the captured forts and occupy the city. Much to Porter's surprise, Welles liked the idea. In fact, the secretary confided, the department had been considering an attack on New Orleans for some time. After the senators left, Welles called for Fox and suggested the three of them go to the White House and discuss the matter with Lincoln.[4]

After the war, Horace Greeley gave credit for the plan to the controversial Benjamin Butler. James Parton, Butler's biographer, credited the idea to both Secretary of War Edward Stanton and Butler. If Parton had checked the calendar, he might have noticed that Stanton did not become secretary until two months later. Welles, who in postwar years developed personal differences with Porter, declared that Porter had no more to do with developing the plan than Butler. The plan, Welles insisted, was developed and designed by the Naval Office. In the scramble for later credit, Fox declared he thought of it first, and some supported his claim. Regardless of who conceived the idea, Porter played a curious but important role in its execution, and nobody put more effort into making it work. Very likely, by the time the plan unfolded, many people contributed to its final formulation.

Historians are undecided on who, if any single person, first conceived the plan to pass Forts Jackson and St. Philip in wooden warships. Nonetheless, the evidence is clear that Porter was shuffled over to the White House with Welles and Fox. Welles would not have taken Porter to the president unless he felt certain the commander had something of value to say. It is reasonable to assume, as Fox later claimed, that the matter had been a topic of discussion in the Naval Office prior to Porter's visit, but if Porter

---

4. Porter, *Incidents and Anecdotes*, 64–65; West, *Second Admiral*, 114. Welles's distrust of Porter appears in his *Diary*, I, 19, 35–37, 88. See also Charles Lee Lewis, *David Glasgow Farragut: Our First Admiral* (Annapolis, 1943), 6–7.

did not conceive the overall plan—which is also likely—he was the only one to recommend the use of mortar schooners. Porter, an innovator with a quick mind, had no doubt suggested the mortars as a way to include himself in an important campaign. Quite possibly Welles had counseled Lincoln earlier about the risks of running the forts. Now he wanted Porter's voice added to the discussion. Porter's novel idea of using mortar schooners might reduce Lincoln's anxiety over the possible prospect of losing most of the Gulf Squadron, and for a campaign this uncertain, Welles needed presidential approval.

As a naval strategy, Porter's proposal sounded plausible to civilians, and to a man who lived most of his life on the prairie, sensible. Neither Welles nor Lincoln could afford another "Pope's Run." Porter's idea of first reducing the forts with a mortar barrage became the key to obtaining approval for the project, and this was probably the reason Welles took him to the White House.[5]

According to Porter, Lincoln paced the floor, "calm and thoughtful," as the junior naval officer discussed conditions at the mouth of the Mississippi and answered questions from decision makers who had never been there. The president, who as a young man had twice journeyed down the river on flatboats, probably remembered the stacked levees along Canal Street and the sailing ships waiting in line to exchange their cargos, but he had never descended to the forts. The plan interested Lincoln, but he admitted to not being a military man. In his *Anecdotes,* Porter recalled Lincoln's comments: "It seems to me what the lieutenant proposes is feasible. He says a dozen ships will take the forts and city, and there should be twenty thousand soldiers sent along to hold it. After New Orleans is taken ... we can push on to Vicksburg and open the river all the way along. We will go to see General [George B.] McClellan and find out if he can't manage to get the troops."[6]

That evening, Welles, Fox, and Porter, joined later by Lincoln, met at the general's residence. At first, despite DuPont's recent success, McClellan—who considered Forts Jackson and St. Philip among the strongest fortifications in the country—argued that wooden warships would be cut to

5. See correspondence between Welles and Fox in the David Dixon Porter Papers, Henry E. Huntington Library and Art Gallery, San Marino, California: Welles to Fox, June 8, 10, and Fox to Welles, June 17, August 12, 1871. Welles made his case in Gideon Welles, "Admiral Farragut and New Orleans," *The Galaxy: An Illustrated Magazine of Entertaining Reading,* XII (November, 1871), 673, 676, 677, 819, 821. For contemporary accounts, see Lewis, *Farragut,* 7; Dufour, *Night the War Was Lost,* 136–38.

6. Porter, *Incidents and Anecdotes,* 64–65.

splinters if they tried to pass the forts. McClellan may have been more concerned about the dilution of his own military force. Fox later remembered McClellan's reaction when he learned only ten thousand troops would be required to hold the city, not the fifty thousand he had imagined. The general, Fox said, came "readily into the agreement."

McClellan sided with Porter on the use of a mortar flotilla as "absolutely essential for success," perhaps believing this strategy would necessitate the use of enough army personnel to give him a share of the credit for any victory. Fox, who claimed somewhat rigidly that "the steamers could pass the forts without reducing or even bombarding them," yielded when the secretary asserted that Porter's proposition "might render assistance and be of no detriment to the expedition."[7]

In this meeting Porter probably performed a more passive role than he portrayed in his flamboyant *Anecdotes*. Nonetheless, he helped launch one of the most important strategies of the Civil War, one that Lincoln insisted be kept most secret. At the time, Welles and Fox were no doubt pleased with Porter's help in obtaining both Lincoln's and McClellan's support. A few days later Porter received the first of many rewards when Welles placed him in command of the mortar flotilla. Porter was delighted. Responsibility for a squadron exceeded Porter's expectations, and he probably sniffed promotion in the offing.[8]

With his customary energy, Porter immersed himself in the details of creating the mortar flotilla. Schooners had to be bought and cut down, their beds reinforced to carry 13-inch mortars and their decks modified to receive heavy carriages on pivots. Several light-draft steamers had to be purchased to tow the schooners around to the Gulf and up the Mississippi. Foundries already backlogged with orders for army cannon received orders to squeeze in twenty big mortars and thirty thousand 13-inch shells. The task could take months.

While Porter scoured navy yards and commercial shipyards for schooners, Welles faced another dilemma. Who would command the attack? Certainly not Porter. In selecting a flag officer, Welles had four dozen senior officers on the Navy Register to choose from, but most of them topped sixty years of age, and Welles probably wondered if any of them possessed the stamina for the assignment. McKean, for example, who was already in the

---

7. Fox to Welles, June 19, 1871, in Gustavus Vasa Fox Papers, Huntington Library; Welles, "Farragut and New Orleans," 678; Dufour, *Night the War Was Lost,* 136–37; West, *Second Admiral,* 115–16.

8. West, *Second Admiral,* 116.

Gulf, came immediately to mind, but he was ill and needed to be replaced.

After the war, both Porter and Fox took credit for suggesting the post be given to Captain David Glasgow Farragut, but it was probably Fox who made the recommendation. At least his brother-in-law, Postmaster General Montgomery Blair, a close confidant of Lincoln, said so. But Porter may once again have been drawn into a decision that put him in the position of recommending his own boss.[9] According to Porter, Fox brought him a list of several candidates, among whom was Farragut. By an odd coincidence, Farragut was Porter's own foster brother, having been adopted at the age of eight, about four years before Porter was born.[10] Farragut, like many of his colleagues, was sixty years of age, but Porter claimed all the other candidates had forgotten that their primary duty was to fight and manifested the same defects as the captains at "Pope's Run." In Porter's version, Fox evidently agreed and took the recommendation back to Welles.

Welles had previously formed a favorable impression of Farragut, but "neither the President nor any member of the Cabinet knew him, or knew of him." Farragut, whose home had been in Norfolk, became a marked man in Welles's mind: when Virginia seceded, Farragut denounced the act and "abandoned the State, leaving his home and property the day following, avowing openly and boldly, in the face of the Rebels by whom he was surrounded, his determination to live and die owing allegiance to no flag but that of the Union." But in his meticulous way, Welles wanted the opinion of somebody besides Fox and Porter. Captain Joseph Smith, who had been chief of the Bureau of Yards and Docks at a time when Farragut was commandant of the Mare Island Naval Yard, replied to Welles's query by writing, "I consider him a bold, impetuous man, of a great deal of courage and energy, but his capabilities and power to command a squadron are a subject to be determined only by trial."[11]

Welles realized no guarantees came with command, but the relationship between Porter and Farragut, along with Fox's encouragement, influenced the secretary's decision. Referring to the opinions of other senior officers, Welles wrote, "Most of them . . . while speaking well of Farragut,

---

9. Montgomery Blair, "Opening the Mississippi," *The United Service: A Monthly Review of Military and Naval Affairs*, IV (January, 1881), 38.

10. The actual date of Farragut's adoption by David Porter, Sr., is obscure, but both Loyall Farragut and Alfred T. Mahan place the time at about 1809. See Alfred Thayer Mahan, *Admiral Farragut* (New York, 1892), 4–8; Loyall Farragut, *The Life of David Glasgow Farragut: First Admiral of the U.S. Navy* (New York, 1879), 9–11.

11. Welles, *Diary*, II, 116, 134–35; Farragut, *Life of Farragut*, 204–205.

doubted if he was equal to the position . . . but yet no one would name the man for a great and active campaign." At this point Welles had said nothing of New Orleans. He followed his own instincts, which were usually pretty good in sizing up character, and decided upon Farragut, admitting that "as Porter himself was to take a conspicuous part in the expedition, it had an important influence."[12]

Welles's only direct contact with Farragut had been a day fifteen years earlier at the Naval Office during the secretary's brief stint as head of the Bureau of Provisions and Clothing. This was during the Mexican War, and Farragut, a much younger naval officer then, had made an impressive presentation to Naval Secretary John Y. Mason. It had been delivered resolutely, earnestly, and in impressive detail. Mason considered the proposal too risky and somewhat visionary, but Welles remembered it well. He wondered if Farragut still possessed the same assertiveness. Instead of inviting him to the Naval Office to find out directly, he once again called upon foster brother Porter to go to New York and "ascertain, in personal interviews and conversations on naval matters and belligerent operations . . . the views of Captain Farragut on the subject of [a] naval attack as was proposed by the Navy Department, without advising him of our object or letting him know that the Department had any purpose in Porter's inquiries or knew of them."[13]

About the middle of December, Porter met Farragut at the Pierpont House in Brooklyn. The two men had not seen each other for ten years, but Porter described Farragut as active and energetic. "Time had added grey hairs to his head, and a few lines of intelligence, generally called 'crow's feet,' round his eyes. Otherwise he seemed unchanged."[14]

Porter's father, who commanded the frigate *Essex* during the War of 1812, had taken nine-year-old Davey Farragut into the navy as a midshipman on December 17, 1810. By the age of twelve he was serving as a prize master. At thirteen he participated courageously in the unequal battle between *Essex* and two British frigates, *Cherub* and *Phoebe,* in the harbor of Valparaiso. At twenty-one he became lieutenant, but soon afterward promotions in the navy slowed down. During the Mexican War he was elevated to commander but spent most of those years on blockade duty. Finally in 1855 he became a captain, only to find twenty-six others in

12. Welles, *Diary,* II, 116–17.
13. Welles, "Farragut and New Orleans," 681, 682.
14. David Porter, "Private Journal," I, 181.

line ahead of him. In a navy that traditionally picked its flag officers by seniority, Farragut probably held low expectations.[15]

The only record of the conversation between Porter and Farragut is an exaggerated account contained in Porter's *Private Journal* and describing a junior officer somewhat harshly interrogating a senior officer behind closed doors. More likely, Porter led Farragut through the questioning in a manner that invited the right answers. Porter cherished promotion, and it was not outside his character to divulge information that another interviewer would have cautiously withheld. Of all the candidates who might command the expedition, certainly no one would feel more obligated to Porter than his own foster brother.

According to Porter, one of his objectives was to determine if Farragut would fight against the South. The captain had been born at Campbells Station near Knoxville, Tennessee, on July 5, 1801, but he had spent part of his early childhood on a farm by Mississippi's Pascagoula River, not far from New Orleans. He had relatives who still lived in New Orleans and a wife who came from Norfolk, Virginia. Because Farragut abandoned his Virginia home, Welles probably had little concern about the man's fidelity to the Union, but he knew there would be others who might criticize the appointment. If Farragut was not wholeheartedly Welles's man, he was certainly Porter's, who left the interview claiming to have said, "You will hear in twenty-four hours what your fate will be." If the truth were known, Porter probably promised his foster brother that he would do everything he could to get him named flag officer, knowing that some day the favor might be returned.[16]

Porter claims to have then wired Fox, "Farragut accepts the command, as I was sure he would," although there is no evidence to suggest that Porter was ever given authority to offer the post. That prerogative belonged to Welles. However, years later Farragut admitted, "My first intimation of that attack [on New Orleans] was a message through him [Porter] from the Department to know if I thought New Orleans could be taken, to which I replied in the affirmative. The next message was to know if I could take it, to which I answered I thought so and, if furnished with the proper means, was willing to try."[17]

---

15. Farragut, *Life of Farragut*, 8–11; Faust (ed.), *HTI*, 254.

16. Faust (ed.), *HTI*, 254; Farragut, *Life of Farragut*, 8–9; Mahan, *Admiral Farragut*, 94. Farragut's first wife also came from Norfolk.

17. David Dixon Porter, "The Opening of the Lower Mississippi," *B&L*, II, 28; Lewis,

Farragut went to Washington a few days after his meeting with Porter and arrived there on December 21. Postmaster General Blair and Assistant Naval Secretary Fox met him for breakfast and laid out the whole plan, including a list of vessels being fitted out for the fleet.

"What is your opinion of it?" asked Fox.

"It will succeed," Farragut answered quickly, but after scanning the list of warships assigned, he added, "I will engage to run by the forts and capture New Orleans with two-thirds of the number."

Fox seemed satisfied with Farragut's reaction and said, "More vessels will be added to these, and you are to command the expedition."

Farragut was delighted. When he left to report to Welles, Fox turned to Blair and asked, "Don't you think Farragut is too enthusiastic?"

Blair replied, "No. I was most favorably impressed with him, and I am sure he will succeed."[18]

Had Porter been in Farragut's meeting with Welles, he might have been shocked to hear his foster brother say, in reference to the mortar flotilla, "I would not have advised this, as these vessels will be likely to warn the enemy of our intentions, and I do not place much reliance upon them. But some of them have already been procured, and they may be more efficient and of greater benefit than I anticipate. So I willingly adopt the [mortar] flotilla as part of my command."[19]

After his meeting with Welles, Farragut wrote home, saying: "Keep your lips closed and burn my letters; for perfect silence is to be observed— the first injunction of the Secretary. I am to have a flag in the Gulf, and the rest depends upon myself. Keep calm and silent. I shall sail in three weeks."[20]

Even after the issue of command had been decided, several members of Congress questioned the decision. Why had Flag Officer Silas Stringham, who had given the navy a victory at Hatteras, or Samuel F. DuPont, who achieved an important victory at Port Royal, not been chosen? Both were Union-born, tried and true. Senator Hale asked Welles if he were certain of his man, "Southern born, a Southern resident, with a Southern wife," plus a brother in New Orleans, a sister at Pascagoula, and now of all things, Captain John Mitchell, the husband of Farragut's cousin, in

Farragut, 11–12. Unfortunately, Farragut's letter was written in 1869 and does not indicate whether Farragut learned of the planned attack on New Orleans before or after his meeting with Porter.

　18. Blair, "Opening the Mississippi," 39.

　19. Welles, "Farragut and New Orleans," 683.

　20. Farragut, *Life of Farragut*, 208n.

command of the Confederate flotilla below New Orleans. Besides, they wanted to know, who really knew Farragut? When word leaked around the upper echelon of the navy, senior officers referred to Farragut as a daring and dashing fellow but of doubtful "discretion and ability to command a squadron judiciously."[21]

But Welles had made his decision and would live with it. He had conducted his own private research into Farragut's qualifications, and not even Senator Hale, who sat on the Naval Affairs Board and favored DuPont for the post, could change his mind. On January 9, 1862, Welles issued orders giving command of the newly constituted West Gulf Blockading Squadron, from western Florida to the Rio Grande, to Farragut, and on March 19 the Senate confirmed his appointment to flag officer.[22]

For Davey Porter, everything was moving in the direction he wanted. Twenty schooners, each carrying one 13-inch mortar, were fitting out in the Brooklyn Navy Yard. Back in the Naval Office, Fox cut orders for officers and crew to man the flotilla. In Pittsburgh, foundries worked around the clock casting giant, keglike mortars and thirty thousand 13-inch shells. For foundry capacity, Porter's principal competitor was Flag Officer Andrew Hull Foote, lately detached from the Brooklyn Navy Yard and loaned to the army to build and fight ironclad gunboats for Major General Henry W. Halleck. The delays were aggravating. Gun carriages had been mounted in the schooners, but the mortars seemed to take forever.

The only other credential missing was a promotion. Certainly an officer in charge of a flotilla deserved a grade higher than commander, but for the present Porter had received something no other commander in the navy had been given—visibility and opportunity. And Davey Porter would make the most of it. [23]

At a time when the Union navy was concentrating its numerous resources on attacking the lower Mississippi and capturing New Orleans, Secretary Mallory sent Flag Officer Hollins and his mosquito fleet upriver to join Major General Leonidas Polk in the Confederate defense of Columbus, Kentucky. The floating battery *New Orleans* was towed along with the fleet and reached Columbus about the same time Welles was selecting Farragut as a Union flag officer. By then, Mallory had received word of several river ironclads under construction by the Union navy at Carondelet and

21. Welles, *Diary*, II, 117, 119.
22. *ORN*, XVIII, 5, 73, Welles to Farragut, January 9, March 21, 1862.
23. *Ibid.*, Welles to Porter, December 2, 1861; West, *Second Admiral*, 118.

Mound City, but by sending Hollins upriver, he left New Orleans without naval protection. The ironclads *Louisiana* and *Mississippi* were still on the ways, the gunboats *Livingston, Bienville,* and *Carondelet* were still in shipyards, and the side-wheel river steamers *Maurepas* and *Pontchartrain* were in various stages of being refitted and reinforced to carry guns. In Algiers, the floating battery *Memphis* languished against the levee, waiting for iron and her full complement of eighteen guns.[24]

Secretary Mallory still shared with the War Department the popular belief that the threat to New Orleans would come from upriver and not from the Gulf. The citizens of New Orleans did not agree. But Mallory had no control over improving the fortifications at Forts Jackson and St. Philip, and because so little coordination existed between the War Department and the Naval Department in Richmond, or anywhere else, Mallory had no reason to believe that General Twiggs was not attending to the matter. What he may not have known was that Twiggs, on October 5, had asked to be relieved of command.[25]

The resulting confusion continued to propagate, and over the next five months it grew steadily worse.

24. Fletcher Pratt, *Civil War on the Western Waters* (New York, 1956), 14–21; *ORN*, Ser. 2, I, 464, Investigation of the Navy Department; New Orleans *Daily Picayune*, November 16, 18, 19, 1861.

25. *ORA*, LIII, 748, Twiggs to Benjamin, October 5, 1861.

SEVEN *Mansfield Lovell's Debut*

*On September 25, 1861, ten days before General Twiggs asked to be relieved, the Con-*federate War Department issued orders for Brigadier General Mansfield Lovell "to repair to New Orleans" and report to the ancient commander. As Twiggs's subordinate, Lovell was charged with "the coast and other defenses of the department." Lovell took his time getting to New Orleans, and when he arrived on October 17, he learned he had been elevated to major general and placed in charge of Department No. 1, which consisted of Louisiana and the southern third of Mississippi.[1]

Some Orleanians looked upon Lovell's promotion with skepticism; others heralded it as a positive improvement over Twiggs. Lovell was born in the District of Columbia on October 20, 1822, which made him thirty-nine years of age and full of the exuberance and energy Twiggs lacked. Ranked ninth in the class of 1842 at West Point, he had received a wound as an artillery lieutenant in the Mexican War, and was brevetted captain. On December 18, 1854, he resigned from the army with his close friend and classmate Gustavus W. Smith, and established a business in New York City that promptly failed. Smith became the city's commissioner of streets and offered Lovell the post of deputy; both men remained with the street commission until September 19, 1861. Through lobbying efforts by Smith in Richmond, the War Department granted Lovell a commission and sent him to New Orleans to help Twiggs execute his responsibilities. When Twiggs asked to be relieved, Lovell was available and already on his way to the city.[2]

1. *ORA*, VI, 643, LIII, 748–49, Withers to Lovell, October 7, and Benjamin to Lovell, October 9, 1861.
2. Faust (ed.), *HTI*, 450–51, 695–96.

Because Lovell had lived in New York and then waited until September to join the Confederate cause, some southerners questioned his loyalty. From her home on Bayou Lafourche, Mrs. Braxton Bragg expressed her sentiments to her husband by writing, "Yesterday's paper informs us that ... *Mansfield Lovell*, never conspicuous that I am aware of, of doubtful attachment to our cause, certainly *very slow* in joining us, has been raised to the same rank as yourself & assumes this important command of two States!" On October 18 she added, "Gen. Lovell has not yet arrived. I presume he will make a great stir when he does come. You know he is very fond of pomp and show."[3]

Mrs. Bragg was correct about anticipating glowing press commentaries. Lovell reached New Orleans on October 17, and the October 18 edition of the *Daily Delta* showered superlatives on the "able and accomplished" young general of "remarkable foresight, knowledge, experience, bravery."[4]

Before Lovell departed from Richmond, he spoke to both President Davis and Secretary Benjamin regarding the question of control over the naval units in New Orleans. He argued that the commanding general should have use of all means of defense, and the only way to defend New Orleans properly was to unify the command. Evidently the president listened without responding, because a few days later Benjamin reminded Davis of an imminent misunderstanding between himself and General Lovell. On October 17, Davis wrote: "The fleet maintained at the port of New Orleans and its vicinity is not a part of your command; and the purpose for which it is sent there, or removed from there, are communicated in orders and letters of a department with which you have no direct communication. It must ... be obvious to you that you could not assume command of these officers and vessels coming with your geographical department, but not placed on duty with you, without serious detriment to discipline and probably injury to the public service." Davis closed by encouraging "unrestrained intercourse and cordial fraternization" with Mallory's navy, words that had no more significance in New Orleans than they had in Richmond.[5]

Lovell arrived in New Orleans five days after Hollins' mosquito fleet drove Pope's intruders out of Head of Passes. With the Confederate navy riding on a crest of praise, Lovell discarded his request for overall com-

3. Mrs. Bragg to Braxton Bragg, October 13, 18, 1861, in Braxton and Mrs. Bragg Papers, University of Texas Archives, Austin, quoted in Dufour, *Night the War Was Lost*, 67.

4. New Orleans *Daily Delta*, October 18, 1861.

5. *ORA*, VI, 645–46, Davis to Lovell, October 17, 1861.

mand, at least for the moment. But as time passed, he would begin to wonder who, if anyone, was really in charge of the navy. Aside from Davis' note excluding the navy from Lovell's purview, the War Department issued no specific instructions to the new commandant beyond doing what was "right and proper." General Twiggs, upon leaving, made no official report on the condition of the department, but he stated verbally that it "was almost entirely defenseless; that [he] had been unable to get anything done, and that at many points we could not make an hour's fight." Twiggs admitted that his "feeble state of health had prevented him from making personal inspections . . . of the department."[6]

For the next several weeks Lovell spent "night and day" inspecting field fortifications and those below the city. "I found matters generally so deficient and incomplete," he said, "that I was unwilling to commit their condition to writing for fear of their falling into wrong hands, and so stated to the Secretary." Forts Jackson and St. Philip had been under the supervision of Colonel Johnson K. Duncan, and Lovell found them in better shape but "still sadly deficient . . . for their full defense, and much of the ammunition on hand was so inferior in quality as to not give more than half range. . . . On inspection I found them armed principally with smoothbore 24 and 32 pounders, there not being in the whole department more than nine guns mounted of a greater caliber than a 32 pounder. . . . Seven of eight of the 32s had been rifled, but there was neither shot nor shell for them. The gun-carriages were generally old and . . . many of them were so decayed that I could insert a penknife with ease into the wood." None of the department's navigable rivers had been obstructed, and the smaller forts located on Lake Pontchartrain and elsewhere had "become much dilapidated . . . crumbling with their own weight," and armed only with old 24-pounders.[7]

Before leaving New Orleans, Twiggs had requisitioned more guns, and Lovell found them piled by the railroad where they had been received from the Gosport Navy Yard. There were "more than 100 old navy guns," Lovell reported, "many of which had been long in use and the others as to be unfit for friction tubes. Many of the guns had been cast more than forty years earlier. There were none larger than a 42-pounder, and a number were 32-pounder carronades, a gun entirely useless except for firing grape and canister at short distances. No carriages, chassis, or implements came with the guns, and none of them were mounted."[8]

6. *Ibid.*, 558, Lovell Testimony, April 7, 1863.
7. *Ibid.*, 559.
8. *Ibid.*

THE CONFEDERATE IRONCLAD "LOUISIANA."
On the way to Fort St. Philip.

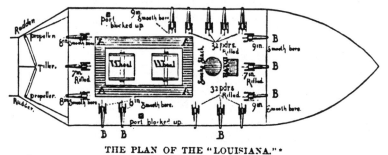

THE PLAN OF THE "LOUISIANA." *
After a sketch made by commander J. K. Mitchell, about the time of the engagement.

A A, Bulkhead around wheels.   B B, Guns used in action.

Sketch and plan of Confederate ironclad C.S.S. *Louisiana*.
From *Battles and Leaders of the Civil War*

Gun Deck of "LOUISIANA" (Confederate) April 24, 1862.

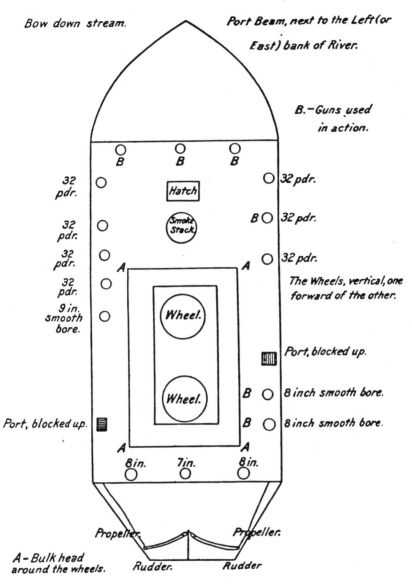

Bow down stream.

Port Beam, next to the Left (or East) bank of River.

B.—Guns used in action.

32 pdr.

32 pdr.

32 pdr.

32 pdr.

9 in. smooth bore.

Hatch

Smoke Stack

Wheel.

Wheel.

32 pdr.

32 pdr.

32 pdr.

The Wheels, vertical, one forward of the other.

Port, blocked up.

8 inch smooth bore.

8 inch smooth bore.

Port, blocked up.

8 in.   7 in.   8 in.

Propeller.   Propeller.

A — Bulk head around the wheels.

Rudder.   Rudder

Gun deck of C.S.S. *Louisiana*.
From *Official Records of the Navy*, Ser. I, Vol. 18

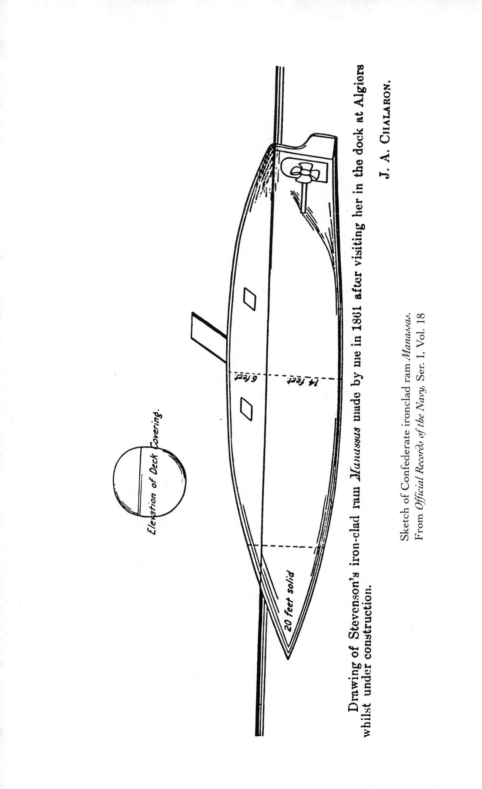

Elevation of Deck Covering.

20 feet solid

14 feet   6 feet

Drawing of Stevenson's iron-clad ram *Manassas* made by me in 1861 after visiting her in the dock at Algiers whilst under construction.

J. A. CHALARON.

Sketch of Confederate ironclad ram *Manassas*.
From *Official Records of the Navy*, Ser. I, Vol. 18

U.S.S. *Hartford*, 1864.
Courtesy U.S. Naval Historical Center

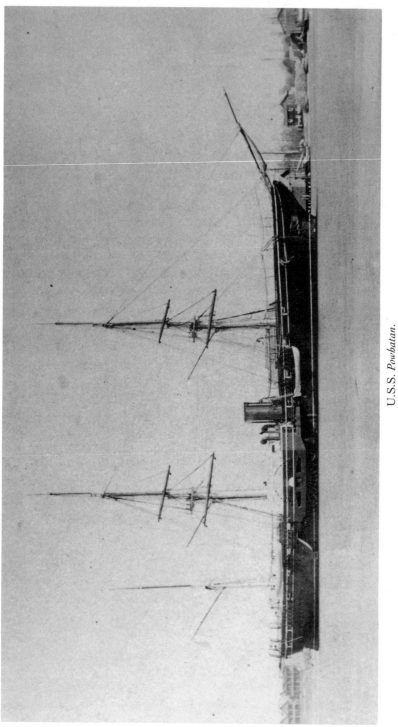

U.S.S. *Powhatan.*
Courtesy U.S. Naval Historical Center

Deck of a mortar schooner in Porter's fleet.
Courtesy U.S. Army Military History Institute

At Forts Jackson and St. Philip, Lovell found large piles of stacked lumber and a few men at work making fire rafts. Much of this material had been floated downriver months earlier when Beauregard suggested that a heavy log barrier be strung across the river and held together by heavy chains. Lovell gathered a list of shortages and requisitioned "all the large chains and anchors that could be had from Pensacola, Savannah, and other places."[9]

During his inspection, Lovell counted only five hundred barrels of powder. He reported some of it "old and unfit" for use, but remanufacturable if a supply of fresh saltpeter could be made available. He estimated that with the powder on hand, he could fire about twenty rounds per gun, "not more than enough for an hour's fight." He wrote Benjamin that if he had one hundred rounds per gun, he would feel "pretty safe." Twiggs, a month earlier, had made a similar request. In the meantime, Lovell activated three mills capable of producing about six thousand pounds of powder a day.[10]

Lovell discovered another problem — manpower. When a regiment enlisted for service in Louisiana, the War Department scooped it up and sent it elsewhere. On November 1, Lovell found five new regiments drilling at Camp Moore, seventy-eight miles north of New Orleans. They were "only partially armed and equipped," and "unfit to take the field." He counted three more regiments stationed along the Mississippi Coast, also poorly supplied, one regiment having "not more than five rounds per man."[11]

Strung around the city, double lines of eight-mile-long entrenchments had been laid out and started by General Twiggs. Another double line, four and a half miles long, was laid out to circle Algiers. Lovell found the lines "unfinished; not a gun was mounted, a magazine built, or a platform laid." The plans called for an exterior line containing a series of forts to defend the various water approaches, and an interior line fortified to repel an attack by land, with the flanks of both lines terminating along impassable swamps. To man the lines, Lovell scraped together twenty miscellaneous infantry companies raised by Twiggs, drilled them in heavy artillery, and fed them into the works. Earthworks, regardless of their strength, meant nothing without a sufficient number of men to defend them.[12]

9. *Ibid.*, 559, 560.

10. *Ibid.*, 560, 746, 754–55, 760, Twiggs to Benjamin, September 26, Lovell to Benjamin, October 23, 25, and Lovell to Davis, October 31, 1861.

11. *Ibid.*, 558–59, Lovell testimony.

12. *Ibid.*, 560.

Medical supplies, clothing, rifles, and even some of the big naval guns were being drained off by Richmond and shipped to Virginia, South Carolina, and Tennessee. Again Lovell appealed to War Secretary Benjamin, suggesting "that the heads of bureaus be requested to order nothing further ... from here until we have provided ourselves with a fair supply for the force required for the defense of this city." Lovell probably wondered who in Richmond was running the war when Benjamin responded, "I cannot restrain the heads of bureaus from purchasing or forwarding supplies from New Orleans. This interference with commerce exceeds my power except in cases of entreme emergency."[13] Lovell could not demonstrate the presence of an emergency, so the dilution of resources continued.

Aside from Colonel Duncan at Forts Jackson and St. Philip, Twiggs seems to have collected all the incompetent officers in the Confederate army and passed them on to Lovell. Brigadier General Daniel Ruggles, by rank second in command, arrived in New Orleans about the same time as Lovell. On October 31, Lovell wrote Davis, "With your permission I will urge strongly upon you the appointment of Col. J. K. Duncan as a brigadier-general; he is worth a dozen of Ruggles. . . . The public service would be advanced by giving him rank enough to direct . . . the colonels of volunteer regiments . . . who require a great deal of dry-nursing."[14]

Benjamin took no action on Lovell's request, because neither he nor President Davis considered Louisiana in imminent danger of attack. But in February, after Lovell had organized and trained a force of ten thousand infantry, Benjamin transferred five thousand of them to reinforce General Albert Sidney Johnston's forces, then being regrouped at Corinth following the loss of Forts Henry and Donelson. Lovell had no choice but to comply. He took the opportunity to send Ruggles with them, but he warned Benjamin, "I regret the necessity of sending away my only force . . . and feel sure that it will create a great panic here."

For the present, the panic existed in faraway Tennessee. General Grant had just captured Forts Henry and Donelson and was pushing General Johnston's retreating army into northern Mississippi. The citizens of New Orleans undoubtedly hoped Grant would be stopped before the Yankee horde reached the uncompleted entrenchments protecting their city. [15]

13. *Ibid.*, 561, 753, 758, 646, Lovell Testimony, Lovell to Benjamin and Benjamin to Lovell, October 18, 29, Gorgas and Gibbon to Lovell, December 17, 1861, January 1, 1862.

14. *Ibid.*, 559, 760, Lovell to Davis, October 31, and to Cooper, December 10, 1861.

15. *Ibid.*, 822, 823, 825, Lovell to Benjamin, February 6, 12, Benjamin to Lovell, February 8, 1862.

Lovell's other complaint, which probably made him unpopular with some of the newly created companies, was that the men had elected as their officers a large number of unskilled and untrained volunteer soldiers. He asked Benjamin if he had the authority to transfer the good men into fighting units and purge incompetent officers, but Benjamin replied that "under the acts of Congress company officers are always elective." He suggested Lovell muster the old units out of the service, form new units, encourage the men to re-enlist, and then "induce" them to elect better officers. Lovell needed every man he had, and with the daily risk of every new unit being transferred to Virginia or Tennessee, men mustering out were not always easy to re-enlist. He decided to get along with the system as well as he could.[16]

But incompetent officers were not the only people to criticize Lovell. Enemies sprang up everywhere. J. B. Jones, a clerk in the War Department who had never held a high opinion of Secretary Benjamin, thought even less of Mansfield Lovell. According to Jones, the public questioned the loyalty of a man who waited until after the Battle of Manassas to join the Confederacy.[17]

Older generals like Braxton Bragg and William H. T. Walker conceived a dislike, and perhaps a ration of jealousy, toward Lovell and publicly expressed it. Bragg, who lived in Louisiana, had been shuttled to a numerically strong but territorially small command at Pensacola. He knew Lovell from the Mexican War and was shocked, but mostly envious, when the War Department elevated the latecomer to major general and assigned him to the much more populous Department of Louisiana and Southern Mississippi. Bragg had defended Louisiana early in the war and felt entitled to defend it again. He believed Governor Moore would agree and wrote: "How do you get along with your new fledged Major General fresh from the lecture room of New York where he has been . . . instructing the very men he will have to oppose? . . . I had confidence in him at one time but he forfeited it all by asking a price before he would come and when it was offered waited to see who was the strongest." In closing, Bragg almost wept tears: "The command at New Orleans was mine. I feel myself degraded by the action of the Government. . . . Had the command been organized under proper hands three months ago, you would now be impregnable. As it is, I tremble for my home."[18]

16. *Ibid.*, 777, Lovell to Cooper, December 10, 1861.
17. J. B. Jones, *A Rebel War Clerk's Diary* (2 vols.; Philadelphia, 1866), I, 89.
18. Bragg to Moore, October 31, 1861, Thomas O. Moore Papers, Louisiana and Lower

Bragg also made an appeal to Benjamin on behalf of General Ruggles, who had served briefly under his command before being transferred to New Orleans. Ruggles was dismayed, Bragg wrote, "to learn that another junior (Lovell), just from the enemy . . . was promoted over his head and assigned to a command the highest and most important in the Southern country. That command includes my home and fireside, and all that is dear to me in life." Perhaps in reference to himself, Bragg added, "You will never preserve the *morale* of this army by thus degrading the commanders they so much love and admire." Benjamin did not reply to Bragg's outburst. Lovell, who may have been aware of Bragg's antipathy but not his letter, found Ruggles lethargic and removed him from the department at the first opportunity.[19]

William "Shot Pouch" Walker used the press to air his grievances. Since entering West Point in 1832, Walker had remained in the United States Army until Georgia, his native state, seceded. Commissioned a brigadier general in the Confederate army, he received command of the Louisiana Brigade but a short time later was unexplicably removed. He interpreted the action as a maneuver by Davis to create a vacancy whereby the president could promote his former brother-in-law, Colonel Richard Taylor of the 9th Louisiana, to brigadier general, although Taylor, ten years younger than Walker, had no previous military experience. Embittered and enraged, Walker resigned, and while castigating both Davis and Benjamin in the press, he included Lovell as another example of Davis' preference for younger men, adding: "Not content with putting my own *countrymen* over me, an office holder (Gen. Lovell, from New York City, who was there under pay of New York when our countrymen were gallantly fighting at Manassas and elsewhere) has been brought to the South and made Major General."[20]

The local press did not entirely agree with Walker. Compared with Twiggs, Lovell had made a good impression, and for the first time the people of New Orleans were beginning to see results. One paper accused Walker of "bad taste" and praised Davis for selecting the best man, regardless of his birth and prior occupation. After all, the new general was visible to the public, tireless in his efforts to improve defenses, and in a

Mississippi Valley Collection, Louisiana State University, Baton Rouge, quoted in Dufour, *Night the War Was Lost*, 95–96.

19. *ORA*, VI, 759, 825, Bragg to Benjamin, October 30, 1861, Lovell to Benjamin, February 12, 1862.

20. New Orleans *True Delta*, November 2, 1861.

short time had created a new atmosphere of confidence. But behind the cautious smile on every native's face was an awareness of Lovell's background, and Walker's attack added more kindling to the public's smoldering suspicions. The newspapers implied that New Orleanians would accept and work with Lovell, who seemed to be their only hope, but they would watch him. Ask any man or woman on the street who should have command of the department, and they would probably say Beauregard or Bragg. Lovell had his work cut out for him, and only part of it concerned military affairs.[21]

The general expected an attack in January, and he worked determinedly to build the city's defenses. By the time 1862 began, he had made progress. When he could not beg or borrow heavy guns from either the Ordnance Department in Richmond or General Bragg at nearby Pensacola, he expanded three local foundries and began casting 8-inch and 10-inch columbiads and 10-inch sea-coast mortars. With Duncan's help, he replaced many of the old 24-pounders en barbette at Forts Jackson, St. Philip, Pike, and Macomb with the best of the 32- and 42-pounders salvaged from the pile received from Gosport. By December, ten companies—about a thousand men—garrisoned Forts Jackson and St. Philip. Fort Jackson boasted six 42-pounders, twenty-six 24-pounders, two rifled 32-pounders, sixteen common 32-pounders, three 8-inch columbiads, two 8-inch and one 10-inch mortars, with two 48-pound and ten 24-pound howitzers—a total of sixty-eight guns. Across the river at Fort St. Philip, work crews expanded the batteries to six 42-pounders, nine 32-pounders, twenty-two 24-pounders, four 8-inch columbiads, one 8-inch and one 10-inch mortars, and three field guns. Not all of the guns were in good working condition, and Lovell continued to reinforce the batteries with heavier guns.

At the entrance to Lake Pontchartrain, Fort Macomb, with a garrison of 250 men, mounted thirty guns, mostly 24-pounders. Fort Pike, with 350 men, had thirty-three guns, four 42-pounders, one 9-inch mortar, one 8-inch mortar, two rifled 32-pounders, and the balance all 24-pounders. On the opposite side of the Delta, Fort Livingston, guarding the entrance to Barataria Bay, had 300 men but only fifteen guns, mostly 24-pounders and 12-pounders, which Lovell admitted were too light to do much good. Several other works spread along the outer Delta had been garrisoned and fortified, including Proctorsville on Lake Borgne, Tower Dupré on Bayou Bienvenu, and Battery Bienvenu where Bayou Mazant flows into

21. New Orleans *Daily Delta,* November 3, 1861.

Bienvenu. By the end of December, Lovell had stationed about 4,500 men along the exterior line of defense.[22]

When Lovell could not get ammunition for the guns, he built mills to produce his own powder, cast shot and shell in local foundries, and established a factory for making his own cartridges by occupying half of the large new Marine Hospital and converting it into an arsenal. At midnight, December 28, an explosion rocked the hospital, rumbling through the city, knocking out windows, and shaking the buildings along the levee. "A pillar of fire shot up to the sky," wrote a reporter. The section of the hospital containing the powder mill lay in rubble. Eight thousand pounds of precious powder erupted in fire and smoke. Citizens hunted through the debris for clues, convinced the explosion was the work of some diabolical "fiend." Flag Officer Hollins grimaced—he had counted on Lovell for his powder because the Naval Department had been unable to fill his requisitions.[23]

From New Orleans to Savannah, Lovell dispatched officers and agents to collect loose chain and anchors to strengthen the log boom across the Mississippi. By the end of December the barrier had been securely chained to both banks, held by fifteen anchors weighing from 2,500 to 4,000 pounds, and laid in twenty-five fathoms of water by sixty fathoms of strong chain. Lovell wrote: "This raft is a complete obstruction, and has enfilading fire from Fort Jackson and direct fire from Saint Philip."[24]

To speed up the movement of materials, supplies, and men, he laid a railway track connecting the city with the Pontchartrain and Mexican Gulf Railroad. To improve communications, he set up telegraph lines to Proctorsville and to Brashear City on Berwick Bay.

Shortly after his arrival, Lovell renewed work on the interior defense lines in the vicinity of New Orleans and Algiers. Soon thousands of blacks bent their backs in the wet winter weather digging entrenchments extending from the Crescent City to Lake Pontchartrain. Where works touched the river above New Orleans, Lovell intended to emplace fourteen 42-pounders, providing he could find them. Below the city, ten 32-pounders had already been mounted. Many of the carronades sent from Gosport went into the interior lines, where they could sweep the entire

22. *ORA*, VI, 559–60, 775, 776, Lovell's testimony, April 8, 1863, and Lovell to Benjamin, December 5, 1861.

23. *ORN*, Ser. 2, I, 657–58, Lovell to Benjamin, December 29, 1861; New Orleans *True Delta*, December 29, 1861.

24. *ORA*, VI, 560, 775, Lovell Testimony, and Lovell to Benjamin, December 5, 1861.

front with grape shot and canister. The entrenchments around Algiers had been completed, except for a battery of ten 32-pounders covering the river.

To man the interior lines, Lovell reorganized scattered infantry companies, scraped up muskets and ammunition to equip them, and used the few qualified officers he had to drill and train the men in artillery. When the War Department began siphoning off his men, he recruited more, knowing those taken would never be returned. By the end of December, he had 3,500 effectives manning the entrenchments, and another 6,000 well-armed volunteers in the city, bringing his total force, including the exterior lines, to about 15,000 men. Lovell felt that he could defend the city "against any force that can be brought, unless we are attacked on all sides at once." [25]

But almost as fast as Lovell developed his own resources, the War Department sent them elsewhere. Forty-six heavy guns needed for the forts and eventually for arming the unfinished *Louisiana* and *Mississippi* were sent to other departments. And that was only the beginning.[26]

Even when Lovell attempted to prepare for a worst-case scenario—a combined naval and ground attack leading to a lengthy siege—his efforts met with frustration. He tried to stockpile ammunition, but war matériel alone was not enough. Neither his army nor the populace of New Orleans could survive a long siege without provisions. He attempted to lay in sixty thousand barrels of flour and enough beef to last two or three months, but he could find no one to finance the project, not in New Orleans and not in Richmond.[27]

What puzzled and annoyed Lovell was the sudden and unexpected departure upriver of Hollins' mosquito fleet. Without it, there were no naval vessels patrolling the river and no means of preventing the enemy from re-establishing itself at Head of Passes. Lovell had been instructed by President Davis to leave matters of the navy to Mallory, and for awhile he followed orders. But on December 25 he discovered Union transports unloading troops on Ship Island, a strip of sand located about midway between the entrances to Mobile Bay and Lake Pontchartrain. He could not divine why the enemy showed such interest in that solitary strip of flea-infested sand and sent a detail to investigate. After reconnoitering for four days, the detail reported that "the enemy has now 22 vessels, large and small, and is landing troops in large numbers. They had been sounding and staking out the channels leading toward the Rigolets and Chef Menteur

---

25. *Ibid.*, 776, Lovell to Benjamin, December 5, 1861.
26. *ORA*, VI, 559–61, Lovell Testimony, April 8, 1863.
27. *Ibid.*, 776.

Pass. . . . They can not take New Orleans with any force they can bring to bear."[28]

But with only two small naval vessels operating on Lake Pontchartrain and the mosquito fleet upriver, Lovell felt vulnerable. Except for Forts Pike and Macomb, he had no way of preventing Union forces from establishing, if they so chose, a beachhead at some strategic point along the lake. He reminded Benjamin that when he was given command of the department, he had asked for his own supporting naval force to prevent such a landing. He revoiced his concern, reminding Benjamin that the navy operated exclusively to its own agenda. They would not cooperate "in connection with the land defenses," and "this is just what has happened." So far, President Davis' suggestion of "unrestrained intercourse and cordial fraternization" had not worked.[29]

Benjamin took just long enough to confer with Davis before responding, "You will impress, immediately, for public service, the 14 ships hereafter named: *Mexico, Texas, Orizaba, Charles Houston, Florida, Arizona, Jewess, Atlantic, Houston, Magnolia, Matagorda, W. H. Webb, Anglo-Saxon, and the Anglo-Norman.*" The following day Lovell seized all fourteen ships. They had many deficiencies, but temporarily, Lovell had the rudiments of his navy.[30]

Curiously enough, it was not Mallory who acted to improve naval defenses but Benjamin, demonstrating that the War Department had much less difficulty getting congressional attention than the navy. To create this special naval force on "Western waters" required the hurried passage of two congressional laws, Nos. 344 and 350, and $1 million. The men recruited for this service were to be steamboat captains and steamboat crews. Each vessel would be fitted out to suit the captains but would carry no more than one stern gun. The bows of the vessels would be clad with iron to enable them to run down at high speed "gunboats and mortar rafts prepared by the enemy for attack on our river defenses." President Davis named James E. Montgomery and J. H. Townsend captains of two of the vessels, leaving Lovell with the task of locating skippers for the others. This was not quite the type of navy Lovell had envisioned when he asked for gunboats. In an attempt at "cordial fraternization," he offered to turn the steamers over to Hollins, who would know better than he what to do with them, but Hollins wanted no part of vessels belonging to the War Department. The so-called River Defense Fleet landed on Lovell's lap at a time when

28. *ORN*, Ser. 2, I, 657, 658, Lovell to Benjamin, December, 25, 29, 1861.
29. *Ibid.*, 659, Lovell to Benjamin, January 7, 1861.
30. *Ibid.*, 662, 667, Benjamin to Lovell, January 14, Lovell to Benjamin, January 18, 1862.

he needed every hour of the day to improve his fortifications elsewhere. He needed reconnaisance ships and well-armed gunboats, and he only needed them because the navy could not provide them and could not get them. From the moment he seized the fourteen riverboats, he had to divert resources to strengthen, man, arm, and clad them. Suddenly, command responsibility for the navy and for the defense of the lower Mississippi became a more confused—if not fatal—mess.

And it happened at the very moment Welles issued orders for Farragut to go to the Gulf and fight his way up to the Crescent City.

EIGHT *Farragut Steams South*

On January 9, 1862, Secretary Welles officially appointed Farragut to command the newly formed Western Gulf Blockading Squadron and ordered him to proceed to Philadelphia, where his flagship, the wooden steam sloop of war *Hartford*, was being fitted out for what evolved into three years of constant service. Of all the big warships in the Union fleet, *Hartford* was among the newest, having been launched at Boston's Charlestown Navy Yard on November 22, 1858. Three similar vessels had been built about the same time: *Richmond*, *Pensacola*, and *Brooklyn*, and all were assigned to Farragut. In 1857, anticipating an outbreak of war with Great Britain, the Navy Department had designed the vessels with gundecks high above the water for ocean fighting in rough seas, a type of warfare quite different from the river where the vessels were headed.[1]

Hartford was anything but a river craft, weighing 2,900 tons and stretching 225 feet in length with a 44-foot beam and a 17-foot 2-inch draft aft. Being a full-rigged three-masted ship, she could develop a top speed of thirteen and one-half knots when under sail and steam, and her twin horizontal direct-acting engines pushed her along at eight knots in a calm sea. She carried twenty-two 9-inch Dahlgren shellguns in broadside, two rifled 32-pounders on the poop and forecastle, and a 12-pounder howitzer behind quarter-inch boiler iron in both the fore- and maintops. With a full spread of canvas, *Hartford* projected a graceful and majestic appearance, looking much like the magnificent sailing vessels built before the advent of steam. All these fine lines would soon be lost with the growth of the

---

1. *ORN*, XVIII, 5, Welles to Farragut, January 9, 1862; Lewis, *Farragut*, 16. Welles split the Gulf Blockading Squadron, and McKean retained command of the Eastern Gulf Squadron with headquarters at Key West.

ugly ironclads. Loyall Farragut, the flag officer's seventeen-year-old son who accompanied him to Philadelphia, said the *Hartford* "was the admiration of all who could see beauty in a ship." Flag Officer Farragut could see it, too, and if he had his way, he would never serve on an ironclad unless forced to do so. And he never did. [2]

For his fleet captain, Farragut chose Commander Henry Haywood Bell, and to captain *Hartford*, Commander Richard Wainwright, both distinguished career officers who had grown up in a time when the old navy had matched its muscle against England's powerful frigates. Bell, a North Carolinian, had joined the navy at the age of fifteen and spent nearly forty years at sea. His adherence to the Union surprised almost everyone but Farragut, who knew the man personally. At the time Farragut requested Bell as fleet captain, the commander was at the Brooklyn Navy Yard fitting up nineteen of Porter's mortar schooners. Everybody expressed confidence in Farragut's selection of Bell but Porter, who described him as an officer who dreaded responsibility and had no confidence in himself. Porter seldom said good things about professional competitors, and with Bell's new responsibilities, he knew the man would soon be elevated to the rank of captain. Paradoxically, after the war Porter took credit for suggesting Bell as Farragut's fleet captain.[3]

The 24-gun steam sloop of war *Brooklyn*, under Captain Thomas T. Craven, had been on blockade duty at Pass à l'Outre since May, 1861. The 23-gun *Pensacola*, under Captain Henry W. Morris, was on station at Key West where she had run aground. With *Pensacola*'s 3,000 tons and 18-foot 7-inch draft, grounding became a constant concern for her commander. The 22-gun *Richmond*, now captained by Commander James Alden, went to the Brooklyn Navy Yard for repairs shortly after Captain Pope fled from Head of Passes on October 12, 1861. Most of the crew remained on board, and on February 13, *Richmond* steamed out of the Narrows and headed for Ship Island.[4]

Besides the four big steam sloops of war, Welles detached twenty-three other vessels from McKean's command and turned them over to Farragut, along with four coal ships. At the time, these vessels were spread from Pensacola to the Rio Grande, and many of them would have to remain at their stations and maintain the blockade until relieved. In his instructions

2. *ORN*, Ser. 2, I, 99, Statistical Data of Vessels; Farragut, *Life of Farragut*, 210.

3. David Dixon Porter, "Private Journal," 48, 114, 116–18, 121, 127–28; Mahan, *Gulf and Inland Waters*, 55–56; Lewis, *Farragut*, 17.

4. *ORN*, XVIII, 27, 39, 45, 729, 764, Farragut to Welles, February 12, Farragut to Morris, February 25, and Farragut to Alden, March 4, 1862, also Log of *Richmond*, Log of *Pensacola*.

to Farragut, Welles was very explicit regarding the blockade. A diplomatic battle was being waged with the British government over the *Trent* affair, and Welles was tormented by the possibility of the English entering the war on the side of the Confederacy. Referring to the possibility of "foreign interference," Welles instructed Farragut, with the force at his disposal, to "interdict communication at every point . . . and thus destroy any pretense for breaking or attempting to break the blockade." He promised to send more ships, and by the end of February, four more arrived. Still, more than half of the squadron's vessels remained sailing ships. Farragut had a thousand miles of coastline to watch, and he needed all his steamers for the planned attack. He could wait a few weeks before summoning all of them. His first obstacle involved the onerous task of getting the deep-draft steam sloops over the bar.[5]

And then there was Porter's flotilla, another twenty-one vessels, each carrying a 13-inch mortar, and on most, a pair of 32-pounders. One of the vessels, *Horace Beals*, was included in the count but did not carry a mortar. When Farragut put to sea from Hampton Roads on February 2, the mortar schooners were scattered from the Brooklyn Navy Yard to Key West, where six of the bomb boats, as Porter called them, waited for the others. In addition, seven steamers had been attached to Porter's command to tow the schooners, among them the fast, six-hundred-ton *Harriet Lane*, Porter's flagship. *Lane*, a shallow-draft sidewheeler, carried three 9-inch guns, a rifled 30-pounder, and a small bronze 12-pounder.[6]

In his orders to Farragut, Welles wrote:

> When these formidable mortars arrive, and you are completely ready, you will collect what vessels can be spared from the blockade and proceed up the Mississippi River and reduce the defenses which guard the approaches to New Orleans, when you will appear off that city and take possession of it under the guns of your squadron, and hoist the American flag thereon, keeping possession until troops can be sent to you. If the Mississippi expedition from Cairo [Illinois] shall not have descended the river, you will take advantage of the panic to push a strong force up the river to take all their defenses in the rear. You will also reduce the fortifications at Mobile Bay and turn them over to the army to hold. As you have expressed yourself satisfied with the force given to you, and as many more powerful vessels will be

5. *Ibid.*, 7–8, 9–10, 40, Welles to Farragut, January 20, 25, 1862.
6. *Ibid.*, 25–26; *ORN,* Ser. 2, I, 99, Statistical Data.

added before you can commence operations, the Department and the country will require of you success. . . . There are other operations of minor importance which will commend themselves to your judgment and skill, but which must not be allowed to interfere with the great object in view, the certain capture of the city of New Orleans.

Destroy the armed barriers which these deluded people have raised up against the power of the United States Government, and shoot down those who war against the Union, but cultivate with cordiality the first returning reason which is sure to follow your success. [7]

Farragut was a man who followed orders. He probably read them several times, tucked them in his pocket, and read them again until he committed every word to memory. And as the war stretched from months into years, there were few commanders who executed their orders as diligently and as thoroughly as Farragut.

Porter left Washington on February 11 and arrived at Key West on February 28. He found the mortar schooners rocking at anchor, waiting for the arrival of the steamers to tow them to the Delta. After seven days passed, Porter grew impatient, put the schooners under sail, and with three steamers, including his flagship, headed into the Gulf. Five days later he arrived safely at Ship Island, but the flag officer was not there.

On March 7, Farragut had grown impatient waiting for Porter's bomb boats and took most of his fleet to the mouth of the Mississippi. Porter, fearing that his tardiness might invite criticism, covered his tracks by surreptitiously writing Fox from Ship Island, "Farragut is not ready for us yet," but to Welles he added the qualifier, "some of the ships being still at Ship Island, lightening to cross the bar." [8]

Ship Island, a sandy strip of barren land eight miles long and barely a mile wide at its widest point, lay about fifteen miles off the coastal town of Biloxi, Mississippi. As a boy, Farragut and his father often sailed by the usually gull-inhabited and insect-infested island as they traveled between New Orleans and the family's farm on the Pascagoula River. Now, blockade-running coastal schooners, protected by a few guns on Ship Island, plied their trade by staying inside Mississippi Sound.

When the first serious battle of the war opened in the summer of 1861,

7. *ORN*, XVIII, 8, Welles to Farragut, January 20, 1862.

8. Thompson and Wainwright (eds.), *Fox Correspondence*, II, 84; *ORN*, XVIII, 72, Porter to Welles, March 18, 1862.

the closest supply point for the Union navy was Key West, Florida. Sheltered harbors like Pensacola Bay, Mobile Bay, and the northern side of Ship Island remained in Confederate possession. In July, 1861, Lieutenant Warley, who later commanded *Manassas*, working with three companies of the 4th Regiment, Louisiana Volunteers, installed an 8-inch navy gun and a 32-pounder to add weight to the few small artillery pieces already in place on Ship Island. Warley considered the island strategically located but poorly defended, and he encouraged General Twiggs to hold it.

On September 17, Lieutenant Colonel Henry W. Allen, CSA, observed "two heavy frigates, two steamers, a brig, and two tenders" bearing down on Ship Island. The five-gun USS *Massachusetts*, under Commander Melancton Smith, had been stationed off Ship Island for much of the summer. Smith fired a few probing shots from his rifled 32-pounder and was surprised to see Confederates set fire to the barracks and evacuate. Smith occupied Ship Island with men from *Massachusetts*, *Preble*, and *Marion*, and from that day the Union navy converted the slender stretch of sand into a naval supply depot. [9]

But Farragut intended to make Ship Island more than just a supply depot for a few Union blockaders. Here he could assemble and organize his squadron and later make the small spit of barren sand available to Major General Benjamin Butler and his army of more than fifteen thousand troops. The island was ideally located for a combined attack on the lower Mississippi, and in the summer of 1864, when Farragut prepared to enter Mobile Bay, Ship Island provided a jumping-off point for Brigadier General Gordon Granger's division to launch its attack on Fort Gaines.

By the time *Hartford* reached Ship Island on February 20, Farragut began to grasp the complexity of his problems. After a week at sea, he complained that his flagship's crew was "most inefficient," but he hoped "Commander Wainwright will get them in condition to do good service before the mortar vessels are ready." In Havana he had observed small schooners loaded with cotton, which had come out of "little places" along the southern coast where it seemed nothing "larger than a rowboat could pass." In Key West he talked to the commanders of *Pensacola* and *Santiago de Cuba* and learned that many "of the gunboats are sadly in want of repairs, and it is thought will have to be sent north." He also discovered that "not a vessel" attached to his command was fit for service in shallow waters, and he

9. *ORN*, 581–82, 677–78, Smith to Mervine, July 9, Twiggs to Walker, July 12, Smith to McKean, September 20, 1861.

wrote Welles requesting steamers with less than six feet draft. Bell remembered six shallow-draft steamers in New York waiting for work, and Farragut asked for them. When he finally caught up with Flag Officer McKean at Ship Island, he received a "miserable account of the condition of the few vessels now on the station" and required for operations. He blamed most of the problems on young, inexperienced engineers who were gradually destroying the machinery and boilers.[10]

Farragut also began to doubt some of his officers. He found a note waiting for him at Ship Island from Secretary Welles, reporting that an informant claimed he had witnessed *Manassas* aground for thirty hours in sight of a Union warship off Pass à l'Outre; Welles wondered why no effort had been made to destroy the Confederate ram. After making inquiries, Farragut identified the Union warship as USS *Mississippi*, under Captain Thomas O. Selfridge, who when questioned, explained that at the time he had been busy giving the bark *Kingfisher* a tow and was in the process of changing his position to prevent *Manassas* from attacking him. He also claimed his vessel had too deep a draft to pass the bar, which was true, but Farragut could not understand why Selfridge did not attack in his launches. He detached Selfridge, which shocked the captain but left no doubt in the minds of other commanders that Farragut meant business.[11] If some of his officers suffered from timidity, Farragut planned to weed them out quickly.

Two days after he reached Ship Island, Farragut dispatched the *Brooklyn*, under Captain Thomas T. Craven, to Head of Passes with orders to take "all the vessels blockading the mouths of the Mississippi that can enter," and "keep your position until further orders from me." He wanted telegraphic wires to New Orleans cut, pilots captured and sent to Ship Island, and all blockade running stopped. He expected the Confederates would try to force Craven's gunboats out of the river, and he did not want another Pope's Run. He instructed Craven to "send down your topgallant masts and keep a lookout during the day from the topmast head, and at night send [a] gunboat at least 1 mile higher up the river with rockets to give you notice of the approach of the enemy's vessels. Let her have lines with a hook ready to take a fire ship or other annoyance in tow, and tow it off the river."[12]

10. *ORN*, XVIII, 28, 30, 31, 33, 34, Farragut to Welles, February 12, 17, 21, and Farragut to Fox, February —, 22, 1862; Thompson and Wainwright (eds.), *Fox Correspondence*, I, 301.

11. *ORN*, XVII, 31, 32, and XVIII, 57, Welles to Farragut, February 6, Selfridge to Farragut, March 7, and Farragut to Smith, March 10, 1862.

12. *ORN*, XVIII, 35, Farragut to Craven, February 22, 1862.

As soon as Craven established his station at Head of Passes, Farragut began dispatching sailing vessels like *Preble* and *Vincennes* from their posts off the passes to relieve the steamers posted on blockade duty around the Gulf. *Mississippi* steamed in from Pensacola, *Itasca* and *Kanawha* from Mobile, and *Pensacola*, with her "worthless" engines, along with *Richmond* and *Kennebec*, from Key West. Vessels waiting for orders at Ship Island got them directly from Farragut, and the whole flotilla steamed over to Southwest Pass, which at the time had the deepest channel of all the passes. Farragut worried about the heavy *Colorado*, under Captain Theodorus Bailey, and her 22-foot 7-inch draft. On March 5 he wrote Welles that they would "be getting some of the vessels over the bar," and he would "do all a man can do to get the *Colorado* over."[13]

In getting his big steamers into the river, Farragut, whose fleet had consumed most of the coal stored at Ship Island, was about to confront the first of many time-consuming obstacles. When Captain Alden arrived on *Richmond*, he reported that Key West was out of coal. Advance units from General Butler's division had begun to arrive at Ship Island and brought with them about eight hundred tons. Farragut borrowed it. He asked the Naval Office for ten thousand tons a month, and Welles assured him three thousand tons were on the way. Farragut hoped it would arrive before his steamers were forced to shake out their sheets.[14]

Oddly enough, while the navy had been mobilizing a force to attack New Orleans, General McClellan seemed to have forgotten his commitment to provide ten thousand troops. Part of this oversight can be blamed on Welles and Fox, who had sworn everybody involved in the campaign to secrecy, excluding McClellan from the tight loop of communications. The general, however, wanted every soldier he could enlist to build the Army of the Potomac to two hundred thousand men for his "On to Richmond" march. When Farragut sailed for New Orleans on February 3, McClellan had neither picked a commander for his share of the campaign nor identified the regiments to go to Ship Island.

On the list of major generals available for assignment, politically influential Benjamin F. Butler of Massachusetts had already distinguished himself as a meddlesome manipulator and vocal critic of McClellan's indolence. Butler, who was bald, slightly cross-eyed, and carried a bulging torso on a pair of thin, chickenlike legs, was a shrewd lawyer and a pow-

13. *Ibid.*, 47, Farragut to Welles, March 5, 1862, and Farragut's orders to various commanders, *ibid.*, 45 and *passim*.

14. *Ibid.*, 49–50, 58–59, Farragut to Welles, March 6, Welles to Farragut, March 12, 1862.

erful Democrat, the kind of person Lincoln would rather have as a friend than an enemy. If Butler disliked a person or for private reasons felt compelled to seek revenge, nobody in politics could contrive more ways to assassinate the character of an adversary.

When presidential candidates were being selected for the 1860 election, Butler, believing that only a moderate southerner could hold the Union together, voted for Jefferson Davis fifty-seven times at the Democratic convention in Charleston, South Carolina, before it adjourned and the Democratic rump convention in Baltimore chose Stephen A. Douglas. Butler then threw his support to John C. Breckinridge and campaigned furiously against fellow Democrat Stephen Douglas and Republican nominee Lincoln. Nonetheless, when the South seceded, Butler sought out Lincoln and offered his services to the Union.

Lincoln wanted Butler's support, not his enmity, and in an act of mollification appointed him the first major general of volunteers, ranking from May 16, 1861. Butler took command of the troops at Fort Monroe and promptly demonstrated his penchant for stirring up trouble. Lincoln was still trying to save the Union, but if war could not be avoided, he did not want to lose the border states. Meanwhile, southern slaves were abandoning plantations and trekking north, filtering daily through Fort Monroe. In the absence of a formal government policy dealing with escaped slaves, Butler declared them "Contrabands of War." Southern slaveholders, including those within the border states, raged over this new policy, regarding it as confiscation of their rightful property. Lincoln attempted to placate the border-state governors without embarrassing his thin-skinned general.

Nor was Butler any more skilled as a commander of troops in battle. His first demonstration of military ineptitude occurred at Big Bethel, one of the first skirmishes of the war, where his troops fled from a small Confederate force, leaving a cannon, muskets, and assorted equipment scattered over the field of retreat. The defeat embarrassed the Union army and provided Lincoln with a good excuse to replace his newly appointed political general, but he worried about Butler's reaction. The goggle-eyed general could give him trouble, and Lincoln preferred to retain Butler's support by keeping him occupied.

Lincoln decided the best way to keep Butler out of civilian affairs was to try him on another military assignment. Supported by Captain Silas H. Stringham's six naval vessels, Butler, with eight hundred troops, invaded Pamlico Sound via Hatteras Inlet, capturing two partially constructed

Confederate forts and collecting 615 prisoners. Lincoln was so pleased with the unexpected victory, for which Butler claimed the lion's share of credit, that he sent the general back to Massachusetts to recruit troops for more coastal engagements.[15]

Butler's troop-raising activities collided with those of Massachusetts Governor John A. Andrew, who, when he discovered Butler granting commissions to political friends of questionable character, refused to sign the commissions. Both Butler and Andrew complained to Lincoln, whose executive patience was wearing thin. Andrew, who had done a creditable job raising enlistments in the past, wrote Lincoln, "General Butler is cross-eyed [which he was]; I guess he don't see things the way other people do." Undaunted, Butler went back to Washington, complained of Andrew's interference, and returned to Massachusetts a few days later as head of the Department of New England, which put six states under his jurisdiction for recruiting purposes. With Andrew squeezed out, Butler had his way. He had little difficulty raising all the troops he wanted and salted his personal staff with friends, relatives, and political cronies.[16]

Once again Lincoln puzzled over where to assign Butler. The reporting relationship between McClellan and Butler was strained because McClellan, as General of the Army, commanded the huge Army of the Potomac, but on paper Butler outranked McClellan by time in grade. McClellan wanted the troops raised by Butler for the Army of the Potomac, but he did not want Butler. Nonetheless, Lincoln deferred the matter of Butler's assignment to McClellan and asked for suggestions. McClellan wanted to send Butler as far away as possible, and when the demand came for troops to support Farragut's attack, he happily sent Butler off to sandy, shadeless Ship Island with more than fifteen thousand freshly uniformed troops. Randolph B. Marcy, McClellan's chief of staff (and father-in-law), celebrated by saying, "I guess we have found a hole to bury this Yankee elephant in."[17]

On February 23, 1862, Butler received orders from McClellan to direct the army's part of the New Orleans expedition, although he had already begun to embark his untrained New England regiments for Ship

15. Benjamin F. Butler, *Autobiography and Personal Reminiscences of Major-General Benj. F. Butler: Butler's Book* (Boston, 1892), 285–87; Robert S. Holtzman, *Stormy Ben Butler* (New York, 1954), 37–52; Faust (ed.), *HTI*, 98–99.

16. *Butler's Book*, 298–309; William B. Hesseltine, *Lincoln and the War Governors* (New York, 1948), 190–91.

17. *Butler's Book*, 298, 307–308, 324–25, 333, 335; Holtzman, *Butler*, 53–61; T. A. Bland, *Life of Benjamin F. Butler* (Boston, 1879), 83.

Island. McClellan referred to the military district as the Department of the Gulf, "comprising all the coast of the Gulf of Mexico west of Pensacola Harbor and so much of the Gulf States as may be occupied." Perhaps because McClellan recognized the futility of controlling Butler's movements, he added that General Butler's "headquarters for the present will be movable, wherever the commanding general may be."

When the Naval Office conceived the idea of passing the forts and capturing New Orleans from below, Welles ordered Farragut to do it and asked Lincoln for about ten thousand troops to garrison the forts and hold the city. The army's role was to occupy enemy positions surrendered to the navy, but McClellan's orders to Butler read, "The object of your expedition is one of vital importance—the capture of New Orleans." He then outlined the naval strategy, reminding Butler of his supporting role. Butler undoubtedly saw another opportunity, similar to the victory at Hatteras Inlet. If New Orleans fell, he could rush in and grab most of the credit, feeling certain that if he extended a helping hand to the navy, Farragut would not mind sharing the glory. But Butler overlooked lowly Commander Porter, whose fiery ambitions raged as fervently as his own.[18]

Just prior to embarking for Ship Island, Butler confided to Secretary of War Stanton that his orders could not be countermanded after he got to sea, for he was "going to take New Orleans or you will never see me again."

"Well," the secretary replied in the presence of Lincoln, "you take New Orleans and you shall be lieutenant-general."

Those being the precise words Butler wanted to hear, he bowed and left.[19]

On February 25 Butler sailed for Ship Island on the steamer *Mississippi* with Mrs. Butler and sixteen hundred troops. Two days later the ship grounded on Frying Pan Shoals off Cape Fear. In the excitement, the crew dropped the anchor with such haste that a fluke ripped open the ship's hull. After repairs at Port Royal, *Mississippi* got underway and ran aground on another shoal. In typical army style, Butler had had enough. He deposed the captain and "took command of the ship." Butler had no trouble taking charge and playing by his own rules. Had he worked for Jefferson Davis, "unrestrained intercourse and cordial fraternization" would have meant nothing to him.[20]

18. *ORA*, VI, 694–96, McClellan to Butler, Thomas to Butler, February 23, 1862.

19. *Butler's Book*, 335–36.

20. *Ibid.*, 336, 341, 346; James Parton, *General Butler in New Orleans* (New York, 1864), 205–208.

Butler, whose penchant for quarreling with peers was notorious, ingratiated himself with Farragut by generously lending him eight hundred tons of army coal at a time when the navy had depleted its store and was attempting to tow its deep-draft steamers over the bar. When Farragut asked whether the transfer of army supplies was not contrary to regulations, Butler replied, "I never read the army regulations, and what is more, I shan't, and then I shall never know I am doing anything against them."[21]

The relationship started affably, although Farragut had difficulty picturing Butler as the typical hard-driving military professional he had hoped to have at his side. He found the general bright, but after their first lengthy conference, Farragut realized Butler did not "have any . . . plan of operations, but simply to follow in my wake and hold what I can take." Farragut was partially correct, but he was accustomed to dealing with people who served their country before they served their own interests. The flag officer had much to learn about the wily political general who came to Ship Island to "hold what I take." Butler, the shrewd opportunist, always had a plan, and alternatives if the first plan did not work.[22]

By early March the stage was set. *Brooklyn* occupied Head of Passes, and light-draft steamers like *Winona, Kineo,* and *Kennebec* steamed upriver, reconnoitering the forts and occasionally drawing a probing shot from a long-range gun. Porter's steamers towed the mortar schooners into the river and lined them up along the bank, where they drilled their guns and waited for orders to move upstream.

On March 13, *Hartford* bumped over the bar and joined *Brooklyn* at the Head. On March 23, Butler reached Ship Island with the balance of his 15,255 men. He moved promptly into his new headquarters, a hastily built shack accommodating Mrs. Butler, her linen, and her dishware.[23] Lincoln was probably pleasantly surprised to learn that Butler's army was not late for the affair. It was Farragut's heavy ships that still lay off the passes, some aground and others waiting to be lightened. The flag officer had found a new enemy—mud—and that battle had only started. He worried that every day lost would narrow his chances of passing the forts and cost him more casualties. The element of surprise was gone. Now the Confederates would be moving at breakneck speed to improve the defenses to New Orleans. And what about those powerful ironclads being built in

21. *Butler's Book*, 355.
22. Farragut, *Life of Farragut*, 212.
23. *ORN*, XVIII, 64–65, 67–68, Farragut to Welles, March 14, 16, 1862.

New Orleans? Deserters often mentioned them.

Farragut probably watched each painful hour pass, staring upriver and wondering what the Confederates were doing to stop him.

NINE   *New Orleans Shudders*

On January 1, 1862, the citizens of New Orleans could not decide how to celebrate the new year. Many felt grateful in being so far removed from the bloodshed and ravages of war. Since Hollins chased Pope out of the river, there had been no more Union incursions into the lower Mississippi. After Mansfield Lovell came to town, work on the fortifications had resumed with noticeable energy. People still worried, but now they felt more secure behind heavy gun emplacements. Downriver, the forts were being strengthened with reinforcements, and every other day people observed big guns departing on barges for Forts Jackson and St. Philip. In the evening, the city's militia marched through town to the parade ground, and for an hour or two people could hear the pop-pop of musket drill or the occasional deep boom of gun crews exercising. They read stories about General McClellan's so-called Army of the Potomac, but that was in faraway Virginia, and in the few skirmishes in Missouri and Kentucky, Confederate soldiers had held their ground.

Military activity had reached a new threshold, but the commerce upon which the city depended remained paralyzed by the war. A few blockade runners slipped into Berwick Bay or Lake Pontchartrain, but traffic through the passes had slowed to a crawl. Prices for food, clothing, and household commodities continued to climb, although beef, cotton, seafood, salt, sugar, and vegetables remained plentiful. Flour, which came from the Midwest, jumped to $20 a barrel, coffee from South America to $1 a pound, and a black market flourished in common toilet articles and medical supplies like quinine and morphine. Men accustomed to working in the warehouses along the levees or crewing steamboats had nothing to do and out of desperation joined the army. And money, especially coins, disappeared from the streets, hoarded and buried by those who had it. Various forms of paper, including tickets in trade, appeared in place of hard money, and local businesses were confounded by forgeries.[1]

John Maginnis, editor of the *True Delta*, offered a solution. Make New Orleans a free city, he said. Put it under the protection of the Confederate government but keep it separate and in all other ways independent from the rebellion. Maginnis' idea probably appealed to some, and if New Orleans had successfully separated itself from both state and country, it would have set an interesting precedent for cities like Mobile and Galveston — even for the entire state of Texas, which often contemplated its own independence.[2]

But New Orleans, guided by the Confederate government, waited for foreign intervention. If Richmond's King Cotton policy did not bring Great Britain and France into the war, the *Trent* affair would. Then British ships would drive away the Union vessels and business would be better than ever. Louisianians still expressed confidence in Jefferson Davis and the Confederate government, so New Orleans would be patient and wait for the Confederacy's foreign policy to work. Besides, the city was safe, at least for a good long while — General Mansfield Lovell, a man of demonstrated energy who knew how to get things done, had told them so.

But Lovell, without the navy to keep him informed, had more problems than he could count. On January 16 he seized fourteen river steamers, but Commodore Hollins refused to take the vessels, pleading that he had no funds to arm or refit them and no men to crew them. Besides, War Secretary Benjamin did not want the navy involved with the army's gunboats. Lovell had asked for the vessels and Benjamin had gotten them for him, so why did Lovell now want to turn army property over to the navy? Benjamin admitted the force was intended as "a peculiar one," but he wanted the vessels "subject to the general command" of Lovell, not Hollins. Had Lovell deceived the War Department by demanding vessels he never expected to get? After appropriating $1 million from Congress, Benjamin was not about to go back and say it was all a mistake. To complicate matters more, Lovell discovered after the seizure that the government of Louisiana had intended to outfit some of the same vessels at state expense. Now they were in his possession, and to some observers it seemed that neither the army nor the navy wanted them. The press poked around for

1. New Orleans *Commercial Bulletin*, January 7, 1862; Dufour, *Night the War Was Lost*, 112–14.
2. New Orleans *True Delta*, January 10, 1862.

answers, assailed Lovell for disrupting the plans of the state, and asked what the War Department wanted with steamships.[3]

What the press failed to discover was that the War Department had grabbed $1 million authorized by Congress for the purchase of "floating defenses for the Western rivers" before the Navy Department had time to think about it. Unlike Mallory, Benjamin could get almost all the money he needed to run the War Department, and when Lovell asked for money so Hollins could "help" refit the vessels, Benjamin came up with another $300,000. But Hollins still wanted nothing to do with refitting vessels unless they fell exclusively under his command. Instead, he suggested reassigning the money to the navy, where he would find better ways to spend it. Hollins was responsible to Mallory, not Lovell. President Davis had neglected to include Mallory and Hollins in his "unrestrained intercourse and cordial fraternization" message to Lovell.

Equally absurd was Congress' authorization of a corps "of not more than 6,000 men" to man the fourteen river steamers. Most of the vessels could carry about seventy men, but the War Department did not know any more about sizing crews than Lovell knew about shipbuilding. However, that issue was partially settled by President Davis, who could not shake the habit of ruling on nearly every matter involving military affairs. Davis reserved the right to appoint the captains, who would then fit out their ships as each "may desire."[4]

Because the vessels were to be manned by civilians and volunteers recruited from the lakes, bayous and rivers, and not by naval personnel, the problem of outfitting the fleet for service and organizing crews fell upon Lovell. He had plenty of other problems and not one of the six thousand men Congress had authorized him to enlist. After Davis named James E. Montgomery and J. H. Townsend captains of two of the vessels, Lovell suggested that the quasi-military gunboat captains with presidential commissions name someone "to have general control of the fleet, in fitting it out and making general rules and orders for its . . . management. Fourteen Mississippi River captains," he warned, "will never agree upon anything after they once get underway."[5]

Lovell proceeded under instructions and appointed a committee, which included naval constructor John L. Porter, to appraise the fourteen vessels

---

3. *Ibid.*, January 16, 1862; *ORA*, VI, 809, 811, Lovell to Benjamin, January 18, Benjamin to Lovell, January 19, 1862.

4. *ORN*, Ser. 2, I, 663–64, Benjamin to Lovell, January 19, 1862.

5. *Ibid.*, 672–73, Lovell to Benjamin, January 28, 1862.

seized by the War Department. The committee reported some of the ships not worth the asking price. Better vessels, they said, could be obtained from the glut of shipping lying idle along the levee. Lovell wanted to replace several of the vessels, but since his orders had originated in the War Department, he wrote Benjamin for instructions. Time dragged, and each day owners "who are clamorous for their money" made visits to the general's office.[6]

In the meantime, Colonel Duncan's promotion to brigadier general arrived. To take some of the load off himself, Lovell put Duncan in charge of all coastal fortifications. To some degree this diluted Duncan's focus on Forts Jackson and St. Philip, but Lovell, who was not blessed with a cadre of energetic officers, had little choice.[7]

New Orleans joined with the general in cheering the news of Duncan's promotion. The new thirty-four-year-old general was born in York, Pennsylvania, graduated fifth in the West Point class of 1849, was a competent engineer, a first-rate artillery officer, and well liked by his men. He had moved to the Crescent City in 1855 to supervise government construction, and by 1861 he was more Louisianian than Yankee and sided with the South when the state seceded. Lovell depended upon Duncan more than any other officer in the department.[8]

Lovell's first inkling of trouble in the Gulf appeared when the Washington *Star* reported Farragut had been named to command a "great expedition that is to operate on the western part of the gulf. . . . The fleet will consist of the *Richmond, Pensacola,* and other large steam frigates . . . and some twenty or thirty vessels carrying mortars and thirty-two pounders. The opinion is expressed in naval circles that few fortified places can hold out against such an expedition." The story was picked up by the Richmond *Examiner* and on January 29 reprinted in the New Orleans *Picayune.* Even if every reader did not believe the news, Welles's carefully guarded plan was beginning to leak like some of his old rotten vessels.[9]

If this news gave Lovell cause to worry, there was not much he could do about it. Even if the War Department's fourteen steamers were outfitted with their one authorized gun apiece, clad with iron on their bows, and manned by crews armed with cutlasses, what could they do against Farragut's mighty sloops of war? Lovell could keep digging entrench-

6. *Ibid.,* 672.

7. *Ibid.,* 660, Benjamin to Lovell, January 6, 1862.

8. Faust (ed.), *HTI,* 229; Ezra J. Warner, *Generals in Gray: Lives of the Confederate Commanders* (Baton Rouge, 1959), 77–78.

9. New Orleans *Picayune,* January 29, 1862.

ments and improving fortifications, but still, he asked, where was the navy?

When Hollins vanished upriver with his mosquito fleet, he left behind *Manassas*, which could barely stem the current, a few small armed steamers, and shipyards crammed to capacity with work. By the end of January, John Hughes & Company launched the light-draft side-wheelers *Bienville* and *Carondelet* into Bayou St. John and began installing on each vessel five old navy smoothbore 42-pounders taken from Lovell's slush pile. Three other vessels—*Maurepas*, *Livingston*, and *Pontchartrain*—were already in service. On February 6, the shell of the mighty *Louisiana*, started by E. C. Murray on October 15, skidded down the blocks and splashed into the Mississippi. The vessel righted herself and to every spectator's delight, floated high in the water like a huge barge stacked high with green timber. She was far from finished; weeks of work lay ahead installing railroad iron, machinery, and guns, and much of the material had not arrived on site. In the adjacent lot lay the Tifts' dormant *Mississippi*, with woodwork complete and boilers installed, waiting for her enormous shaft to arrive from the Tredegar Works in Richmond, Virginia.[10]

Originally, the Tifts had promised to deliver *Mississippi* to the Confederate navy by December 15, 1861, and E. C. Murray had promised *Louisiana* by January 25, 1862. Both vessels were being built on a four-acre tract owned by Laurent Millaudon, who loaned the property to the Confederate government until February 1. The contracts for both ironclads contained penalties for late delivery, but they also contained escape clauses based upon the availability of materials, and the only material readily available in the vicinity of New Orleans was lumber.[11]

The forty-four-foot center shaft for *Mississippi* exceeded the forging capabilities of the Tredegar Works, and because of its size, there was no other factory in the South that could handle it. The Gosport Navy Yard had better forging facilities, but most of its efforts were being consumed by rebuilding *Merrimack*. A shaft was located on the burned hulk of the *Glen Cove*, a steamer resting on a bank of mud in the James River just below Richmond, and Tredegar agreed to salvage the shaft, modify it, and as quickly as possible ship it to the Tifts. Because of its size and location, riggers from Tredegar lost weeks attempting to extract the shaft from the hulk, and once it was out, they lost more time hauling it by oxen through the mud. As one detail worked to fish the shaft out of the steamer, another

10. *ORN*, Ser. 2, I, 249, 250, 454, 540–41, Statistical Data, and Investigation of Navy Department.

11. *Ibid.*, 433–34, 601, 602, Investigation of the Navy Department.

gang of mechanics built special cranes, furnaces, and a railroad car to handle it. The shaft finally reached Tredegar on January 5, but by then the Tifts had already passed their delivery date.

Secretary Mallory tried to nurse the shaft through the factory by making morning visits. At first men worked around the clock, but the blacksmiths struck for higher wages, and for three weeks work stopped. The shaft was finally shipped from Richmond on March 26; three weeks later it arrived in New Orleans. Jackson & Company routed the shaft into their shop, machined the couplings, and fitted the propellers, which took more time, then the shaft had to be installed before the vessel could be launched. By then, Farragut's warships had arrived in the river, and the city was girding for the attack.

Other delays plagued the Tifts. Simple items like bolts, spikes, and iron plates dribbled in from all over the Confederacy. By mid-February the woodwork was finished, boilers installed, and the frames and doors for gunports cut and ready for installation. In the yard, tons of iron plating lay heaped in a pile waiting for the vessel to be launched. Until the machinery arrived, there was little the Tifts could do.

In early April the Tifts offered Jackson & Company, who were already four months late, an extra $5,000 if they would deliver the machinery by April 25. This was not good enough for the Committee of Public Safety, which approached the Tifts demanding the vessel be launched. The Union navy had forced its way into the river, the committee argued, and they expected an attack on Forts Jackson and St. Philip any day. The Tifts refused. Even Naval Constructor Pierce recommended the vessel be launched. The river was high, Pierce said, and if not launched immediately, the vessel would "settle on her ways." But the Tifts remained adamant. If the engines and shafting had to be installed with the vessel in the water, another month would be lost.[12]

Murray had better luck with *Louisiana,* but not much. He knew his way around New Orleans and had issued purchase orders for all the material available locally, leaving the Tifts with enormous supply problems. His biggest obstacle was getting the money to pay for what he had ordered. To cloud the matter more, the Tifts claimed title to Murray's iron. When it arrived on-site the two builders bickered over ownership while the iron sat idle in a pile between the two shipyards waiting for Governor Moore, General Lovell, or Commander John K. Mitchell to resolve the issue of ownership. Murray appealed to the Committee of Public Safety, who told

12. *Ibid.,* 637–39, 766–68, 773–75; *ORA,* VI, 595, 625–27, Nelson Tift testimony.

him to "go and take it, and they would back [him] up with 2,000 muskets if necessary." It seems the only local authority eager to complete at least one of the ironclads was the committee.

When Murray took possession of the iron, the Tifts did not object. By then they accepted the harsh fact that their shaft was weeks away from delivery, and the Union navy was in the river. Besides, iron could not be fastened to their vessel until after she was launched and her machinery installed. Work on *Mississippi* came to a virtual halt, and in the interest of completing *Louisiana*, the Tifts offered Murray whatever help he needed.[13]

In late January, when the *Picayune* tipped off its readers that the Union navy was coming in force, leading citizens of New Orleans got the jitters. To them, construction on the ironclads had moved at a lethargic pace, regiments raised for local defense had been shipped to Kentucky and Tennessee, defense preparations were still incomplete, and Hollins' mosquito fleet, except for the sluggish *Manassas*, was somewhere upriver. No one seemed to be in overall charge of the Crescent City's defense, and the builders of *Louisiana* and *Mississippi* were outsiders who, beyond finishing the vessels, had no stake in the future welfare of the city. About sixty concerned and influential citizens had taken matters into their own hands and formed the Committee of Public Safety. Where money was a problem, they would raise it. They would tolerate no more delays.[14]

Neither E. C. Murray nor the Tifts ever received any help from the governor, or for that matter, from General Lovell or Flag Officer Hollins, who had no specific directives in that regard. What little help the builders got came from influential members of the Committee of Public Safety, who kept pressure on the builders, also expedited work through the various local contractors responsible for providing machinery, fittings, and other components. The committee discovered that many local shops concentrated their resources on work for which they were paid, and the Navy Department was not paying its bills. So the committee raised $250,000 in local capital and when work on *Mississippi* ground to a standstill, it "proposed to the Messrs. Tift money without limit."[15]

On February 26, committee members expressed their concern directly to President Davis. We find, they wrote, "that the naval department at this station, as far as finances are concerned, is in a most deplorable condition,

13. *ORN*, Ser. 2, I, 754–58, Investigation of the Navy Department.
14. New Orleans *Picayune*, January 29, 1862; *ORA*, VI, 575–76, D. W. Brickell testimony.
15. Brickell testimony, *ORA*, VI, 575; *ORN*, Ser. 2, I, 755, Investigation of the Navy Department.

retarding by this course the manufacture of all kinds [of implements] for that department; also, preventing the enlisting of men for that branch of . . . service." Members of the committee had audited unpaid bills and estimated naval arrearages between $600,000 and $800,000, and they cited cases where some businesses had refused to do further work for the navy. For several months a sign reading No Funds had been hanging over the door of the navy paymaster's office. "Unless a proper remedy is at once applied," the committee warned, "workmen can not longer be had." [16]

Davis seemed surprised by the letter and sent it to Mallory for "prompt attention and report." Why had Mallory not brought the problem to Davis' attention before? Was he so oblivious to the problems in New Orleans that he had taken no action? Or was Davis so preoccupied with military affairs that he ignored naval matters until the public clamored for action? And where was Mallory when Benjamin was lobbying for $1 million to buy fourteen riverboats for the army and another $300,000 to refit them? Did Mallory spend too much time expediting shafts at the Tredegar Works and not enough attending to administrative affairs?

From the correspondence in the *Official Records*, the problem seemed to arise from the personalities and decisions of administrators with different agendas. President Davis was a busy man organizing and equipping the army, and he left naval matters to Mallory. His secretary of the Treasury, Charles G. Memminger, had the responsibility of paying for the war from funds authorized by the Confederate Congress. Memminger could sell bonds and print money, but to maintain the integrity of the government's credit he could not glut the market with worthless paper. By a prior presidential edict, money flowing into the Treasury from the sale of bonds was disbursed first for the army. This left little for the navy, although funds had been authorized and approved by Congress. In an effort to placate New Orleans creditors, the Treasury Department made payments in Confederate bonds, payable in Richmond, instead of in bank notes, which protracted payments by as much as two months. Because of Memminger's policy forbidding creditors from sending their bonds back to Richmond for payment, bondholders had to sell their bonds to local third-party investors. Creditors wanted money; they did not want to get into the business of selling bonds at a discount and lose a share of their profits. [17]

Since the fall of 1861, Mallory had become increasingly critical of

16. *ORN*, Ser. 2, I, 713, Committee to Davis, February 26, 1862.
17. *Ibid.*, 481, 732–36, Mallory/Memminger correspondence, various dates in investigations of Navy Department.

Hollins' unauthorized expenditures, and he blamed his flag officer for buying ships and making "contracts for ordnance and ordnance stores amounting to about $500,000." Mallory failed to mention that if Hollins had not done this, the mosquito fleet would not have had guns, coal, ammunition, and provisions when it went upriver to Columbus, or that when Hollins attacked Pope in the lower Mississippi, he did so without enough ammunition to follow up the advantage won. Mallory also refuted the Committee of Public Safety's claim that as much as $800,000 was past due to New Orleans contractors, asserting that "if the Treasury Department has sent . . . the money for its [Navy Department's] requisition of the 1st of March for $300,000 they have funds in hand more than sufficient to meet every cent due by the department."[18] Mallory tended to be timorous in Davis' presence and probably said nothing about the $1.3 million given to Benjamin to buy and refit riverboats for the army.

When Mallory wrote Davis that by March 1 the navy paymaster in New Orleans would have funds to "meet every cent due by the department," he shifted the president's attention away from the problem by telling Davis exactly what he hoped to hear. But did Mallory believe it himself? A few days earlier he had advised Memminger that "the operations of this [Navy] Department are much embarrassed and the credit of the Government damaged by the delays incurred in placing funds in New Orleans to meet expenditures." Evidently Davis was satisfied, because he sent a copy of Mallory's explanation to the Committee of Public Safety and dropped the matter.[19]

After the committee's appeal to the president, nothing changed. In the water, *Louisiana* waited for more iron plates and the balance of her machinery. On land, *Mississippi* waited for all her machinery and iron. But even if both vessels had been complete and ready for service on March 1, neither had guns, nor were any immediately available.[20]

Mallory did make some changes, but not necessarily for the better. Commander John K. Mitchell was sent to New Orleans in December as Hollins' right-hand man. Mitchell had been born in North Carolina and lived in Florida, and no one questioned his loyalty. At the start of the war, he resigned from the Union navy and received a Confederate commission. When Mallory sent Hollins upriver, he put Mitchell in charge of the re-

18. *ORA*, VI, 844–46, Mallory to Davis, March 8, 1862. Also in *ORN*, Ser. 2, I, 736–38.

19. *ORA*, VI, 846, Harrison to Committee, March 6 [8], 1862; *ORN*, Ser. 2, I, 736, Mallory to Memminger, February 22, 1862.

20. *ORN*, Ser. 2, 1, 467, 511–12, Investigation of the Navy Department.

maining naval force at New Orleans, but at the time (about February 1) the scope of Mitchell's responsibilities excluded any involvement with the ironclads. [21]

On February 24, Mallory, out of patience with his two contractors, ordered Mitchell to "stimulate" both Murray and the Tifts into completing the vessels and to make "all possible exertions to have the guns and carriages ready." Mitchell advised the builders of his instructions, and workmen were transferred from *Mississippi* to *Louisiana*. Three weeks later, on March 15, Mallory again demonstrated his restlessness by ordering Mitchell to consult with General Lovell, who had no responsibility for the ironclads, and to take *Louisiana* out of the hands of the contractors. "Complete her yourself," he told Mitchell, if the contractors were not doing "everything practicable to complete her at the earliest possible moment." Mitchell thought the work was progressing slowly, but he did not feel much could be done to accelerate it and left the work with the contractors. [22]

A week later, Mallory became even more nervous. With Farragut straining to get every Union ship over the bars, Mallory began to sense a need for more than one qualified naval officer present in New Orleans. He transferred Commander Arthur Sinclair to New Orleans with orders "for the command" of *Mississippi*. Sinclair, a Virginian who spent forty years in the old navy, twenty of them at sea, had been building gunboats in Wilmington, North Carolina. When he arrived at the Tifts' yard, *Mississippi* was still on the ways. Sinclair lacked the authority to take over construction of the vessel, but he visited the building site "three or four times a day" superintending construction. The vessel was still waiting for shafts and propellers, and Sinclair agreed that to launch her then would have "retarded her completion." [23]

But Mallory was still dissatisfied with his organization, and on March 29, 1862, ordered Captain William C. Whittle to take command of the New Orleans station. Whittle was another old navy man. Born in Norfolk in 1805, he went to sea as a midshipman at the age of fifteen, fought in the Mexican War, and had lived much of his life on sailing ships. He had a lithe, muscular frame, a frank, businesslike manner, and looked much younger than his fifty-seven years. What he found waiting for him in

---

21. *Ibid.*, 453, Investigation of the Navy Department.

22. *Ibid.*, 453; *ORN*, XVIII, 824, 834, Mallory to Mitchell, February 24, March 15, 1862.

23. *ORN*, XVIII, 351, 836, Sinclair testimony, and Mallory to Sinclair, March 15, 1862; also, *ORA*, VI, 608.

New Orleans was a small ragtail flotilla of armed riverboats, two incomplete ironclads, and the Union fleet pressing into the river.[24]

Whittle may never have understood the intended scope of his responsibilities, but that was more Mallory's fault than his own. With Mitchell to command *Louisiana* and Sinclair *Mississippi*, it might have been obvious to Whittle, the ranking officer, that someone should take charge of the overall naval force, much as Hollins, his predecessor, had done. But Whittle had just arrived on the scene, and in naval protocol command of a station did not involve responsibility for "anything afloat that does not appertain to repairs." Traditionally, Whittle said, "when an officer is in command of a station he commands nothing more." Flag Officer Hollins, who was upriver defending Island No. 10 and New Madrid with eight gunboats, still held command of all vessels afloat, including *Manassas* in New Orleans. However, neither Hollins, Whittle, nor Mallory had any control over Lovell's River Defense Fleet, and Captains Montgomery, Townsend, and Stevenson, who had returned from obscurity to command it, "refused to be placed under the orders of naval officers."[25]

The River Defense Fleet was rapidly becoming one of Lovell's headaches. He had spent most of the appropriation on advances for fitting up, arming, and provisioning the fleet and still owed the original owners $563,000. The civilian captains acted independently and demonstrated "no system and no administrative capacity whatever." The whole enterprise was turning into a waste of Confederate resources, Lovell complained, and "unless some competent person, of education, system, and brains, is put over each division of this fleet, it will, in my judgment, prove an utter failure."[26]

On the brink of confronting Farragut's powerful Union squadron and with Butler's force of more than fifteen thousand troops camped on Ship Island, the Confederate navy passed each day in a quaqmire of command confusion. By early April, Lovell had not warned Mitchell, Sinclair, or Whittle that he believed the enemy's fleet was strong enough to pass the forts. Lovell may not have reached that conclusion himself, but the possibility must have occupied his thoughts. Lovell recognized Whittle's limited responsibilities as a handicap and begged the new secretary of war, George W. Randolph, to confer with Mallory and leave Hollins "in command afloat, at least until he can strike a fair blow at the enemy." But Randolph,

24. Scharf, *Confederate Navy*, 300; *ORN*, Ser. 2, I, 435, Investigation of Navy Department.

25. *ORN*, Ser. 2, I, 435. See also *ORA*, VI, 611, 612, Whittle and Mitchell's testimony.

26. *ORA*, VI, 876, Lovell to Randolph, April 15, 1862.

who had replaced Benjamin as war secretary on March 17, 1862, had limited knowledge of the situation in New Orleans; moreover, although Davis had picked Randolph for the job, he did not support him on military matters.[27]

Prior to Benjamin's exodus from the War Department to the post of secretary of state, he had arranged for Lovell to receive forty-four thousand pounds of powder and a number of 10-inch columbiads and sea-coast mortars to beef up the defenses of the forts. A few days later, Randolph stepped into the War Department and had no idea what guns Lovell was asking about.[28]

To compound the confusion, Governor Moore had purchased with state funds 1,880 rifled muskets and thirty thousand cartridges to arm new troops. When Benjamin transferred five thousand of Lovell's volunteers, along with General Ruggles, to Corinth, Mississippi, they took their small arms with them. Once again, Lovell had new recruits but no weapons. Because the Mississippi was blockaded, muskets had to be landed in Florida and transported overland. Governor John Milton of Florida, who needed arms for his own troops, seized the shipment and sent half of it to Pensacola. When Governor Moore learned his precious weapons had been pilfered by a brother governor, he angrily wired Davis, "in God's name . . . I ask you to order them to be sent to me immediately." Randolph, of course, knew nothing of the matter until Davis handed him the telegram. He promised restitution, but a few days later he admitted having no jurisdiction over Governor Milton's actions and lamented that he could do nothing about the muskets. Evidently, between Confederate governors, possession of military supplies defined ownership.[29]

With public nervousness building to a crisis, Governor Moore and several prominent New Orleans citizens asked Lovell to declare martial law, but the general hesitated. Merchants were refusing to accept Confederate currency except at huge discounts, and speculators were stashing away necessities in hopes of doubling their profits later. Lovell felt that martial law would only make matters worse. But Randolph had just stripped eleven regiments from the department and sent them to Tennessee, forcing Lovell to call upon the governor for ten thousand more volunteers as re-

---

27. *Ibid.*, 608, 650, Whittle testimony, and Lovell to Randolph, April 17, 1862; Faust (ed.), *HTI*, 613.

28. *ORA*, VI, 866, Benjamin to Lovell, Benjamin to Jones, March 23, Randolph to Lovell, March 29, 1862.

29. *Ibid.*, 869, 870, 874, Moore to Davis, April 1, Randolph to Moore, April 2, 14, and Lovell to Randolph, April 3, 1862.

placements. Lovell complained to the War Department, "Persons are found here who assert that I am sending away all troops so that the city may fall an easy prey to the enemy." Besides speculators, the city had attracted spies, and Lovell finally agreed that martial law was the only alternative.

On March 13 a directive from President Davis ordered martial law, and two days later Lovell assigned provost marshals to the parishes of Orleans, Jefferson, Saint Bernard, and Plaquemines. Thereafter, all white males above the age of sixteen were required to take an oath of allegiance to the Confederate States, and all persons, "whether foreigners or not," who were "unfriendly" to the Confederate cause received orders to leave the district. Bars closed at 8 P.M., and citizens were required to have passports when traveling into or out of the four parishes.[30]

Lovell was becoming as nervous as the public. In early March the great raft below Forts Jackson and St. Philip began giving way. Never had the Mississippi seemed so high, and tons of drift piled up behind the barricade. Huge trees ripped from the banks, and heavy barges swept away by the current tumbled downriver at five miles an hour. Lovell sent Montgomery's steamboats downriver to remove the debris, but hundreds of workmen on boats could not keep ahead of the drift. Finally, section by section, the great barrier upon which so much depended snapped. Had Farragut's vessels been poised for attack, they could have passed the forts that day.

As soon as the chains broke, Lovell appealed to the city council for financial assistance and promptly received $100,000. He sent Colonel Edward Higgins down to the forts with Montgomery's steamers to restore the raft, but too much of it had broken loose and was gone, and there were no more heavy chains or anchors to restore the original barrier. Higgins recovered a portion of the original raft and filled the empty spaces with the hulls of old schooners, but Lovell was not satisfied with the new barrier, which would be much easier to breach. As added protection, he had "forty or fifty" fire rafts built, piled high with lightwood mixed with cotton, rosin, and tar oil, and placed them both above and below the barrier. And when Confederate commitments at Pensacola were slashed, Lovell telegraphed General Bragg asking for more heavy guns. Bragg, who hesitated to help the man who had stolen his command, replied that he "regarded the points above Memphis as the best for the defense of New Orleans."[31]

30. *Ibid.*, 872, 877.
31. *Ibid.*, 562, 842, 847, 856, 857–58, 860–61, Lovell to Benjamin, March 6, 9, Davis to Moore, March 13, 1862, and Lovell's General Orders Nos. 10 and 11.

By March 22 the second raft had been strung across the river. Lovell's scouts reported thirteen enemy vessels near the mouth of the Mississippi and several large steamers inside, which, he wrote, "in my opinion only await the arrival of the mortar fleet to attempt to come up the river to New Orleans."[32]

But on April 1, 1862, Flag Officer Farragut was still trying to get his vessels over the mud, and the Battle of Shiloh had not yet been fought. General Albert Sidney Johnston thought he could beat Grant's army at Pittsburg Landing before Major General Don Carlos Buell's Army of the Ohio, marching overland from Nashville, arrived, and he positioned his force to do just that. If Johnston could whip Grant, a victory might change the whole complexion of Farragut's plans in the river. Hollins could return with the mosquito fleet, take it downriver, and give Farragut the same trouble he had given Pope.

For a few days, New Orleans had hope. They knew a little about Grant, who had pushed Johnston out of Kentucky and most of the way through Tennessee. Grant bothered them. They knew nothing about Farragut, but they were about to find out.

A few days later, the news became worse. On April 6–7, near a small Tennessee church named Shiloh, General Grant defeated Johnston's Confederate army. For a few days, President Davis forgot about the problems in New Orleans and exchanged bitter telegrams with Moore, pressing both the governor and Lovell for more troops to send to Corinth.[33]

Lovell had no choice but to comply.

32. *ORA*, VI, 562–63, Lovell testimony.
33. *Ibid.*, 865, Lovell to Benjamin, March 22, 1862.

TEN *Out of the Mud*

Farragut felt vulnerable. It was the middle of March, and half his fleet was in the river and the other half still outside the bar. At any hour he expected to hear the guns of Confederate gunboats, led by *Manassas* or perhaps the two new ironclads about which he had heard so much, all steaming down-river to contest his possession of the passes. He had just received news from the East that on March 8 the Confederate ironclad *Virginia (Merrimack)* had sunk USS *Congress* and USS *Cumberland* in Hampton Roads and on the following day fought an inconclusive engagement with USS *Monitor.* Farragut detested the idea of a navy composed of floating iron, but if New Orleans was about to launch two more *Virginia*s, he had no monitors to protect his wooden vessels.[1]

He must be vigilant. He posted fast picketboats several miles above Head of Passes, but all was strangely quiet. The only sign of Confederate activity occurred on March 12 when *Winona, Kineo,* and *Kennebec* sighted a steamer coming downriver and gave chase. The cotton-carrying side-wheeler sheered back upriver and was joined by another, which had been following about three miles behind. Both vessels backtracked to the protection of Fort Jackson's guns. At two and one-half miles, *Winona* and *Kennebec* tried the range of their 20-pounder Parrotts, firing two rounds each, but could not see where the shots fell.

Aside from this occurrence, Farragut could not understand why the Confederate navy allowed him to bring his heavy vessels into the river without a show of resistance. Perhaps they were waiting for the Union ships to concentrate in the river where they could be boxed in and destroyed, or maybe he had underestimated the strength of the forts where

1. *ORN,* XVIII, 59, Welles to Farragut, March 12, 1862.

a special kind of hell awaited his fleet. He knew that the raft barricade strung across the river had broken and been repaired. To pass the forts he would have to break it again. But in mid-March, with half his squadron stranded outside the bar, the enemy was too quiet, almost smugly indifferent to his presence. To Farragut, a fighting man, the quiet was worrisome, but before he could battle Confederates he had to fight another enemy—mud.[2]

In other years the bars had been deeper, but without the steady flow of maritime traffic to keep the passes open, dredging had stopped and the channels filled with mud. Heavy ships like *Brooklyn*, which drew fifteen feet of water, and *Hartford*, which drew about the same, had to steam around to Southwest Pass where the channel was deepest.

At Head of Passes was Pilottown, a small village of fisherfolk who lived in a dozen shacks built on poles above the river. A company of marines occupied the town and paroled the inhabitants, whom Farragut found "ill-treated by both parties." They had no way to send their catches to market and complained that "to sell to [Yankees] is death by the law of Louisiana." The village, although infested with mosquitoes and midges, provided a handy storage place for sails, spars, and other supplies. On the lone flagpole at Pilottown, Farragut raised the Stars and Stripes and said, "Our flag is now, I hope, permanently hoisted on Louisiana soil."[3]

If the words "I hope" sounded tentative, Farragut had good reasons. He did not want to engage the forts without the heavy broadsides of *Pensacola*, *Mississippi*, *Richmond*, and *Colorado*, and none of those vessels could get over the bar. He ordered them all back to Ship Island to be lightened, which created another delay. As each vessel finally came into the river, all her guns, carriages, shot, shell, and coal had to be restored before the ships could protect themselves from attack.

Of the four big warships, Farragut doubted whether *Colorado* could be lightened enough. She drew twenty-three feet, compared with *Brooklyn*'s sixteen, and in crossing the bar *Brooklyn* grounded and had to be pulled off by *Hartford*. Farragut decided not to waste time trying to lighten *Colorado*, but James Alden, captain of *Richmond*, claimed it could be done. Theodorus Bailey, captain of *Colorado*, disagreed. "If I thought it possible to lighten this ship sufficiently to cross the bar," he said to Farragut, "I [would] have asked . . . permission to do so long since. If Captain Alden thinks that he can lighten the *Colorado* and take her over the bar, I beg that

2. *Ibid.*, 62–63, Bell to Farragut, March 13, 1862.
3. *Ibid.*, 64–65, Farragut to Welles, March 14, 1862.

you will order him to change ships with me and try it." Bailey was certain Alden would not make it, even with a swept hold and the masts removed, and added, "Then, with the *Richmond*, I will be most happy to serve as your second in command up the river." When Captain Melancton Smith and Commander Porter agreed with Bailey, Alden changed his mind, but by then, more time had been wasted.[4]

Bailey took *Colorado* back to Southwest Pass and offered the vessel's guns, supplies, and men while Farragut's steamers tugged and struggled with *Pensacola* and *Mississippi*. Both vessels had been lightened of everything but enough coal to carry them to the pass, and they still drew about eighteen feet. Farragut calculated that several tugs would be required to pull one vessel through "1 foot of mud."[5]

Alden scoffed at his colleague's hesitation to cross the bar. With enough momentum, Alden claimed, the big vessels could plow through the mud and force their own channel. He would show them how to do it. On March 22 he steered *Richmond* toward nearby Pass à l'Outre, gathered steam, and lunged into a mound of mud, shaking the masts and upsetting half of the crew. After grounding three times, he backed off and was about to give up when a fresh breeze enticed him to try once more. The wind was right, and all he needed was another knot or two of speed. Alden ordered all sail set, called for full steam, made a wide circle to gather speed, and with a tremendous jolt crashed into the bar one last time. Late in the afternoon he got off, retreated into deeper water, and anchored. In the morning he weighed anchor and headed for Southwest Pass, where he found the gunboat *Sciota*, under Lieutenant Edward Donaldson, with a draft of only twelve feet, fast in the mud and waiting for a tug.

Alden sighted the buoy marking the channel and decided to try that route. This time he sounded his way toward the channel, working slowly. Caution paid dividends, but in a small way. When the vessel thudded against the bar, he was able to back off. After trying three or four more times, night fell, and he finally gave up.

The following morning, March 24, Alden tried again, this time slamming into the shoal with force. He was still fast on the bar when *Pensacola* and *Mississippi*, steaming in from Ship Island and riding high in the water, came to anchor behind him. Red-faced and burning with embarrassment, Alden paced the quarterdeck, hollering orders to the engine room. By now the whole fleet had probably heard of his offer to get the deeper-

4. *Ibid.*, 64–65, 66, Farragut to Welles, March 14, Bailey to Farragut, March 9, 14, 1862.
5. *Ibid.*, 71, Farragut to Welles, March 18, 1862.

draft *Colorado* over the bar, and here he sat in his own ship, grounded and running out of coal. Alden had been so confident that *Richmond* would glide smoothly into the pass that he had barely bothered to lighten his ship. Now with the crews of *Pensacola* and *Mississippi* watching, professional credibility dictated that he show the others how it was done. Early in the afternoon and with all eyes watching, he backed off the mud, steamed into the Gulf, got a good running start, and with engines throbbing under full steam smacked into the bar with just enough momentum to carry him over. He had the satisfaction of proudly noting in the ship's log, "The *Pensacola* and [*Mississippi*] did not get over the bar last night."[6]

Getting *Mississippi* and *Pensacola* into the river presented no easy task, and the effort spawned an amazing sequence of correspondence from Porter criticizing his foster brother. Farragut knew nothing of Porter's secret letters to the Naval Office, and had he been made aware of them, he probably would not have believed Porter capable of such duplicity. After all, was it not Porter who had recommended him to Welles and Fox? Without Porter's steamers, Farragut may not have dragged the two heavy sloops of war off the mud, but for that dual accomplishment Porter did not deserve all the credit and Farragut none.

Farragut lost ten days pulling the lightened *Mississippi* over the bar and another four for *Pensacola*, and what occurred during those fourteen days revealed Porter's insatiable appetite for recognition. Assistant Naval Secretary Fox was as much to blame for the sub rosa correspondence as Porter. A month earlier Fox had misunderstood one of Farragut's requests for light-draft vessels, assuming they were wanted for the attack. Mystified by Farragut's reasoning, he wrote Porter, "I trust we have made no mistake in our man, but his dispatches are very discouraging. *It is not too late to rectify our mistake.* You must frankly give me your views from Ship Island, for the cause of our country is above all personal considerations. . . . I shall have no peace until I hear from you."

Fox erred in stimulating Porter's ambition by suggesting he spy on his boss, but he had no way of visualizing the situation on the lower Mississippi and he knew senior naval officers had a way of altering facts to cover their own ineptitude. He trusted Porter to keep him informed and perhaps felt justified because of their past relationship. But ambitious Davey Porter, sniffing opportunity and promotion, and—if Farragut slipped— maybe even a greater role, was a horrible choice to cast loose as an inside

6. *Ibid.*, 72, Log of *Richmond*. Alden erroneously wrote *Brooklyn* instead of *Mississippi; Brooklyn* was already in the river. See *ibid.*, 758.

informant. The navy frowned upon junior officers disparaging their seniors, but here the assistant naval secretary had encouraged it. Perhaps Fox had more confidence in Porter's integrity than the commander deserved.[7] Unfortunately, Farragut did not explain until March 27 that he did not want light-draft steamers for his river flotilla but for blockade duty off the many bayous and deep inlets along the coast. By then, Porter was already sending Fox disturbing reports filled with damaging innuendoes.[8]

On March 18, a few days before *Richmond* entered Southwest Pass, Porter began towing his mortar squadron up Pass à l'Outre. By March 20, all twenty-one schooners and Porter's seven gunboats were across the bar. They anchored near Pilottown and began stripping for action. When *Pensacola* and *Mississippi* arrived at Southwest Pass on March 24, Farragut did not have enough shallow-draft steamers to pull the big ships over the bar and asked Porter for help.[9]

Porter rolled up his sleeves and pitched right in. Unlike the screw steamer *Richmond*, the side-wheeler *Mississippi* could not be tilted and dragged through the mud on her side because her huge, slashing side-wheels sucked at the soft mud along the bottom and created a vacuum, holding the vessel fast. Porter attached heavy cables to four steamers, and by tugging in unison, they inched the heavy *Mississippi* through the mud. On April 4, after eleven days and nights of hard labor, the crews cheered as they watched the big side-wheeler float free.

Pensacola did not cross the bar until April 8, partly because of the obstinacy of her captain, Henry W. Morris. Porter's steamers worked the vessel through the worst part of the bar, but as soon as *Pensacola* cleared, Morris waved Porter off and cranked up his steam. Morris had witnessed Alden's plunge across the bar and probably figured if Alden could do it, so could he. Porter, who knew more about the channel than Morris, cautioned against it, but Morris was captain and demanded his way. Moments later, *Pensacola*, with clouds of black smoke spewing from its funnel, steamed full ahead, bungled into a mound of mud, and crashed into a sunken hulk a hundred yards from the main channel. The vessel hit with enough force to nose over and lift her screws clear of the water. Porter was livid and wanted nothing further to do with either Morris or his sloop of war. Morris asked Farragut for Porter's help, but Farragut registered his disgust

---

7. Fox to Porter, February 24, 1862, in David Dixon Porter Papers, Manuscript Division, Library of Congress.

8. *ORN*, XVIII, 86, Farragut to Welles, March 27, 1862.

9. *Ibid.*, 71–72, 717, Porter to Welles, March 18, 1862, and Log of *Hartford*.

and told him to ask Porter himself. He did, finally, and Porter's steamers, aided by a strong southerly breeze, pulled him into the river. But more time had been lost.[10]

Although Farragut had his own steamers involved in liberating *Missis-sippi* and *Pensacola*, he left these matters pretty much in Porter's charge. He concentrated on learning more about Confederate preparations up-river and gathering intelligence needed to prepare his attack. In the mean-time, Porter worked night and day rigging his mortar ships and supervis-ing work out on the bars.

On March 28 Porter wrote a long, curious letter, filled with partial truths and many exaggerations, to his friend Fox. "If as you suppose," he wrote, "there is any want of the proper qualities in the Flag Officer it is too late now to rectify the mistake; but as yet I see no reason why he should not be competent to do all that is expected of him. I never thought Far-ragut a Nelson, or a Collingwood; I only consider him the best of his rank . . . but men of his age in a seafaring life are not fit for the command of im-portant enterprises, they lack the vigor of youth."

After hurling a few barbs at Farragut, Porter turned his attention to Morris (and others) and wrote, "We are hauling the gun boats out of the mud, which got there for the want of common intelligence. I really don't know where the officers have been brought up, they go wandering about here as if the river was deep all over." Then he returned to Farragut, casting himself in the role of savior to a flag officer who somehow bungled through each day. "I have not spoken six words to Farragut, so anxious have I been to get the ships over, and all my time has been spent on the bar. What his plans are I don't know. . . . He talks very much at random at times, and rather underrates the difficulties before him without comprehending them. I know what they are and appreciate them, and as he is impressible [I] hope to make him appreciate them also." For a person who had not spoken six words to the flag officer, it may have seemed a little inconsistent to say in the next breath that Farragut talked "very much at random at times." Where was Porter during these alleged ramblings if not with the flag of-ficer?

After assuring Fox that Farragut would listen to his advice, Porter reemphasized the difficulty for a man of Farragut's age to find himself in com-mand of so large a force. The enterprise had not been "well managed. To be successful," Porter wrote, "we must have young men in command, these young 1st Lieutenants out here should be commanding frigates, then an

10. *Ibid.*, 109, Farragut to Welles, April 8, 1862.

Mortar steamers attacking the water battery of Fort Jackson.
From *Battles and Leaders of the Civil War*

U.S.S. *Brooklyn* attacked by the Confederate ram *Manassas.*
From *Battles and Leaders of the Civil War*

U.S.S. *Mississippi* attempting to run down C.S.S. *Manassas.*
From *Battles and Leaders of the Civil War*

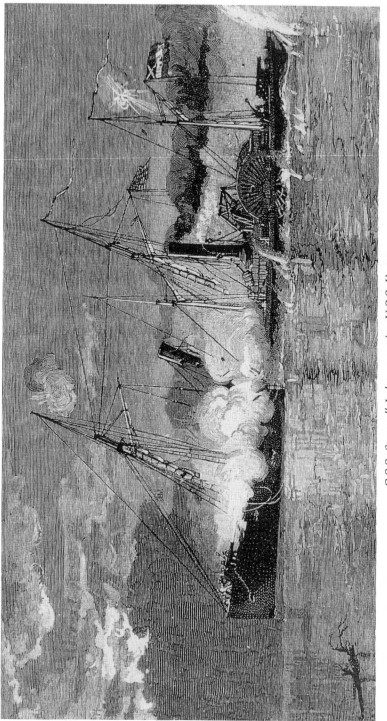

C.S.S. *Stonewall Jackson* ramming U.S.S. *Varuna*.
From *Battles and Leaders of the Civil War*

U.S.S. *Pensacola* disabling C.S.S. *Governor Moore*.
From *Battles and Leaders of the Civil War*

C.S.S. *Governor Moore* in flames.
From *Battles and Leaders of the Civil War*

U.S.S. *Cayuga* breaking through the Confederate fleet.
From *Battles and Leaders of the Civil War*

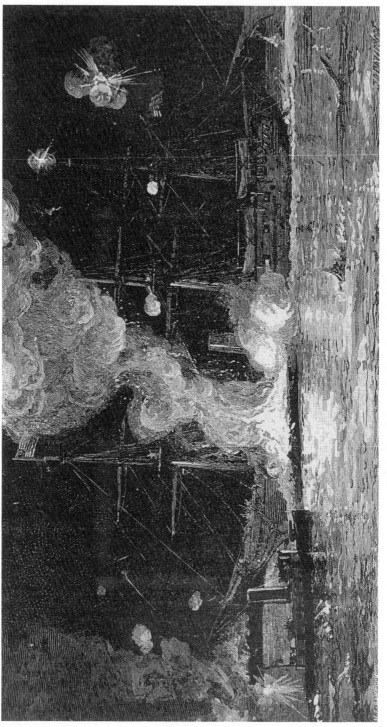

U.S.S. *Hartford* attacked by the *Mosher's* fire raft.
From *Battles and Leaders of the Civil War*

Explosion of the Confederate ironclad *Louisiana*.
From *Battles and Leaders of the Civil War*

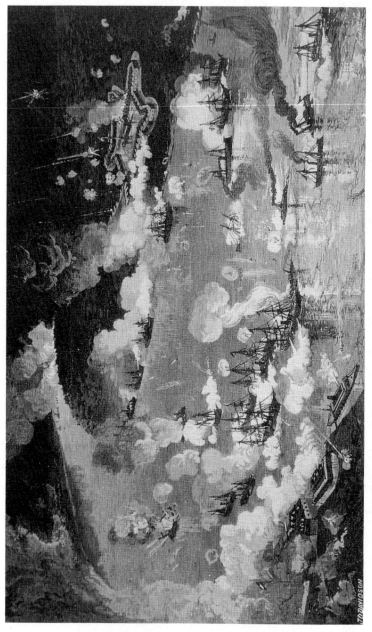

Bird's-eye view of the passage of the forts below New Orleans, April 24, 1862.
The Second Division in action, 4:15 A.M.
From *Battles and Leaders of the Civil War*

elderly Flag Officer could get support. The rank now is so near alike that a Flag Officer has no force, and every old fogy out here is trying to play Commander if left a day by himself." But Porter found a few words to soothe any doubts he had spawned in the Naval Office. If all else failed, he wrote, "I have great hopes for the Mortars. . . . Don't be uneasy yet; though we are behind time, Farragut will bring up lee way when we get the ships across. I hope yet to add a postscript saying that all is right." Again Porter left the impression that Farragut could not think for himself by adding, "the Flag will be urged to move at once, the moment we get the bar clear of ships."[11]

Farragut did not know of Porter's private correspondence with Fox, and one wonders what action he might have taken had he known. Porter probably did not know how little reliance Farragut placed on the mortar boats, or that he had accepted them as a part of his command because some of the schooners had already been purchased. Having them, Farragut had said to Welles, "would probably do no harm." What neither Porter nor Farragut admitted openly to each other was the likelihood that they were pleased to have each other as a part of the expedition.[12]

Ten days later Porter wrote to Fox again, reporting "the *Mississippi* and the *Pensacola* are over the bar and up to Pilot Town," adding that "without us they would have been still at anchor, outside the bar." Then he fired another round at Farragut by writing, "He is full of zeal and anxiety, but has not administrative qualities, wants stability, and loses too much time in talking. . . . In his proceedings he will, he says, be governed by the councils of his officers. He should have adopted that plan the day he took command. Put down the attack for the 20th of April. What the result will be remains to be seen."[13]

Whether Fox was influenced by Porter's correspondence is not known. There is nothing in Welles's diary to suggest that Fox shared the information with the naval secretary, who had already decided that Porter was an able but a somewhat divisive opportunist. Six months later Welles called Porter to the Navy Department and with some misgivings promoted him over dozens of senior officers to the rank of acting rear admiral and placed him in command of the Mississippi Squadron. Porter thereby skipped two grades in which other commanders customarily spent years, if not entire careers, and he had no one to thank more than his foster brother.[14]

11. Thompson and Wainwright (eds.), *Fox Correspondence*, II, 89–95.
12. Welles, "Admiral Farragut and New Orleans," 683.
13. Thompson and Wainwright (eds.), *Fox Correspondence*, II, 96–99.
14. *ORN*, XXIII, 388, Welles to Porter, October 1, 1862.

For two weeks Farragut's steamers subsisted off eight hundred tons of coal borrowed from Butler's army, but that was nearly gone. When *Mississippi* and *Pensacola* crossed over the mud, they had barely enough coal in their bunkers to steam up the pass. On March 30 Butler wrote Farragut: "I am now ready to put on board ship six regiments and two batteries and will be able to be in the Passes in twelve hours. If the navy is not to be ready for six or eight days, I ought not to sail, as my coal is running short and I can not carry more than eight days for sailing." Farragut told him to wait.[15]

Porter also needed coal. In his letter to Fox, he growled: "I don't know whose fault it is, but we are *without coal.* The *Mississippi* put out her fires today having burnt her last pound, the *Clifton* has five tons, the *Westfield* ten, the *Harriet [Lane]* 20, *Pensacola* 20, *all* the gun boats short, and but for the *Richmond* to draw upon, and some I brought in the Mortar vessels, we should all have been at a standstill long ago. I think McKean is in a measure to blame for this, as Farragut could not know the wants of this squadron. It is true that a wise head would have provided against all contingencies, but as I said before I only considered Farragut the best of his rank, his administrative abilities are not of the first order."[16]

Porter probably knew Farragut had coal coming, as much as he needed, but it was late in arriving. Coal vessels were sailing ships, mostly old brigs bought or contracted by the navy to carry supplies. Their speed depended upon the direction of the wind and the enthusiasm of the crew, and it was not until April 14 that Farragut could say, "I have been more fortunate than I supposed in getting coal. Our vessels are nearly all coaled and we are only deficient a few hundred tons."[17]

For a period of two weeks the Confederate navy may have missed an opportunity to upset Farragut's plans. Commander Whittle sent a telegraphic dispatch upriver to Hollins stating that the enemy was in force at the mouth of the river, and begged Hollins to come to New Orleans. At the time, Hollins' five gunboats were below Island No. 10, and according to the flag-officer, they had only "twenty minutes powder." But Hollins was game, and he proceeded posthaste to New Orleans. In an attack on the Union squadron, the guns of his mosquito fleet, along with boats from Lovell's River Defense Fleet, would be pointed downriver, and Hollins knew Far-

15. *ORN,* XVIII, 88, 90, Butler to Farragut, Farragut to Bailey, March 30, 1862.
16. Thompson and Wainwright (eds.), *Fox Correspondence,* II, 92.
17. *ORN,* XVIII, 128, Farragut to Butler, April 14, 1862.

ragut's large vessels would be out of position to engage their big broadsides. Hollins had another advantage; the bows of his vessels were ironplated. General Duncan had prepared forty fire rafts already topped with twelve thousand cords of lightwood and large quantities of combustibles. Towing a fire raft alongside each of his gunboats, Hollins intended to drive them right into the midst of Farragut's fleet and then light them. "I knew they were there in such numbers," Hollins said, "that if I attacked . . . they would run afoul of each other and become so confused as to render them unable to do me serious injury. I felt perfectly safe in going down. . . . I would have caught them at their anchors."

Hollins wired Mallory for permission to make the attack. When Mallory rejected the plan, Hollins took it to Governor Moore, hoping for enough support to change Mallory's mind. By then the entire city was jittery. Moore, Lovell, and Whittle sent an urgent appeal to the Naval Office asking Mallory to let Hollins "remain and make a dash at the enemy." There was no answer, although Hollins waited for twenty-four hours before returning upriver. A few days later Mallory recalled Hollins to Richmond and without further explanation assigned him to the innocuous position of president of the board to examine midshipmen.[18]

Mallory, along with the War Department, still believed the threat to New Orleans came from Flag Officer Foote's Union squadron upriver, not from Farragut's wooden warships. At the time, nobody in New Orleans or Richmond knew Farragut was running out of coal, but Hollins, in the spirit of a commander advancing to the point of attack, had committed a small transgression. Without Mallory's knowledge, he had left his post at Fort Pillow to help save New Orleans. His vessels could do nothing against Foote's ironclads, and Hollins knew it. He had left Commander Robert F. Pinkney in charge of the mosquito fleet during his brief absence, but Mallory's patience toward his independent-minded flag officer had finally reached its limit, and Hollins was gone.

What damage Hollins might have done to Farragut's fleet is open to speculation. Despite Porter's self-serving opinion of his commanding officer's faults, Farragut was a thorough man, leaving nothing to chance that could be prevented. A week before Porter arrived, Farragut had set the stage by issuing orders to all his skippers, stating in specific detail how he expected each commander to prepare his ship against attack. Farragut recognized his squadron's vulnerabilities and ordered each captain to "mount

18. *ORN*, Ser. 2, I, 473–76, 519–20, Investigation of the Navy Department.

one or two guns on the poop and topgallant forecastle; in other words, be prepared to use as many guns as possible ahead and astern . . . bearing in mind you will always have to ride head to the current, and can only avail yourself of the sheer of the helm to point a broadside more than three points forward of the beam."

For added protection, Farragut wanted boat howitzers mounted on carriages in the fore and maintops so they could fire in any direction. Under any circumstance, he insisted every vessel be pointed upstream. Although Hollins was certain that the Union ships if attacked would become hopelessly entangled, Farragut was protecting against the same by ordering, "Should any injury occur to the machinery of the ship, making it necessary to drop down the river, you will back and fill down under sail or drop your anchor and drift down, but in no case turn the ship's head downstream."

Farragut knew about the fire rafts and expected them to be used, so he wanted plenty of grapnels in the ships' boats "to hook onto, and to tow off the fire ships." He also wanted each steamer trimmed "a few inches by the head, so that if she touches the bottom she will not swing head down the river." After covering every other detail, from fighting fires to plugging holes, he remembered Pope's Run and added, "No vessel must withdraw from battle under any circumstances without the consent of the flag-officer."[19]

Despite the odds, Mallory may have been short-sighted when he ignored Hollins' recommendation to attack the Union fleet. Mallory knew more time was needed to finish *Louisiana*, which was in the water, and *Mississippi*, which was still on the ways. If nothing else, Hollins' plan offered an opportunity to upset Farragut's timetable, and a courageously led, damaging night attack might have done it. Besides a coal shortage, Farragut had lightened his vessels to get them over the bar, and before he could launch an attack, guns had to be reinstalled and shot, shell, and top hamper returned to *Mississippi* and *Pensacola*. Instead, Mallory recalled Hollins, presumably for rushing to Whittle's aid at a time of crisis.

Hollins was familiar with the river defense system on the lower Mississippi, and Whittle, who had arrived in New Orleans at the end of March, had never been as far as the forts. But by acting independently and ignoring red tape, Hollins had embarrassed Mallory too many times over expenditures, so the man who might have made a difference in the defense

---

19. *Ibid.*, 474; *ORN*, XVIII, 48–49, Farragut's General Orders.

of New Orleans was finally ordered to pack his bags and return to Richmond.[20]

Two Union ironclads had passed Island No. 10, and Mallory still believed the threat to New Orleans was from Foote's force and not Farragut's. On April 11, three days after the surrender of Island No. 10 and its seven thousand defenders, Mallory ordered *Louisiana* upriver to meet Foote's attack. The ironclad was not ready; she had most of her iron and part of her battery, but the guns were poorly mounted and not sighted in. The engines were still being tested, and the vessel's steerage was unpredictable, and Whittle believed the vessel would not be ready for service for "at least six weeks, if not two months." Mitchell, who commanded *Louisiana*, claimed his ship "was without sufficient motive power even to stem the current of the Mississippi without the aid of her two tenders." There was no evidence that anyone had transmitted this bad news to the naval secretary.[21]

For some reason Mallory paid little attention to Farragut's build up in the passes, and his instructions to Whittle made Lovell, who was already critical of the Navy Department, livid. "With 40 vessels in the lower river," Lovell wired War Secretary Randolph, "please protest in my name against sending the *Louisiana* up the river. If she must go, let her leave here two 7-inch rifles, now at Fort Jackson. . . . We have not now as many guns of heavy caliber as at Mobile."[22]

The 7-inch guns had come from Pensacola, and Lovell borrowed them from the navy because of the inferiority of his own stockpile. General Duncan had rebuilt an old water battery directly across from Fort Jackson and bomb-proofed the shell rooms and magazines, and now he needed two heavy 7-inch rifled guns to give it a power-punch. Duncan wanted a battery across from Fort Jackson for two reasons. First, if Porter anchored his mortar schooners on the west bank, they could not be seen from the fort, but could be seen and be fired upon by the water battery. Second, if Farragut attacked with his fleet, the water battery would provide heavy enfilading firepower.

There is strong indication that President Davis had his hand in most of these decisions, even to the extent of adjudicating who got the two 7-inch guns. In this ruling, the navy got the guns, and Mallory countermanded his order to send *Louisiana* upriver.[23]

20. *ORN*, Ser. 2, I, 441, 444, Investigation of the Navy Department.
21. *Ibid.*, 455, 456; *ORA*, VI, 611, Mitchell's testimony.
22. *ORN*, XVIII, 844–45, Lovell to Randolph, April 11, 1862.
23. *ORN*, XVIII, 845, Davis endorsement.

While Richmond deliberated, Porter moved his bomb boats into position below Fort Jackson and ranged in his mortars. Lovell reported "no harm done. Twenty-seven vessels in sight from forts."[24]

But Lovell knew what was coming.

24. *Ibid.*, 847, Lovell to Randolph, April 15, 1862.

ELEVEN   *Twenty-One Bummers, All in a Row*

*In far-off Richmond, Jefferson Davis and Naval Secretary Mallory met in the pres-*ident's office, discussed the latest intelligence from New Orleans, and speculated on the Union's intentions. Lovell had repeatedly told them that Forts Jackson and St. Philip would repel any attack by Farragut. But now camped on Ship Island was Butler's army of more than fifteen thousand men with a flotilla of transports. If Butler cut through the marshes and pounced on the rear of the forts in a joint attack, the lower Mississippi could fall. From their detached location, neither Davis nor Mallory could see through the fog of confusing correspondence rattling over the telegraph lines between New Orleans and Richmond, and neither could adjust his thinking to accept the possibility of the Union's wooden warships passing the forts. For good reason, perhaps, they discounted Butler's command as an imminent threat.

Davis probably considered Butler a bungling political general of no military consequence, and Mallory, despite his naval background, knew little about Farragut. Despite General Lovell's repeated warnings, Governor Moore's angry telegrams, and Captain Whittle's inexperience, Davis held to his belief that wooden ocean-going warships could not navigate in the river effectively enough to pass the forts, although other heavy vessels had already done so at Port Royal and Island No. 10.

By the first week of April, 1862, Flag Officer Farragut probably knew as much about Forts Jackson and St. Philip as if he had attended to their construction himself. In the 1840s, Brigadier General John G. Barnard, now chief engineer for the Army of the Potomac, had collaborated with Beauregard rebuilding Fort St. Philip and strengthening Fort Jackson. In January of 1862, at the request of Secretary Welles, Barnard prepared a lengthy narrative describing both forts in elaborate detail and supplying sketches showing gun emplacements, bombproofs, and ditches. "Fort Jackson is a bastioned pentagon," he wrote, "with fronts of about 110 yards. It is built of brick and is in good condition. Its scarp walls are 22 feet high," surrounded by wet ditches flanked by 24-pounder howitzers in casemate on each of the ten flanks. "There is not much room for musketry fire around the flanks," Barnard advised, but "the faces of the bastions may be lined with infantry, as the bastions are hollowed out, leaving the top of the scarp to serve as a parapet."

Farragut received the documents in February, studied them, and began to plan his tactics for utilizing Porter's mortar boats. He was less concerned about musket fire and more interested in the two curtains bearing on the river, because each mounted eight guns. Above, parapets had been arranged to carry twenty-two channel-bearing guns, with the other fronts of the pentagon each carrying sixteen more, many of those also bearing upon the channel. Nine more guns were sighted on the channel and covered by a *glacis coupé* with a covered way. Another branch of the covered way leading from the west front had been designed to carry thirty-one guns, but Barnard did not know how many had been emplaced.

At the time Barnard left Louisiana, work had been started but not completed on an earthwork designed to carry another twenty-five guns. In his memorandum, the general estimated that Fort Jackson carried as many as 127 heavy guns with 111 bearing on the channel and the others bearing on the rear. This total did not include the 24-pounder howitzers on the flanks. From the salient on the north bastion of Fort Jackson to the opposite shore of the river was about 840 yards.

Since it was Porter's job to demolish the fort, he probably took special interest in Barnard's description of the bombproofs. The general had built a decagonal barrack in the center of Fort Jackson with a capacity for sheltering about five hundred men. When Barnard left Louisiana, the Confederates had started to cover the ceiling, built of solid one-foot square beams, with a thick layer of earth. "Beside a great deal of bombproof shelter in the casemates and galleries," Barnard wrote, Fort Jackson "is well sheltered from a bombardment."

Fort St. Philip, situated across the river and seven hundred yards upstream from Jackson, had been established by the Spaniards and brought to its present irregular quadrilateral shape of 150 by 100 yards during the War of 1812. The scarp wall fronting the river rose to about fifteen feet, and the work was surrounded by a ditch ranging from three to six feet deep. All the walls had been strengthened by Barnard, who also added flanking parapets. "The main work of St. Philip," he wrote, "is arranged to receive . . . 20 heavy guns bearing directly upon the channel, besides some dozen or more bearing upon the land."

Two external water batteries faced with six-foot wet ditches fanned out from both sides of the main fort. Each had been designed to carry twenty-two heavy guns on the water faces and another half dozen 24-pounders on the extremities and rear. In total, Barnard believed Fort St. Philip could bring seventy-two guns to bear upon the channel. "The two works," he wrote, "mount together 177 channel-bearing guns."

Barnard reported that at the time he left the area, he counted only fifty-two mostly small-caliber guns arranged about the forts and many without carriages. He suggested that heavier guns had been supplied by now, but based upon the inventories captured at Gosport and Baton Rouge, he doubted if many of the guns exceeded 32-pounders. He warned, however, that the batteries of both forts had furnaces and that 32-pounder hot shot, if used, could cause extensive fire damage.

About passing the forts, Barnard had this to say: "From a point in the river 1 ½ miles from the lowest battery of Fort Jackson to another 1 ½ miles above the nearest upward-bearing batteries we shall find a distance of 3 ½ miles to be traversed, 2 miles of which under the fire of 100 to 125 guns, and the other 1 ½ miles under that of from 50 to 100. Now, against the current of the river this distance will not be performed by the majority of steamers . . . in less than twenty-five minutes or a half hour. With hot shot thrown . . . even though by 32 and 24 pounders, I should look upon the daylight passage as too hazardous to be undertaken. . . . Such an attempt should be made at night, when the distant fire must be very uncertain."

Barnard suggested that Farragut lay "two to four" of his heavy sloops of war, armed with 9-inch or 11-inch guns, alongside each fort, and by "firing spherical case or canister . . . make all of these batteries untenable, even those of the casemates." However, Barnard warned, the forts could be more heavily armed than he anticipated, and it might be wiser to pass them, capture New Orleans, and take Forts Jackson and St. Philip with a land force. But this strategy presented another problem. Barnard felt it would take a large land force to capture New Orleans, and before that happened, Farragut's squadron might run out of supplies and be forced to run the gauntlet again.

In Barnard's opinion, capturing Forts Jackson and St. Philip with a land force would be extremely difficult because of the topography. The level of the river was normally high during the months of April through June, so there would be very little firm ground to move troops across, and the higher ground was well covered by guns from the forts. "If an attack on these forts was feared," Barnard warned, "and the river up, probably all the levees would be cut" and every approach to the forts inundated.

Barnard then reverted to his original suggestion that Farragut not pass the forts but force their surrender, using, if possible, four ironclads. Farragut had no ironclads and at this stage of the war could not wait to get them.

"The plan I would suggest," Barnard wrote, "[is] based upon the fact that the batteries of the forts are all, except sixteen guns of Fort Jackson, *en barbette*; that they are very low; that they can be approached to within 200 yards, and . . . while Fort Jackson is a very strong work Fort St. Philip is comparatively weak. Fort St. Philip once fallen into our possession, [and] its own batteries enfiladed or taken in reverse, all the downstream bearing barbette batteries of Fort Jackson . . . can be enfiladed and the scarps of the two water fronts breached." Along a line of sixteen hundred yards stretching between the upper and lower batteries of Fort Jackson, Barnard proposed deploying twelve Union warships and wrote if "these vessels can be laid out without danger of fouling; and if they averaged ten guns to a broadside they would bring one hundred and twenty guns to bear on the fort, and it will be seen that they will enfilade every barbette battery and take most of them in reverse."

In reference to the barrier below Fort Jackson, Barnard warned if "any obstructions (such as rafts) be anchored in the river (difficult, I think, to maintain in the high or even moderately high stages), the forcing of a passage would be almost impracticable. Here, again, ironclad vessels would be very useful for reconnoitering or destroying rafts."[1]

Farragut could hardly have received more complete information on the forts without having spent several days there himself. But a long span of time had elapsed since Barnard left Louisiana, and Farragut wanted to know to what extent the fortifications had been improved. A steady flow of deserters from upriver brought newspapers from New Orleans and detailed observations from the city's shipyards. Two fishermen slipped out of New Orleans by way of Bay Rondo and reported that the chain, supported by "six or seven schooners," had been thrown across the river at the forts,

1. *ORN*, XVIII, 14–15, 15–24, Welles to Farragut, February 10, and Barnard enclosure, January 28, 1862.

"leaving a passageway close to St. Philip, and that the schooners are anchored [and work crews] taking their masts out. . . . A guard is kept on
both banks to watch the chain." The fishermen also reported that Hollins'
mosquito fleet had "been sent up the river and their guns landed for the
army," and that the "old ram" *Manassas* was "giving out." Two ironclads
were being built above New Orleans, and one had been launched but was
still tied at the dock with men working on her.[2]

Farragut was far from satisfied and on March 28 sent Captain Bell on a
reconnaissance. Bell climbed on board *Kennebec* and steamed up the river
in company with *Wissahickon* for a closer look at the forts. About noon,
and at a range of one and one-half miles, Fort Jackson opened with four guns
and Fort St. Philip with two. All the shots fell short, and Bell edged closer.
"Their projectiles seemed to be all shells," Bell noted, "exploding by concussion . . . not more than four or five failing." The guns at Fort St. Philip
appeared to have a slightly greater range and were better served. Lieutenant John H. Russell of *Kennebec* counted twenty-eight shots. Bell reported that the information provided by the fishermen was accurate: eight
dismasted schooners were stretched across the river about twice their
lengths apart; at one end was a large raft and beside it a single small opening to allow the passage of ships. Bell watched the Confederate steamer
Star nosing through the opening, but a single shot from *Kennebec*'s 20-
pounder drove her back inside the barrier. After completing his observations, Bell returned down the river, followed by *Wissahickon*.[3]

When *Mississippi* finally rumbled over the bar on April 4, and with *Pensacola* expected to follow in another day or two, Farragut decided he had
better look at the forts himself. On April 5 he shifted his flag to *Iroquois*
and started upriver, accompanied by Bell and a small flotilla of Union gunboats. For two hours *Iroquois* maneuvered below Fort Jackson. Farragut
and Bell sat undisturbed on the horse block and watched seven Confederate shells splash into the river a few yards from the vessel. Farragut appeared to be amused by the reaction of some of the younger officers. He
would point skyward and shout, "There comes one! There! There!" and as
the shot arced toward the vessel the "quarter-deck party" bobbed about
nervously until the missile plunged into the water. "Ah, too short," Farragut remarked, "finely lined though!" After observing everything first-
hand, he signaled for the squadron to withdraw, only to observe *Hartford*

2. *Ibid.*, 684–85, Diary of H. H. Bell.
3. *Ibid.*, 686, Bell to Farragut, March 28, 1862; *ibid.*, 806–807, Log of *Kennebec*.

and *Brooklyn* steaming rapidly upriver in response to the firing. They backed off and followed *Iroquois* back to their stations at Head of Passes.[4]

Pensacola navigated over the bar on April 8, and a few days later coal began to arrive. Farragut now had all the vessels in the passes he was going to get, and Porter, who impatiently marked time, wanted to test the effectiveness of his mortar boats. He had not forgotten his hasty prediction to Welles and Fox that he would reduce both forts to a rubble in forty-eight hours.

Farragut doubted it. He was willing to let Porter try, but he would not allow a squadron of flimsy wooden bomb boats to take unnecessary risks. On April 13, he steamed up to the forts again, this time on *Harriet Lane* with Porter and Bell. Trailing a short distance behind were four of Porter's steamers, *Westfield, Clifton, Owasco,* and *Miami,* followed by six of Farragut's warships. The Coast Survey steamer *Sachem,* commanded by F. H. Gerdes, led the squadron slowly upriver. Gerdes had arrived at Porter's request on April 11 with four experienced assistants, J. G. Oltmanns, T. C. Bowie, Joseph Harris, and R. E. Halter, all civilians. Farragut's main objective was to establish with precise accuracy the range of the Confederate guns and then let Gerdes determine where Porter should place his bomb boats.

Porter sent *Westfield,* under Commander William B. Renshaw, after a steamer that was holding to the bank well below the chain, but the vessel darted upriver and joined a cluster of gunboats lying under the guns of Fort Jackson. Renshaw opened with his rifled 100-pounder, sending a shot through the hull of one of the River Defense gunboats. The vessel sustained considerable damge and was later scuttled.[5]

Porter then sent *Clifton* forward to draw the enemy's fire, enabling Gerdes to determine the exact range of the forts' guns. With shells splashing around *Clifton,* Porter advanced *Harriet Lane* so engineers could work out the coordinates. Farragut noticed that four of the dismasted schooners making up the chain barrier were clustered against the east bank as if they had broken loose. He spotted a huge pile of logs and debris jammed up against the cable and behind it many fire rafts stacked with four feet of wood. Farragut returned downriver but left Gerdes and his crew of surveyors behind with four of Porter's gunboats for protection.[6]

On April 13 Gerdes and his four assistants began an elaborate survey of the river beginning with Forts Jackson and St. Philip and extending for

4. *Ibid.,* 755–56, 791, 799, Logs of *Sciota, Kineo,* and *Iroquois*; Lewis, *Farragut,* 35.
5. *ORN,* XVIII, 389, Renshaw to Porter, May 5, 1862.
6. *Ibid.,* 423, 686–87, Gerdes Report to Bache, Diary of H. H. Bell.

several miles downriver. For five days they labored, often under fire from the forts or from sharpshooters who crept through the brush and popped away at the men working in the boats. The gunboats chased away the sharpshooters with 32-pounders loaded with canister, but a half hour later they were back again.

At first, markers driven in the ground by the survey team were pulled up and carried away at night by the watchful sharpshooters. Gerdes resorted to numbering his posts and then camouflaging them with weeds and reeds so they could not be found by the enemy. Wherever necessary, because footing was so treacherous along the banks, Gerdes' four assistants hung flags from branches or mounted small theodolites from the chimneys of deserted shacks. Each night Gerdes returned to his cabin on *Sachem* and under a dim lantern recorded every detail on a master map, and every morning his men replaced the stolen markers.

At Porter's request, the surveyors staked out points along the shore for positioning each mortar boat, leaving a distance of from 100 to 150 meters between each. Two weeks later Porter praised the survey team by writing Superintendent Alexander D. Bache, "The position that every vessel was to occupy was marked by a white flag, and we knew to a yard the exact distance [from] the hole in the mortar [to] the forts, and you will hear in the end how straight the shells went to their mark."[7]

Porter had good reason to praise Gerdes. On April 15 he towed three schooners into position at three thousand yards to test his "chowder pots" as well as Gerdes' markers. The "bummers," as the men in the bomb boats were called, opened a slow fire on Fort Jackson. According to Porter, Pierre Soulé and a party of his friends from New Orleans were at the fort enjoying a look at the Yankee fleet. When the first mortar thumped in the distance, they stood calmly on the parapet and watched the shell first rise and then begin its descent. As it drew nearer, they raced for cover just before it exploded right next to the parapet. Porter claimed that "a second shell," fired a few minutes later, fell on the drawbridge and nearly destroyed communications with the mainland. "I don't know what effect it had on General Lovell," Porter added, "but he and his friends made no more visits to the fort."[8] What Porter said of the others may have been true, but Lovell returned to the forts the night of the attack.

On the day Porter ranged in his mortars and chased Pierre Soulé from

---

7. *Ibid.*, 394, 424–25, Gerdes to Bache, and Porter to Bache, April 26, 1862.

8. Porter, "Private Journal," April 15, 1862; West, *Second Admiral*, 128. Lovell did make other visits to the fort, but they are not mentioned in Porter's account.

the ramparts, he made another observation. On April 13 he had noticed a large raft aground a short distance below the chain barrier. He remembered seeing it at the end of the barrier and surmised that it had broken loose, but the raft had only shifted a few yards downriver and still anchored one end of the chain. On the night of April 15, he and Julius H. Kroehl, who had charge of submarine operations on the Mississippi River, rowed up to the raft and placed a fifty-pound charge underneath it. They then eased off, running out a pair of wires attached to a galvanic battery. When safely away, Kroehl gave it the spark and in the morning the raft was gone, but several Confederate steamers had gathered hurriedly to recover the chain and replace the raft. Porter tucked the experiment away in his mind, knowing that sometime soon the chain would have to be broken for good.[9]

On April 17 activity off Fort Jackson began to heat up. The Confederates sent several gunboats below the barrier to fire at the surveyors, only to be chased away by *Westfield* and *Clifton*. A short time later, the watch on *Westfield* reported several fire rafts coming through the barrier and headed toward *Sachem*. Porter's gunboats intecepted the first raft and took it in tow after it drifted down to *Hartford*. At 1 P.M. three steamers of the River Defense Fleet ventured downriver and began shelling Porter's guard boats. Captain Bell signaled *Varuna* and *Kineo* to give chase, and for a half hour guns boomed below the barrier. Most of the shells fell harmlessly into the river, but one shot disabled a two-masted Confederate steamer, and the other two gunboats towed her to safety. That evening another fire raft came around the point. *Clifton* hooked onto it and hauled it to shore.[10]

On the morning of April 18, Porter towed his mortar schooners upriver and placed them in positions marked by the surveyor's tiny white flags. The bummers dressed their masts with brush and cottonwood boughs, and the tops blended perfectly with the trees along the shore. Some of the forward vessels observable from Fort St. Philip covered their exposed broadside with a few long branches. The Confederates had failed to follow Beauregard's advice and felled trees only as far as the lower limit of Fort Jackson's casemate fire, leaving a natural screen for Porter's schooners. Gerdes had picked an ideal spot for Porter to hide his boats. In order for gunners at Forts Jackson or St. Philip to reach Porter's

---

9. *ORN*, XVIII, 428, Kroehl to Welles, June 2, 1862.

10. *Ibid.*, 389, 692, 791–92, Diary of H. H. Bell, Renshaw to Porter, May 5, 1862, Log of *Kineo*.

schooners, they had to fire blindly into three hundred yards of vine-snarled woods through which a shot or shell could hardly pass without hitting some object.

As the bomb boats fell into line and opened with their mortars, amused observers on Farragut's ships predicted "the bloody bottoms of the 'bummers' will drop out at the tenth fire!" When that failed to happen, somebody commented, "The 'bummers' think this is a damned holiday."[11]

The thirteen-man crews had had plenty of time to practice while Porter's steamers were getting Farragut's warships over the bar. They rammed home twenty-pound powder charges, cut fuses, loaded 216-pound shells into the "chowder pots," and lobbed the missiles into swamps. As the manual instructed, the crew stood on tiptoe and held their mouths open to lessen the shock of the discharge and the impact upon their eardrums. In shallow water the recoil often drove the schooners into the mud, where they remained stuck for several minutes before popping free. Occasionally, a mortar recoiled off its turntable, driving the rear of the carriage into the waterways and listing the vessel over about ten degrees. The test firing knocked doors off their hinges and toppled roundhouses. By the time the bomb boats moved into position, carriages had been reinforced and doors taken below.[12]

Lieutenant Watson Smith commanded the first division of Porter's mortar flotilla. On the morning of April 18, Good Friday, *Clifton, Miami,* and *Westfield* towed Smith's squadron, consisting of the schooners *Norfolk Packet, Oliver H. Lee, Para, C. P. Williams, Arletta, William Bacon,* and *Sophronia* into position behind the screen of woods along the west bank. Based upon Gerdes' calculations, the head vessel lay 2,850 yards from Fort Jackson and 3,600 yards from Fort St. Philip. Before every bomb boat had snugged into position, the first vessels in line commenced firing, shaking the treetops along the river and covering them with fine black dust.

The third division under Lieutenant K. Randolph Breese fell into line behind the first. As soon as *Horace Beals, John Griffith, Sarah Bruen, Racer, Henry Janes, Dan Smith, Sea Foam,* and *Orvetta* (of the second division) settled into position, eight more 13-inch mortars opened on Fort Jackson. Observers tied to the top masts of each schooner peered over the treetops as the first of the big shells arced their way skyward and descended into

11. *Ibid.,* 362–63, Porter to Welles, April 30, 1862; West, *Second Admiral,* 128.
12. George W. Brown, "The Mortar Flotilla," *Personal Recollections of the War of the Rebellion* (New York, 1891), 175–76.

the fort with a thump. The observers on the west bank had a good view of the fort and blended so completely with the foliage they could not be seen by spotters on the parapets.

The second division under Lieutenant Walter W. Queen was not so fortunate. Porter placed Queen's boats on the east bank where they were exposed to an unobstructed view from both forts. *T. A. Ward, Maria J. Carlton, Matthew Vassar, George Mangham, Sidney C. Jones,* and *Adolph Hugel* had orders to direct their fire against Fort Jackson, located about 3,680 yards from the first vessel in line. Because of its exposed position, Queen's division attracted most of the fire from both forts.

While Queen deployed his schooners, Porter sent *Owasco,* under Lieutenant John Guest, ahead to draw the fire of the forts. For an hour Guest maneuvered back and forth in midstream, occasionally firing an 11-inch shell at Fort Jackson while shot and shell from both forts fell all around him. Porter steamed over to Captain Bell and asked for support, and a half hour later *Iroquois, Cayuga,* and *Wissahickon* moved into position and joined *Owasco.* This gave Fort Jackson's gunners more targets and diverted much of the fire from Queen's schooners, but Porter had seen enough. He went aboard *Owasco* and ordered Guest to withdraw and resupply his ammunition before his ship was blown to pieces. The others steamers followed, leaving the mortar boats mostly on their own.[13]

Each schooner lofted a shell into Fort Jackson at intervals of ten minutes while both forts targeted all available guns on Queen's exposed division. St. Philip's batteries were barely in range and for the most part ineffective, but Fort Jackson's gunners found the range and concentrated their fire on *T. A. Ward,* the schooner at the head of the line. Queen had barely gotten the schooner into position when he reported, "at 9 a rifle shot struck us, cutting our port main swifter, passing through the wardroom, and over the magazine and out through the starboard quarter at the water's edge." He slipped cable and dropped down the river three hundred yards to make repairs, resuming his station about two hours later. By then, fires could be seen inside Fort Jackson.[14]

A few minutes later the schooner *George Mangham,* under Acting Master John Collins, Jr., received a shot in her port bow that passed through the galley and lodged in the mortar bed. *Mangham* continued to work her mortar, but *Maria J. Carlton,* under Acting Master Charles E. Jack, was

---

13. *ORN,* XVIII, 363–64, 693, Porter to Welles, and Diary of H. H. Bell, April 30, 1862. See also reports from Smith, Queen, and Breese, and Log of *Owasco, ibid.,* 378, 397, 406, 413.

14. *Ibid.,* 408–409, Log of *T. A. Ward.*

not so lucky. At 10 A.M. the following day, a shot from Fort Jackson struck the quarterdeck, broke through a beam, swept away some carlines, plunged through the magazine, and went out the starboard side. The vessel filled rapidly, and boats rushed to bring off the crew. Three men were wounded, and the others transferred elsewhere in the fleet.[15]

By noon on April 18, the concentration of fire on Queen's division became intense. Porter, who had been rowing back and forth between the schooners to keep an eye on the foundations of the mortars, ordered some of the vessels to shuttle back a few hundred yards but to keep up their fire while doing so. At 5 P.M. pillars of black smoke could be seen rising from Fort Jackson, and firing had ceased from the parapets. The bummers kept arcing mortars into the fort until Porter called a halt at sunset. Most of the bomb boats had exhausted their ammunition, and the men had had nothing to eat or drink since daylight. Porter inspected the first and third divisions for damage and found nothing of consequence. A lone 8-inch solid shot had knocked the trucks off the mortar on *Arletta* and mortally wounded Seaman James Lebar, but it did not disable the gun. By contrast, Queen's division was battered, and Porter decided to move it. At 2 A.M. Queen's vessels started across the river and by 8:30 in the morning were back in action, this time sheltered by the same thick stand of cottonwoods that masked Smith's and Breese's commands.

The most accurate mortar fire had come from Queen's division when it lay along the east bank. The gunners could follow the big shells as they dropped into the fort, or if they missed, make a slight adjustment for their next round. From the tottering masttops of the first and third divisions, spotting the shell and following it was not so easy, especially when the spotter seemed half dazed by the concussion of the discharge. About the time he recovered his senses, he found himself immersed in a huge cloud of black smoke, and by the time it passed, the mortar shell had dropped out of sight. When Queen's division shifted to the west bank, Porter lost much of the accuracy the bummers had enjoyed on the first day of fire. He lamented later that had he known the damage done that first day, he would have continued the bombardment throughout the night, although the wind had changed direction and freshened enough to affect the trajectory of the shells.[16]

While the bummers slept on deck, Porter moved up the river to take a

15. *Ibid.*, 407, 410, Queen to Porter, May 3, 1862, and Logs of *Maria J. Carlton* and *George Mangham*.

16. *Ibid.*, 364–65, 404, Porter to Welles, April 30, 1862, Log of *Arletta*.

closer look at the fires in the fort. His bomb boats had fired more than 1,400 shells. At first he believed they had ignited some of the fire rafts, but as he drew closer he could see flames inside the fort and correctly speculated that the barracks and citadel had caught fire. He had missed an opportunity to annoy the enemy at a critical stage by giving them time to control the fires. Porter kept the blunder to himself, resolving thereafter to keep up the bombardment both night and day, but the bummers never matched the first day's marksmanship.

On April 19, the second day, and with no schooners on the east bank to draw fire, Fort Jackson's gunners sighted in on the puffs of black smoke rising above the treetops along the west bank. Some of the camouflage had been knocked off the schooners' masttops, making visible targets for Fort Jackson's gunners. Smith's division, closest to the forts, suffered mostly mast and rigging damage, and one man on *Norfolk Packet* was injured when a shell burst near the mainmast head. Porter suggested that Smith move his vessels more to the rear, but Smith, Porter wrote, "seemed determined not to withdraw until something was sunk." Smith stayed at the head of the line for the next four days, firing sometimes at twenty-minute intervals and at other times ten. At night, as the days began to pass, the divisions took turns firing through the watches as others tried to sleep.[17]

Union ammunition proved to be almost as defective as Confederate shells, which seldom burst. Porter's bombs exploded prematurely because of the varying speeds at which fuses burned. Porter gave up trying to divine the burn-through rate and ordered some of the bummers to use full-length fuses. He could not see what effect this had on the fort, but he knew if his shells hit the ramparts rather than exploding before they arrived, the parapets and the casemates would be damaged. What he could not see or imagine was the demoralizing effect of shells plunging as much as twenty feet into the soft, wet earth, exploding moments later, and lifting tons of earth upward in a boiling mass, only to fall back again in a cloud of dust and debris. To the men inside the fort, it felt like an earthquake.[18]

Once again Farragut sent several warships upriver to give Porter support by engaging the forts, but when the vessels cut across the river to present their broadsides, the strong current swung them out of firing position. Every time a Union vessel nosed around the bend, Fort Jackson's

17. *Ibid.*, 364–65, 398, Porter to Welles, April 30, Smith to Porter, May 3, 1862.
18. *Ibid.*, 365.

guns opened with accuracy. *Oneida,* under Commander Samuel P. Lee, could not get close enough to bring her bow gun into range. The pivot guns, even when fully elevated, could not reach the fort because of the sheer of the vessel. Fifteen minutes after the action opened, a shot from Fort Jackson tore *Oneida's* jib stay away. Two 10-inch shots hulled her starboard side, penetrated the waterways, and sprung several outer planks, and a third shot struck on the port side, tore up the after pivot-gun carriage, and sent splinters flying across the deck, wounding nine men. During the same action, *Itasca,* under Lieutenant Charles H. B. Caldwell, reported shot flying briskly about the ship. One struck the billethead and bowsprit, and another hit forward beneath the waterline, causing a leak.[19] Farragut's warships managed to deplete their ammunition every day, but because most of the firing was done at long range they probably did little damage to the forts.

On April 20 the powder-blackened bummers greeted Easter Sunday with a stepped-up fusillade. A light rain streaked their faces, giving them a ghoulish appearance, and some of the men, overcome with fatigue, dropped to the deck between rounds and fell asleep. When they came off watch, they curled up on the deck and slumbered through the steady roar of the mortar, oblivious to the jolt that followed every discharge at ten- or twenty-minute intervals. Porter noticed that the accuracy of mortar fire improved when the bummers had their rest, but he was beginning to feel the agony of failure. He had promised to reduce the forts in forty-eight hours, and that had not happened.

Porter became more encouraged when a tattered deserter in a mud-stained red cap and dirty shirt hailed *Norfolk Packet* early in the morning and asked to come aboard. When Lieutenant Smith learned the man had come from Fort Jackson, he rushed him over to Porter's flagship. The deserter, who claimed to be a Pennsylvanian with Dan Rice's traveling show, had been performing in New Orleans when the war broke out and he was impressed into Confederate service. The previous night, a shell had exploded outside the magazine door at Fort Jackson, tearing away protective cotton bales, starting fires, and threatening to explode the magazine. While everyone rushed about putting out fires, the deserter slipped across the moat in a skiff, and with flashes of light from the mortars to guide him, made his way through the swamps to the Union flotilla. The deserter

19. *Ibid.,* 776, 812, Logs of *Oneida* and *Itasca.*

asurred Porter that hundreds of bombshells had fallen into the fort, breaking in casemates, setting fire to buildings, and dismounting guns.[20]

At first, Porter was a little reluctant to accept all the good news at face value, but he sensed Farragut's impatience with the protracted bombing and dispatched the deserter to *Hartford* so Farragut could hear his story. Farragut had never had much faith in Porter's mortars, and now, restless over delays, he wanted to force the action. If the deserter was telling the truth, so much the better.

At 10 A.M. on Easter morning Farragut signaled all his officers to the flagship. The time had come to lay out his plans. Let Porter continue to pound the forts and keep up the pressure, but Farragut had seen enough. He now believed, without a shred of doubt, that mortars alone would never force the surrender of the forts. Besides, General Butler had come up the river with seven thousand men, eager for a piece of the action and a slice of the credit.

At Fort Jackson, Brigadier General Duncan wondered when the shelling would end. He felt the steady thump of exploding bombshells, and he sensed the imminence of impending disaster.

---

20. *Ibid.*, 367, 399, Porter to Welles, April 30, 1862, Log of *Norfolk Packet*; Dufour, *Night the War Was Lost*, 238–39.

TWELVE *Recipe for Disaster*

On April 18, Good Friday, rumors of Porter's bombardment began to filter upriver to New Orleans, seventy miles away by river and fifty by air, where people crowded into their churches and offered fervent prayers. From the foot of Canal Street they listened for the rumble of distant cannon, but all they could hear was the gurgle of high water lapping against the levee. On St. Charles Street another crowd gathered, pressing each other for the latest news. As anxiety built, men began to appear on the levee armed with old squirrel guns and shotguns. When evening came, the crowds were still milling about the town, shuffling back and forth from the riverfront, swinging lanterns, asking questions, and offering opinions. Most agreed — New Orleans was in serious peril. "The defense of the river," reported the *Delta* on April 19, "should at this conjuncture be the paramount . . . concern. Upon its defense hangs the fate of New Orleans and the Valley of the Mississippi."[1]

On Ship Island, sixty miles to the northeast across Chandeleur Sound, Mrs. Benjamin F. Butler detected the "distant sound of heavy artillery." The general had left with his men, and Mrs. Butler could not be certain whether the firing came from the Mississippi or Mobile Bay. In a letter to her daughter, she wrote, "I think the firing must be at Mobile, some vessels, maybe, trying to run the blockade. It would seem impossible that the sound would reach us from the Mississippi."[2]

By Easter Sunday, the third day of the bombardment, the citizens of New Orleans began to gird themselves for the worst. In the quiet morning

1. New Orleans *Daily Delta*, April 19, 1862.
2. Benjamin F. Butler, *Private and Official Correspondence of General Benjamin F. Butler During the Period of the Civil War* (5 vols.; Norwood, Mass., 1917), I, 416.

hours the sounds of deep-throated distant firing was heard at Chalmette, a few miles south of the city. Refugees from around Quarantine dribbled into New Orleans, bringing with them a few possessions and words of despair. By now, jittery New Orleans was asking itself why there was no news from the forts.

On April 19, a small crowd watched *Louisiana* leave the levee and start downriver, towed by two tenders. They questioned the effectiveness of the ironclad, which had no motive power, but they prayed their naval officers would use her well. With her heavy casemate and powerful guns, *Louisiana* looked ugly and awesome, but impregnable.

The following day, after a long argument between the Tift brothers and the Committee of Public Safety, *Mississippi* finally splashed into the river. At this stage she was still a partially finished hulk without an engine, and some of her machinery still lay in local shops. Port frames and doors had not been fitted, iron cladding would not be completed before the end of the month, and the shaft and propellers were still on the ground, waiting to be rigged and set in the vessel. Her guns had not arrived, and on April 17 the Tifts wired Mallory asking, as they had so many times before, "When shall we get them? We still hope to have the vessel ready for service by the end of the month."[3]

With the Union navy pounding the forts with heavy shells around the clock, the citizens of New Orleans expressed little optimism as they watched *Mississippi* slide down the bank and splash into the river, but they still had hope. From an allegedly reliable source at Fort Jackson, the *True Delta* reported that the enemy had expended 370,000 pounds of gunpowder and one thousand tons of metal, but had "accomplished nothing." New Orleans could relax, the reporter implied; there was nothing to fear from the mortar boats. Their shells had upset a little earth in Fort Jackson, but no damage had been done to Fort St. Philip, and Confederate ability to resist an invasion had not been reduced by the bombardment. In fact, the *Commercial Bulletin* reported, "the enemy has made very little progress . . . while we have sunk or disabled quite a number of his boats."[4] The source of that information was not published, but intoxication ran rampant among the crews of the River Defense boats.

For a few more days the city's populace and public officials still speculated with frail optimism that everything would turn out for the best. After all, General Lovell had given his word that the forts were impregnable,

3. *ORN*, Ser. 2, I, 597–98, N. and A. F. Tift to Mallory.
4. New Orleans *True Delta*, April 22; New Orleans *Commercial Bulletin*, April 21, 1862.

and after four days of incessant bombardment, not a Union vessel had ventured beyond the barrier. With *Louisiana*'s guns added to the firepower of Fort Jackson and Fort St. Philip, New Orleanians hoped the odds would improve. If Farragut could be stalled for another two weeks, *Mississippi* would join the fleet, and then the city would be spared. All they needed was a little more time.

But neither the citizens of New Orleans nor Porter's bummers had an accurate picture of what 13-inch shells had been doing to Fort Jackson. When the batteries at the fort lapsed into sporadic firing on the first day of the bombardment, Porter did not know that General Duncan had ordered his gunners down from the parapets to help put out fires. The Union commander's only intelligence came from observations at a distance of about two miles and reports from deserters whose information lacked consistency and often credibility.

General Duncan, who remained at Fort Jackson throughout the bombardment, had a clear picture of what was happening to his forts. On April 18, the first day of Porter's shelling, Duncan noted that his guns could not be elevated enough to drive off the mortar boats. The gun closest to Porter's flotilla, a 10-inch sea-coast mortar charged with extra powder, could not reach the nearest schooner, whereas shells from the Union bomb boats had no trouble arcing over the trees and exploding in the bastions. On the first day of the bombardment, Duncan's observers counted 2,997 mortar shells lobbed at the forts. That day, the men's quarters in the bastions and around the fort burned, and afterward barely a shred of bedding or a change of clothing could be found anywhere.

The citadel in the center of the fort burst into flames early in the shelling, and every time Duncan's men extinguished the fire, another shell struck. Eventually, the structure became an uncontrollable inferno, threatening the magazine, and Duncan ordered men down from the parapets to douse it before flames reached the powder. He described the first day's shelling as "accurate and terrible, many of the shells falling everywhere within the fort and disabling some of our best guns."

On April 19, the second day, Porter moved Queen's schooners from the exposed east bank to the west bank. The accuracy of the shelling suffered slightly, but not the intensity, and Duncan reported losing five heavy guns in the fort and two rifled 32-pounders in the water battery. The *terreplein*, parade plain, parapets, and platforms were "very much cut up," and severe damage was done to the casemates. Twice a shell came within inches of penetrating the magazines.

Over the next two days, shells disabled more guns and by then Duncan reported Fort Jackson "in need of extensive repairs almost everywhere." The only good news was the arrival of *Louisiana*, which anchored above Fort St. Philip. Duncan's optimism that the ironclad's heavy guns could help buy time for the fort to make repairs lasted until the following morning, when Captain Mitchell, who came down the river with the vessel, informed Duncan that the ironclad lacked motive power and could not "be regarded as an aggressive steamer" if Farragut attempted to pass the forts.[5]

Day and night, mortar shells fell upon Fort Jackson and to a lesser degree on Fort St. Philip, but another battle raged inside the forts between different adversaries — General Duncan, commanding the army, and Captain Mitchell, commanding the navy. The issue concerned the tactical placement of *Louisiana*. Duncan wanted the vessel with her sixteen heavy guns moved to the eastern shore where she could be deployed as an impregnable battery *below* the raft. From this position, the ironclad could engage Porter's schooners, which through most of the shelling remained screened behind trees and protected from Fort Jackson's guns. Then if Farragut attacked, Duncan argued, *Louisiana* would be in position to shell and rake the leading vessels before they rounded the bend in the river and came in sight of the forts. As the Union vessels approached the barrier, they would be forced to pass through three cross-fires simultaneously. But Mitchell refused to move the ironclad. Mechanics were still working on her, he replied, and he did not want the ship placed in range of Porter's guns until her engines worked. For two days the bickering continued without resolution while *Louisiana* remained safely out of range above Fort St. Philip. The balance of Mitchell's small squadron congregated around the ironclad and waited for the commander to decide what to do.

Under orders from General Lovell, Duncan turned everything afloat over to Mitchell, including his towboats, fire rafts, and the River Defense Fleet. He also gave up 150 of his best gunners and sharpshooters to man the ironclad.

Prior to Mitchell's arrival, Duncan had repeatedly given Captain John A. Stevenson (also spelled Stephenson) of the River Defense Fleet nightly instructions to send down fire rafts. Stevenson proved his ineptness by cutting the rafts loose too soon and allowing them to drift against the banks directly under the fort. One or two of the blazing rafts got loose, drifted into the schooners securing the barrier, and set them on fire. Stevenson,

5. *ORA*, VI, 525; *ORN*, XVIII, 265–67, Duncan to Pickett, April 30, 1862.

Duncan wrote, succeeded in "firing our wharves and lighting us up, but obscuring the position of the enemy." After that debacle, Duncan turned the fire rafts over to Captain Renshaw, the senior naval officer present, along with Stevenson and his boats. Stevenson reminded Duncan that his men and their boats had been commissioned by the War Department and could not be put under the command of a naval officer. After Mitchell arrived, Stevenson temporized, agreeing to cooperate with the navy "to the best of my ability, but in my own way as to . . . the handling of my boats."[6]

Mitchell had enough problems without dealing with Stevenson's independence. He knew little about the river and had not had the opportunity to acquaint himself with the defensive characteristics of the forts. He could not decide how to deploy his own vessels if attacked, so he relied on the views of Commander Charles F. McIntosh and Lieutenants Huger and Warley. Instead of trying to augment his own force with Stevenson's boats and benefiting from Stevenson's knowledge of the river, Mitchell refused to accept responsibility for the River Defense Fleet and passed it back to Duncan on April 23. He advised Duncan that "notwithstanding General Lovell's order to him [Stevenson], this letter so qualifies my authority as to relieve me from all responsibility as to the movements of the vessels of the river fleet." Although Stevenson had made an effort to cooperate with the navy, neither Mitchell nor Duncan now wanted his help.[7]

Time was running short for both Duncan and Mitchell. After midnight on April 24 Duncan made one final appeal to Mitchell to move *Louisiana* farther down the river and again asked that the ironclad be placed behind the raft along the shore below Fort St. Philip, where her heavy guns could be employed with the greatest effect. Duncan knew that Farragut had to be stopped before he passed Fort Jackson. If two or three Union warships got beyond Fort St. Philip, Duncan hoped to separate them, thereby trapping them upriver, but this strategy depended upon repulsing the bulk of Farragut's fleet. With *Louisiana* positioned downriver, her guns could begin to cripple Farragut's vessels before they reached Fort Jackson, but in her present position above Fort St. Philip, the ironclad could not fire at Union vessels until after they had passed the forts. Duncan also recognized the risk of gunners on the ironclad missing their targets, firing into Fort Jackson or accidently engaging their own gunboats.

6. *ORN,* XVIII, 265, 368, Lovell to Stevenson, April 21, and Duncan to Pickett, April 30, 1862; *ORA,* VI, 535–36, 540, Duncan to Stevenson, April 9, Renshaw to Higgins, April 18, Mitchell to Duncan, April 22, and Stevenson to Mitchell, April 21, 1862.

7. *ORN,* XVIII, 328–29, Stevenson to Mitchell, April 21, 1862; *ORA,* VI, 539, Mitchell to Duncan, April 23, 1862.

After rejecting Stevenson and his half dozen gunboats, Mitchell found himself without enough tugs. He complained that on one of his own tugs, *W. Burton*, the volunteer troops were all intoxicated, and on the other, the men were in a hopelessly "exhausted condition." Duncan suggested that he use *Defiance* or another gunboat under Stevenson's command. Mitchell replied that if *Defiance* "comes within reach I will deprive her captain of his command by force, if necessary," but he did not bother to send someone to find her or any other gunboat. Meanwhile, Farragut ran the gauntlet, and the repositioning of *Louisiana* was no longer a matter of great importance.[8]

Duncan regretted placing his carefully prepared fire rafts in Mitchell's hands. Throughout the evening of April 23 and into the early morning hours of the following day, Mitchell failed to release the fire rafts according to Duncan's schedule, making it difficult for observers in the forts to see Union preparations downriver or to harass Farragut's deployment. "To my utter surprise," Duncan wrote, "not one single fire barge was sent down the river. . . . In consequence of this criminal neglect the river remained in complete darkness throughout the entire night."[9]

Lieutenant George S. Shryock, CSN, brought a message to Duncan on the night of April 23 that *Louisiana* would be ready for service "by the next evening, the evening of April 24." Duncan pointed downriver where Farragut was assembling his fleet and said, "to-morrow would in all probability prove too late . . . the final battle was imminent within a few hours." He needed *Louisiana* repositioned to meet the attack now, engines or no engines. Shryock could not move *Louisiana* without Mitchell's approval, and Mitchell had already refused.[10]

The ram *Manassas*, under Lieutenant Warley, lay at anchor above Fort Jackson with her single fixed and virtually useless carronade, a gun that could only be aimed at a target by first maneuvering the vessel into position. The most Warley could hope to accomplish would be to swing into the current and ram the first Union vessel through the barrier. *Manassas* could barely stem the current, and for all practical purposes the vessel had become expendable except to the thirty-five men who comprised her crew.

Captain Renshaw had taken CSS *Jackson* upriver to contest the landing of General Butler's troops in the upper canals. This left Lieutenant Huger's CSS *McRae*, which lay against the east bank a short distance above

8. *ORA*, VI, 540, 541, Duncan to Mitchell, Mitchell to Duncan, April 24, 1862.
9. *ORN*, XVIII, 268, Duncan to Pickett, April 30, 1862.
10. *Ibid.*, 268.

Louisiana, and five of Stevenson's gunboats anchored farther upriver, *Warrior, Stonewall Jackson, R. J. Breckinridge, Defiance,* and *Resolute,* all steamers made partially shot-proof with cotton bulkheads and fitted with iron prows and a bow gun each. They were commanded by Captains Stevenson, Phillips, McCoy, and Hooper respectively. Two State of Louisiana steamers, *Governor Moore* and *General Quitman,* commanded by Captains Beverly Kennon and Alexander Grant, made up the balance of the Confederate squadron. They were anchored on the western side of the river a short distance above *Manassas.* Unlike Stevenson, Kennon and Grant willingly agreed to serve under Mitchell without demanding special conditions. Fire rafts and tugs lay along both sides of the river, and before dark on April 23, the barrier of schooners and chains stretching across the river below Fort Jackson was still intact.

Unfortunately, Captain Mitchell had done little to organize communications between the three flotillas and seemed content to let the various commands operate under their own initiatives. Duncan, aware of the confusion, tried to intercede, but Mitchell refused to listen to anybody but Warley, Huger, McIntosh, and Renshaw, all of whom probably felt as impotent as their captain.

As a last resort Duncan, now aware that the command of the navy was hopelessly disorganized, appealed to General Lovell. If the various naval commanders could not decide who was in charge, at least Lovell might be able to convince Commander Whittle to issue an order to Mitchell to post *Louisiana* below the barrier.

In a final attempt to achieve "unrestrained intercourse and cordial fraternization," Lovell approached Whittle with appropriate delicacy, but Whittle, whose title was officially commandant, still considered himself in charge of naval affairs on land and not naval vessels in the water. Lovell explained that Fort Jackson had been heavily damaged, guns dismounted, magazines exposed, and sally-ports rendered useless. The fort was vulnerable, Lovell explained, and to compensate for the loss of firepower, heavy guns must be placed below the barrier. This could only be accomplished, Lovell insisted, by moving *Louisiana* downriver without further loss of time.

Whittle demurred, stating that he had every confidence in Mitchell to command the fleet and "that he did not like to interfere with them." Besides, Whittle added, he was certain that if the vessel were placed below the barrier, she would be lost. Lovell explained he did not want the vessel "to be sent down amid the enemy's fleet, but . . . towed down and placed in position as a battery. The necessity," he added, "was such that it was better to lose the vessel than the city of New Orleans."

Whittle agreed to send a telegram to Mitchell, in which he asked Mitchell to "strain a point" to placate the general. He then asked Lovell if "that would do," but Lovell insisted that nothing short of moving the ironclad immediately would solve the problem. He planned to go down to the forts the next day and invited Whittle to accompany him, but Whittle refused, claiming that his business in the office was such that he could not spare the time.[11] It is difficult to understand what business in Whittle's office was more important than the salvation of New Orleans.

Duncan made one more attempt to reposition *Louisiana* and prepare for the attack. He observed the enemy staking white flags on the Fort St. Philip side and wrote Mitchell that "it is the probable position of [Farragut's] ships in the new line of attack, which, in my opinion, he contemplates attacking Fort Jackson in his large vessels." By moving the ironclad downriver, *Louisiana* would be in perfect position to receive the attack. Almost any naval commander could see the logic of the request but Mitchell. "Please keep the river well lit up with fire rafts," Duncan added, "as the attack may be made at any time."[12]

Lieutenant Colonel Edward Higgins, attached to General Duncan and in command of Fort Jackson, sent three urgent messages to Mitchell on the evening of April 23, each reporting that Farragut's vessels were moving into position and uniting with Porter's mortar schooners for an attack expected that night. Independent of Duncan's appeals, he asked that *Louisiana* be placed below Fort St. Philip so "she could infilade the mortar fleet, thereby enabling the men in the forts to stand to their guns," and resist the passage of the enemy's vessels. After receiving no response, Higgins crossed the river to Fort St. Philip and found Mitchell arguing with Duncan. When Mitchell finally agreed to send *Louisiana* downriver "in twenty-four hours," no sooner, Higgins turned to Duncan and said, "Tell Commander Mitchell that there will be no to-morrow for New Orleans unless he immediately takes up the position assigned to him . . . if he does not do so the city is gone, and he will be responsible to the country for its loss." According to Higgins, Mitchell "turned a deaf ear to all our warnings," so Higgins made one last request. If Mitchell would not move the ironclad below the barrier, would he move her into a position where she would

11. *ORA*, VI, 569, S. L. James testimony; *ORN*, XVIII, 329, Whittle to Mitchell, April 23, 1962.

12. *ORN*, XVIII, 329, Duncan to Mitchell, April 23, 1862.

draw the enemy's fire? Mitchell replied that he had but "two weeks provisions," and that "he was not bomb-proofed above, and a shell might hit him." Whittle's telegram asking Mitchell to "strain a point" had done no good.[13]

At 3 A.M. on April 24, the Confederacy had eleven vessels and some tugs stationed along the banks of the Mississippi above the barrier. Mitchell, by his own choice, commanded only four of them: *Louisiana,* under Commander Charles F. McIntosh, and *McRae,* under Lieutenant Huger, along the east bank, and *Manassas,* under Lieutenant Warley, posted along the west bank. CSS *Jackson,* under Captain Francis B. Renshaw, had not returned from her mission upriver to harass the landing of Butler's forces in the upper canals, although early that evening, Duncan had sent a dispatch boat to recall her. Mitchell also had command of two state gunboats, but there is little evidence that he exerted any control over their movements. Posted along the east bank and above *McRae* lay the five gunboats of the River Defense Fleet: *Warrior,* under Captain John A. Stevenson; the *Stonewall Jackson,* under Captain George M. Phillips; *Defiance,* under Captain Joseph D. McCoy; *Resolute,* under Captain Isaac Hooper; and *R. J. Breckinridge,* under Captain James B. Smith. All these men were riverboat captains commissioned by the War Department. Two vessels commissioned by the State of Louisiana lay off the west bank above *Manassas: Governor Moore,* under Lieutenant Beverly Kennon, formerly of the United States Navy; and *General Quitman,* under Captain Alexander Grant, another steamboat captain. Also clustered around the forts were numerous fire rafts, tenders, and tugs, some belonging to the navy and some to the army.

Because Mitchell refused to incorporate the River Defense Fleet into his command and showed faint interest in assuming responsibility for the State of Louisiana's vessels, he had developed no overall plan of battle. Although most of the vessels were armed lightly, they still had firepower. The riverboats each carried one or two guns, seldom heavier than light 32-pounders. *Louisiana* carried sixteen guns but had no more than ten in serviceable condition, including two rifled 7-inch guns, three 9-inch shellguns, four 8-inch shellguns, and seven 32-pounders. *McRae* carried six light 32-pounders and one 9-inch shellgun in pivot. *Governor Moore, General Quitman,* and *Jackson* each carried two rifled 32-pounders. By consolidating all the vessels and firepower under his command, including the armed steam launches, Mitchell had about thirty-eight guns, 1,648 men, and eighteen fire rafts.

13. *ORA,* VI, 590, Higgins testimony.

Louisiana could discharge more firepower than all the other Confederate vessels combined, so it is easy to understand why Duncan wanted the
ironclad below the barrier, not only to engage the enemy fleet but to draw
fire away from the men serving the guns in the fort. In defense of Mitchell,
Duncan may not have understood how shabbily *Louisiana* had been designed and constructed. Besides having no motive power, four of her guns
had been mounted on the wrong carriages and could not be fired. One 8-
inch shellgun had been mis-mounted and was useless, and the remaining
guns were manned in part by a company of artillery from the Crescent
Regiment who had no experience in the use of heavy naval guns. Lieutenant William H. Ward of *Louisiana* regarded the vessel "a total failure" but
agreed with Duncan that the vessel could have been used effectively "as
a floating battery."

Finally, at 3 A.M. on April 24, Duncan made one last appeal to Mitchell,
but to no avail. A few minutes later, hell broke loose on the lower Mississippi.[14]

14. *ORN*, XVIII, 263, Duncan to Pickett, April 30, 1862. See also Farragut's prize case, *ibid.*,
249, 329, 330; Statistical Data in *ORN*, Ser. 2, I, 254, 255, 257, 258, 259; *ORA*, VI, 607–608, Ward
testimony.

Thirteen   *Seventeen Mighty Warships, All Ready to Go*

On Easter Sunday, April 20, scattered showers carried by a chill northerly wind spit from low clouds into the faces of Porter's bummers. Forty-eight hours had passed since the mortar schooners had opened fire on Fort Jackson, and still the Confederate flag fluttered defiantly over the bastion. Porter was in a foul mood: the forts had not fallen as he had promised, and worse, he had no reliable information as to their damage. But when *Norfolk Packet* picked up the red-capped deserter from Fort Jackson and delivered him to *Harriet Lane*, Porter cheered up. From the deserter, who claimed to be an impressed Pennsylvanian, he learned for the first time of "hundreds of bombshells falling into the fort, casemates broken in, citadel and out-buildings burned, men demoralized and dispirited, [the] magazine en-dangered, and the levee cut." In addition, the deserter mentioned that an-other six or seven hundred men like himself had been forced to serve in the forts and would escape if they could. Porter's observers could have seen none of this from their posts downriver. The news was so good that Porter rushed the deserter over to Farragut. In the meantime, the bummers kept lofting bombshells into the forts.[1]

Although Farragut seldom attached much credibility to statements made by deserters, this was the kind of news he wanted to hear. He still doubted that Porter's mortars could bring down Fort Jackson's casemates, but Porter remained hopeful. If the deserter's information was accurate, Farragut saw no reason for further delay. Besides, if the mortars contin-ued to consume ammunition at the present rate, there would be none left for running the gauntlet. Farragut wanted to make his move, but not with stiff northerlies blowing into the face of his fleet.

1. *ORN*, XVIII, 67, Porter to Welles, April 30, 1862.

At 10 A.M. he signaled his captains to come on board *Hartford*. Porter and three other skippers were upriver with the mortar boats and missed the meeting. It is likely that Farragut explained his plan to Porter beforehand, because Lieutenant Jonathan M. Wainwright of *Harriet Lane*, Porter's second in command, attended the meeting. But Porter, using his backdoor access to the Naval Office, later grumbled to Fox, "Tho Farragut has been pleased to consider me an 'outsider,' and has not deigned to invite me to his public councils, I don't want to do anything that may look like pique."[2]

When everybody was seated in Farragut's cabin, he unfolded his charts of the river and the forts, and for the first time explained in detail the proposed plan of attack. Midway through the discussion, Commander James Alden of USS *Richmond* interrupted and asked permission to read a rather lengthy memorandum that he said Porter had asked him to present. This memorandum had been prepared prior to the time Farragut's ships had crossed over the bar, but Porter still believed his tactics were sound, or he would not have asked Alden to propose them.

"In my opinion," Porter wrote, "there are two methods of attack—one is for the vessel to run the gantlet of the batteries by night, or in a fog, the other to attack the forts by laying the big ships close alongside of them . . . firing shells, grape and canister into the barbette, [and] clearing the ramparts." The smaller, more agile gunboats would move about and throw in shrapnel, clearing the parapets and dismounting the guns, while the mortar schooners would continue to stand off and hurl shells into the forts.

Porter disliked the idea of Farragut's ships running past the forts, emphasizing that it would "leave an enemy in our rear, and the mortar vessels would have to be left behind," presumably unprotected. If the forts were to be passed, he wanted his mortars "towed along," admitting, however, that it would slow the fleet. Porter clearly did not want to be left out of the action, and if Farragut reached New Orleans, he wanted a share of the glory.

Alden completed the reading of Porter's proposal, folded it, and placed it in his pocket. Captain Bell asked if it would be proper to leave the document with the flag officer. Alden agreed and handed it to Farragut.[3]

The memorandum evidently stimulated conversation among the commanders. Earlier in the morning Porter had recommended that the bar-

2. *Ibid.*, 136, Farragut's unfinished report, April 20, 1862; Thompson and Wainwright (eds.), *Fox Correspondence*, II, 100. There were two Wainwrights in Farragut's flotilla, Commander Richard Wainwright, captain of *Hartford*, and Lieutenant Commanding Jonathan M. Wainwright, skipper of *Harriet Lane*.

3. *ORN*, XVIII, 145–46, 695, Proposition of Commander D. D. Porter, Diary of H. H. Bell.

rier boom be broken that night, a prerequisite to attack, and Farragut agreed. Many of Farragut's commanders doubted that their vessels could run the forts without becoming disabled or entangled, and others argued that circling their vessels between the forts in the hope of forcing their surrender before advancing upriver invited disaster. No one but Lieutenant Wainwright, Porter's emissary, liked the idea of towing the mortar schooners.

On March 28, Captain Bell with Lieutenant Russell had made a reconnaissance of the forts in *Kennebec* and returned with the opinion that the forts could not be passed by ships alone. This meant waiting for Butler to invest the forts from the rear. *Hartford*'s surgeon, Jonathan M. Foltz, who considered Farragut "a bold, brave officer, full of fight but evidently does not know what he is going about," sided with the doubters. "If the attempt is made," he wrote, "we shall probably have another disaster at a moment when all north of us is progressing so favorably."[4]

Farragut listened attentively, but he had already made his decision. Despite Porter's objections to leaving the bomb boats behind, Farragut envisioned no danger to the mortars after the fleet had passed the forts. Porter had plenty of his own gunboats, and Farragut agreed to leave them below the forts to provide protection. To commanders who worried about being disabled while engaging the forts, Farragut assured them that the flow of the river would drift them out of danger. They could make repairs after joining Porter's flotilla.

Farragut argued that a successful land attack on Fort St. Philip depended upon having gunboats available to cover the landing of Butler's troops five miles upriver at Quarantine. It would be hazardous, some of the commanders complained, to go above the forts, "as being out of the reach of supplies." If we don't go now, Farragut argued, we will soon be out of ammunition, and if Butler's troops are landed safely, there will be no further need to worry about the forts. "I believe in celerity," he said, and that ended the discussion.[5]

Later that day Farragut circulated a general order to all commanders reminding them that "whatever is to be done will have to be done quickly, or we will be again reduced to a blockading squadron without the means of carrying on the bombardment, as we have nearly expended all the shells and fuzes and material for making cartridges. . . . The forts should be run,

4. Jonathan M. Foltz, *Surgeon of the Seas: The Adventurous Life of Surgeon General Jonathan M. Foltz in the Days of Wooden Ships* (Indianapolis, 1931), 214.

5. *Ibid.*, 213; *ORN*, XVIII, 695, Bell's Diary.

and when a force is once above the forts to protect the troops, they should be landed at Quarantine from the Gulf side by bringing them through the bayou, and then our forces should move upriver, mutually aiding each other, as it can be done to advantage." He then issued preliminary sailing instructions to the commanders of the seventeen vessels participating in the attack.[6]

Over the objections of many of his commanders who had not anticipated running the forts before they had been reduced, Farragut made a tough decision and shouldered all the responsibility himself. He also wrote a report to Secretary Welles complaining about his lack of supplies. "The officers do their duty well," he wrote, "but I regret to say that I do not find myself half supplied with anything. My shells, fuzes, cylinder cloth and yarn to make the cylinders are all out and should be at this moment entirely unable to continue the bombardment, so far as my squadron is concerned, were it not for the fuzes, etc., sent to Commander Porter." In another letter he added that "the medical department is miserably supplied for the care of the wounded."[7] Another commander may have used these shortages as an excuse to delay his attack, but not Farragut.

Welles was conditioned to complaints from his naval officers, but he was not prepared to accept how Farragut solved his supply problems. "I find myself dependent upon the Army for everything," Farragut added, "and General Butler has been most generous — he gives everything in his power. I mention these facts to show I am driven to the alternative of fighting it out at once or waiting and resuming the blockade until supplies arrive."[8]

Charles Lee Lewis, Farragut's biographer, described Welles's probable reaction to the memorandum and wrote: "Poor Mr. Welles; if that letter had reached him before the victorious news, he would have torn off his newest glossiest wig and trampled it under foot in his consternation and agitation." Nobody in the Naval Office felt any professional warmth toward General Butler, Lincoln's political general, who had a penchant for dramatically claiming praise by stealing laurels earned by his fellow officers. At this early stage of the war, Butler was known for granting small favors and expecting a tenfold return. Welles wanted no part of becoming obligated to him. But as events unfolded, Butler's cooperation led to Farragut's success and did much to improve Welles's reputation as a capable naval administrator.[9]

6. *ORN*, XVIII, 160, 162, Farragut's general orders.
7. *Ibid.*, 135, 136, Farragut to Welles, April 20, 21, 1862.
8. *Ibid.*, 136.
9. Lewis, *Farragut*, 48–49.

Captain Bell volunteered to break the boom on the night of April 20. At nine o'clock he went on board *Pinola*, commanded by Lieutenant Peirce Crosby, accompanied by Captain Julius Kroehl, an experienced submarine torpedo man loaded down with apparatus. The obstruction consisted of a heavy chain buoyed up by demasted schooners, stretched across the river a short distance below Forts Jackson and St. Philip. *Pinola* was to take the west end of the obstruction and *Itasca*, under Lieutenant Charles H. B. Caldwell, the east end. After stressing to the officers of both vessels the importance of destroying the barrier, Bell ordered the vessels underway.

Kroehl's equipment consisted of five 180-pound charges, batteries, and several reels of insulated wire. Nobody, including Bell, showed much confidence in Kroehl's devices, but the torpedo expert scoffed at breaking a chain with a hammer and chisel when a couple of kegs of explosives could accomplish the same result quickly and thoroughly. Men on *Pinola* were instructed to board the hulk on the far end from the shoreward side, attach Kroehl's torpedoes to the bow and stern, and fasten a third device, a hundred-pound keg of powder with a five-minute fuse, to the forward chain amidship. *Itasca*, carrying two fifty-pound kegs of powder with five-minute fuses, was to move upriver and locate the hulks on the opposite end of the barrier. A picked crew of thirty men was to board the second hulk from the eastern end, attach the explosives, activate the fuse, and get out of the way.

At ten o'clock both vessels started upriver. In support, Porter's bummers increased the tempo of their bombardment, hoping to drive the fort's gunners deeper into their bombproofs. There was no moon, and a thin haze mixed with drizzle had settled over the river. Bell hoped to accomplish the mission unseen, but after the ships passed Porter's picket boats, Fort Jackson flashed a signal light, answered by a rocket from Fort St. Philip. Lieutenant George B. Bacon, executive officer on *Itasca*, wrote: "It was apparent that we were discovered. In a moment a sharp fire was opened upon us from the water batteries and Fort Jackson, nearly all the shots passing over us." At first the engines slowed, but Lieutenant Caldwell ordered all ahead fast, and *Itasca* made a dash for the hulks. *Pinola* headed for the opposite shore, and soon both the vessels lost sight of each other.

Itasca struck the second hulk from shore on the starboard side, threw out grapnels, and shut down her engine. The strong current swung the gunboat astern of the hulk, tearing loose the grapnels and ripping away some of the hulk's upper works. Caldwell ordered the engine restarted and moved *Itasca* to the port side of the first hulk. This time he kept the engine running to ease the strain on the grapnels.

When Bacon climbed on board with his kegs of powder, he was surprised to find the hulk unmanned. Through the haze he could see seven hulks about one hundred yards apart, each weighing around two hundred tons and anchored separately. A large, heavy chain was lashed to the anchor cable outside the hulk, near the hawsepipe, and triced up well under the bows. The anchor chain had been passed several times around a windlass, and Bacon discovered that by slipping the anchor cable, the heavy barrier chain would follow it to the bottom of the river. Without using any explosives, Acting Master Johnson knocked away the bitts, and the chain dribbled into the water. The hulk swung loose and drifted downriver, carrying *Itasca* with it. Before Caldwell realized what was happening, *Itasca*, still attached to the hulk with grapnels, swung around and ran bows-on into the bank close to and just below Fort St. Philip. Fortunately, the enemy had lost sight of *Itasca*, assuming that both the hulk and the gunboat had gone downriver.

"Our position," Lieutenant Bacon wrote, "now was very critical; every means in our power were used to back the vessel off, but of no avail, we could not move her an inch. Her bow seemed to be securely held in the mud of the bank. A short distance above us could be seen the Confederate gunboats signaling, and every moment we expected them down upon us."

Lieutenant Caldwell looked across the river but could not see *Pinola*. If *Itasca* were discovered, she would be a sitting duck, so Caldwell reluctantly made preparations to abandon ship. The hulk still lay alongside, and if attacked, Caldwell planned to transfer his crew to the hulk and set it adrift downriver. A slow match was made ready to fire the magazine, and the men waited, expecting to be attacked at any moment. But no attack came.

Through the haze a lookout spotted *Pinola* steaming slowly toward them. *Pinola* had had her own difficulties. At 10:30 P.M. Crosby had mistaken a raft for a hulk, ran into it with a noisy crash, and backed off. The hulks were all to starboard. Crosby made an adjustment and closed on the port quarter of the second hulk from the far left. Ten minutes later, explosives were in place over the bow and stern moorings, with a barrel of powder attached to the midship cable. *Pinola* attempted to back away, but the vessel's starboard cathead caught on the hulk's port quarter. "The cable and anchor were finally slipped," Bell wrote, "the steamer glided off, and the engine immediately stopped. I called for the operator [Kroehl] to explode. He replied that his conductor was broken. There being two conductors, I called for him to explode the second, and, after a little while, it was answered that that also was broken."

Bell had heard no explosion from the other end of the boom and began wondering if *Itasca* had been hit or just "given it up." He asked Captain Kroehl to bring up two more torpedoes and ordered Lieutenant Crosby to bring his vessel alongside the hulk again. Crosby made a wide swing and spotted *Itasca* along the west bank. At this point Caldwell hailed Crosby and said he was fast aground.

Crosby tried to pull *Itasca* free with a 9-inch hawser tied to *Pinola,* but the line parted and Crosby headed downriver to get another. Sporadic and searching gunfire from the forts splashed nearby, and when *Pinola* did not return, Caldwell became nervous and dispatched a boat to *Hartford* for help. Soon after the boat left the ship, *Pinola* reappeared out of the mist with a heavier hawser. A lookout on *Itasca* reported a fire raft in sight and trending toward them. The men hurriedly fastened an 11-inch hawser to *Itasca* and Caldwell backed engines, but the line snapped. Finally, a heavy 13-inch hawser was strung between the vessels, and with help from *Pinola,* *Itasca* broke free, cast loose the hawser, dodged the fire raft, and headed upriver.

At first Caldwell stayed close to the shore, hiding his ship in the backdrop of the trees. When the vessel reached the lower end of Fort St. Philip, Caldwell sheered into the main current, called for full steam, and headed his bow into the chain connecting the second and third hulk. The chain broke, setting the hulks adrift and making a clear passage for the Union fleet.

Pinola followed *Itasca* upriver and when well above the chain crossed the river close under the guns of Fort Jackson. Kroehl reported that visibility had become so poor "we could not see half a ship's length ahead." Lieutenant Crosby swung into the current and rammed through the cable fastened to the third hulk from the western shore, cutting it loose.[10]

The fire raft that threatened the grounded *Itasca* may have been the same raft that drifted downriver and awakened Farragut's slumbering fleet at 2:30 in the morning. Alarm bells sounding the call for fire quarters brought

10. *ORN,* XVIII, 696, Bell's Diary; *ibid.,* 812–13, Log of *Itasca; ibid.,* 429–30, Report of Julius H. Kroehl, June 2, 1862; George B. Bacon, "One Night's Work, April 20, 1862: Breaking the Chain for Farragut's Fleet at the Forts Below New Orleans," *Magazine of American History,* XV (1886), 305–307.

men to the decks. Farragut had just retired, and now he was up again. The northerly wind had increased, and the huge raft blazed furiously as it passed between *Hartford* and *Richmond*. Flames licked mast high, and the men on both ships could feel the intense heat as the raft drifted by.

Below the flagship, sailors on *Kineo* and *Sciota* slipped their cables and scrambled to get clear of the raft. *Kineo* became entangled with *Sciota* and knocked down her mainmast, then in the confusion both vessels drifted into *Mississippi*. With a loud crunch of splintering boards, *Sciota* lost her launch and cutter. Then the fire raft caught *Sciota* on the port bow, setting the ship on fire, but all hands brought hoses forward and extinguished it. During the turmoil, Commander James S. Palmer sent two boats from *Iroquois* to tow the raft away from the fleet. While everybody crowded on deck to watch the operation, which had attracted about fifty boats from other vessels, *Westfield*, one of Porter's steamers, ran into *Iroquois*.[11]

If one fire raft, properly placed, caused this much havoc among Farragut's fleet, General Duncan's irritation over Commander Mitchell's inept handling of dozens of prepared fire rafts was justified. One can wonder what might have happened had Hollins' mosquito fleet, now far upriver, followed behind a dozen fire rafts and worked its guns on the tangled and disorganized Union squadron. Despite Farragut's earlier orders to his commanders on how to maintain formation or withdraw in the event of an attack, one fire raft had created enough confusion among them to cause several collisions.

On April 22, General Butler had seven thousand troops anchored on transports below the fleet. Butler's presence made Farragut intensely impatient. He planned to attack that night but delayed because all the ship carpenters on *Mississippi* had gone down the river to repair *Sciota*, and Captain Melancton Smith did not want to go into battle without them.

On the afternoon of the same day a party of French and English naval officers whom Farragut had allowed to proceed to New Orleans came back down the river and stopped aboard *Hartford*. They warned Farragut that his ships would never withstand the fire of the forts. When Porter came on board *Hartford* and Farragut related the recent conversation, Porter waged all his old clothes that the fleet would get through to New Orleans without losing more than one vessel. "Ah, Porter!" Farragut said.

---

11. *ORN*, XVIII, 738, 756, 800, Logs of *Richmond*, *Sciota*, and *Iroquois*.

"I'd give a great many suits of new clothes to think and feel as you do!"[12]

During the same meeting, another conversation occurred, this one related by Farragut's signal officer, B. S. Osbon. After four days of bombardment, which Osbon called useless, the signal officer claimed he overheard Farragut say to Porter, "We are wasting ammunition and time. We will fool around down here until we have nothing left to fight with. I'm ready to run those forts now, tonight."

"Wait one more day," Porter urged, "and I will cripple them so you can pass with little or no loss of life."

"All right," Farragut replied. "Go at 'em again and we'll see what happens by tomorrow."

On the morning of April 23, Porter was back on *Hartford*, described by Osbon as downcast but still eager to continue the bombardment.

"Look here, David," Farragut said. "We'll demonstrate the practical value of mortar work." Turning to Osbon, he said, "Get me two small flags, a white one and a red one, and go to the mizzen topmasthead and watch where the mortar shells fall. If inside the fort, wave the red flag. If outside, wave the white one."

Farragut recalled that Osbon had joined *Hartford* at Porter's suggestion and said, "Since you recommended Mr. Osbon to me, you will have confidence in his observations. Now go aboard your vessel, select a tallyman, and when all is ready, Mr. Osbon will wave his flags and the count will begin."

Osbon climbed the mizzenmast, took his post, and for a while they "kept me busy waving the little flags and I had to watch very closely not to make any mistakes." Farragut sat aft and every so often hollered up for the score. "At last," Osbon reported, "the tally sheet was footed up and the 'outs' had it, by a large majority."

When Porter reboarded *Hartford*, Farragut waved the paper in his face and said, "There, David. There's the score. I guess we'll go up the river tonight."[13]

In Porter's report of the events leading to the passage of the forts, he wrote Welles that on April 23 he had "urged Flag-Officer Farragut to commence the attack with the ships that night, as I feared the mortars would not hold out. The men were almost overcome with fatigue, and our supply ships laid a good ways off." The second statement was probably

12. West, *Second Admiral*, 131–32.

13. Albert Bigelow Paine (ed.), *A Sailor of Fortune: Personal Memories of Captain B. S. Osbon* (New York, 1906), 182–84.

true, but on May 10 he wrote his confidant, Assistant Secretary Fox, asking that the first sentence be deleted from his report. Porter's pen was beginning to prick his own hand. Welles declined to change the record or delete the statement, stating after the war that Farragut "needed no urging from anyone to move, certainly not from one who from the first advised that the forts should be reduced before the passage of the fleet was attempted."[14]

On the afternoon of April 23, Farragut went from ship to ship to make certain his orders were clearly understood. The battle plan had been laid out carefully in his cabin, but he wanted no confusion once the attack began, no misunderstanding among the commanders if a vessel were disabled and forced to fall out of line.

The First Division of gunboats under Captain Theodorus Bailey, flying red pennants, would lead the way with *Cayuga* first, followed by *Pensacola, Mississippi, Oneida, Varuna, Katahdin, Kineo,* and *Wissahickon.* Bailey's division would pass up the eastern side of the river and concentrate its fire on Fort St. Philip. The second or Center Division of ships, flying blue pennants, would carry Farragut on *Hartford* at the head of the division, followed by *Brooklyn* and *Richmond.* These ships were to engage Fort Jackson on the left, followed immediately by the Third Division under Captain Bell, carrying red and white pennants. Bell's division, whose objective was also Fort Jackson, consisted of the following ships in order of formation: *Sciota, Iroquois, Kennebec, Pinola, Itasca,* and *Winona.* That made seventeen ships in all.

Porter's bummers were not excluded. When the action started, the bomb boats would open along the western shore and throw shells into Fort Jackson as fast as the mortars could be reloaded and fired. Farragut placed *Portsmouth,* an old sailing vessel, behind Porter's gunboats with orders to engage the water battery below Fort Jackson the moment the fleet got underway. Farragut's instructions were clear, rehearsed, and included every vessel in his command.[15]

Late in the afternoon of April 23, an observer on one of the picket boats reported that the Confederates had stretched another chain across the river at the same location. After spending the day preparing the attack, the last thing Farragut needed was another variable. He signaled Cald-

14. *ORN,* XVIII, 367, Porter to Welles, April 30, 1862; Thompson and Wainwright (eds.), *Fox Correspondence,* II, 100; Welles, "Admiral Farragut and New Orleans," 827–28.

15. *ORN,* XVIII, 156, 164, Farragut to Welles, May 6, 1862.

well over to *Hartford* and ordered the flagship upriver. Both men climbed the maintop and each with a glass studied first the shoreline and then the breadth of the river. They climbed back down admitting they could not see a chain, but Farragut wasn't satisfied and wanted Lieutenant Crosby to go up in *Pinola* and take a closer look. Instead, Caldwell volunteered to go at dark in *Hartford's* gig.

With a picked crew, Caldwell pulled up to the hulks strung along the west shore and found nothing. Several shells from the fort dropped into the water nearby but failed to explode, and Caldwell ignored them. He ordered the gig to cross the river slowly, giving the men sufficient time to search for chains and take soundings. When they reached the opposite shore they found the river clear. At 11 P.M. the gig signaled Farragut that the river was open. "Soon after," Lieutenant Bacon wrote, "another signal was run up by the flagship for 'fleet to form in line of battle.'"[16]

Signal Officer Osbon, who always seemed to be at Farragut's side, reported the signal had been acknowledged. No doubt in a reflective mood, Farragut turned to him and asked, "What do you estimate our casualties will be?"

Osbon, who had answers for everything, replied, "Flag Officer, I've been thinking of that, and I believe we will lose a hundred."

Farragut seemed surprised, reminding Osbon that there were four thousand men in the fleet. "No more than that?" he asked. "How do you calculate so small a number?"

Osbon thought a moment and replied, "Well, most of us are pretty low in the water, and, being near, the enemy will shoot high. Then, too, we will be moving and it will be dark, with dense smoke. Another thing, gunners ashore are never as accurate as gunners aboard a vessel. I believe a hundred men will cover our loss."

Farragut nodded uncertainly. "I wish I could think so," he said. "I wish I could be as sure of it as you are."[17]

The hammocks had been piped down at dark, and the crews told they would be called to quarters without the usual noisy signals around midnight. The men probably got little sleep. If they were to die in the morning, sleep now had little meaning to them. Off in the distance they could hear the thump

16. Bacon, "One Night's Work," 307.
17. Paine, *Sailor of Fortune*, 186. B. S. Osbon had the advantage of writing his account of the battle years after it had taken place. By then, many of the eyewitness accounts had been published and Farragut was deceased.

of Porter's mortars sporadically lobbing shells into Fort Jackson. Most of them probably hoped the bummers had done their job well—but nobody knew, and it made them restless.

The watch was on deck, but the ships were quiet. Even the officers had hunkered down in their cabins.

All but one, Davey Farragut, and he stared into the darkness upriver and offered a silent prayer.

FOURTEEN   *Running the Gauntlet*

Shortly after midnight on April 24, activity began to stir aboard the Union fleet. The mates made their rounds with carefully hooded lanterns. Men wiped sleep from their eyes, stowed their hammocks, dressed quickly, and went topside for a ration of hardtack and coffee. The night was clear but dark and moonless, with a sharp chill coming off the river. The men ate quickly and then went to work, each to his own station. Gun crews stripped to the waist, leaving nothing but monkey jackets tied loosely around their necks. They shivered as they cast loose the guns, checked the lock strings and sanded the decks. Then they stacked buckets filled with sand behind the guns to be spread on the decks when blood made them slippery. Others prepared tubs of water to put out fires, and carpenters cut plugs to patch holes if enemy shells penetrated the chain-armored hull.[1]

At five minutes before 2 A.M., Farragut ordered two red lanterns hoisted to the mizzen peak of *Hartford*. Slowly the vessels moved into formation, with *Cayuga*, under Captain Bailey, taking her position at the head of the squadron. For nearly an hour Bailey waited for *Pensacola*, which could not haul up her anchor, to fall in behind. Signal Officer Osbon, who had been tolling off the vessels to Farragut as they filed into position, reported that *Pensacola* had not come into line. "Damn that fellow!" Farragut blurted, referring to Captain Morris. "I don't believe he wants to start." But other vessels had similar problems, and the fleet was not ready to move until nearly 3:30 A.M.[2]

1. Farragut, *Life of Farragut*, 229; Bartholomew Diggins, "Recollections of the Cruise of the U.S.S. *Hartford*, Admiral Farragut's Flagship in Operations on the Mississippi River," Manuscript Division, New York Public Library, 78.
2. Paine, *Sailor of Fortune*, 191; *ORN*, XVIII, 156, Farragut to Welles, May 6, 1862.

Keeping to starboard, Bailey led the way. *Cayuga* acted as a pilot boat, guiding the bigger *Pensacola* and the six warships behind her toward Fort St. Philip. When *Wissahickon*, the last vessel in Bailey's First Division, passed the Second Division, Commander Richard Wainwright fell in behind with *Hartford*, keeping to port and followed by *Brooklyn* and *Richmond*. Bell's division, led by *Sciota* under Commander Donaldson, fell in closely behind *Richmond*, but slightly farther to port.

Porter's bummers looked up from their guns and watched the fleet pass. For the first time in four days, an odd silence fell across the river. There was no sound but the swirling of the river and the pulsation of the passing fleet. Bummers checked their loads and stared upriver, waiting for the first sound of gunfire. On *Harriet Lane*, Porter waited for the signal to move up his gunboats. At 3:28 it came. *Harriet Lane* moved forward a short distance to port of *Hartford*, followed by *Westfield*, *Owasco*, *Clifton*, and *Miami*. Fifteen minutes later Porter anchored his gunboats five hundred yards below Fort Jackson and opened fire on the water battery with shrapnel. The old sailing ship *Portsmouth*, towed by the gunboat *Jackson*, passed to starboard and anchored off the point just below Porter.[3]

Captain William B. Robertson of the 1st Louisiana Artillery had taken command of the water battery below Fort Jackson on April 15. The battery had no casemates or covered ways but was enclosed on three sides by earthen breastworks and surrounded by two moats. It was strictly an outwork mounting six guns and facing downriver. During Porter's earlier bombardment, two of the guns had been dismounted but repaired and returned to service.

At 3:30 A.M. Sergeant Herman reported to Robertson that he detected several black, shapeless masses barely distinguishable from the surrounding darkness moving silently but steadily up the river. "Not a light was visible anywhere," Robertson observed. "Not a torch had been applied to a single fire-raft, and not one of them had been started from its moorings. As soon as I caught sight of the moving objects, I knew they were the enemy's vessels, and I ordered the guns to be trained on the two in the lead, and to open fire on them." At 3:40 A.M. the guns of the water battery roared into action, followed by those from Forts Jackson and St. Philip. "The Federal vessels replied with their broadsides," Robertson observed, and "the flashes of the guns from both sides lit up the river with a lurid light that revealed the outlines of the Federal steamers more distinctly. I do not

3. Farragut, *Life of Farragut*, 229; *ORN*, XVIII, 360, 822, Wainwright to Porter, April 25, 1862, and Log of *Portsmouth*.

Approaches to New Orleans from the Gulf of Mexico

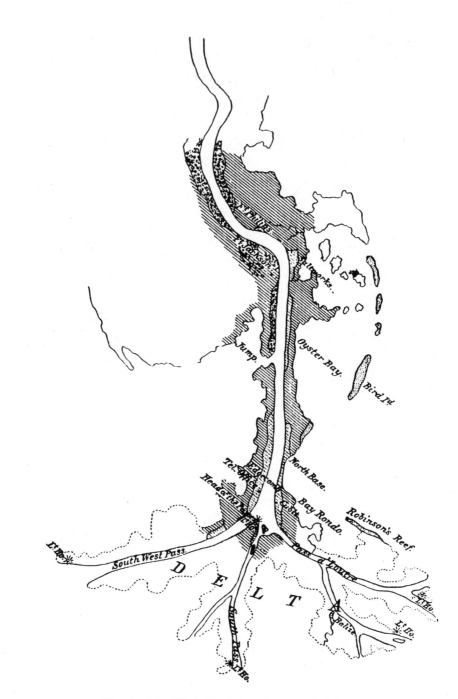

Sketch of the Mississippi River above Head of Passes,
showing firm soil, beach, and marsh.
From *Official Records of the Navy*, Ser. I, Vol. 16

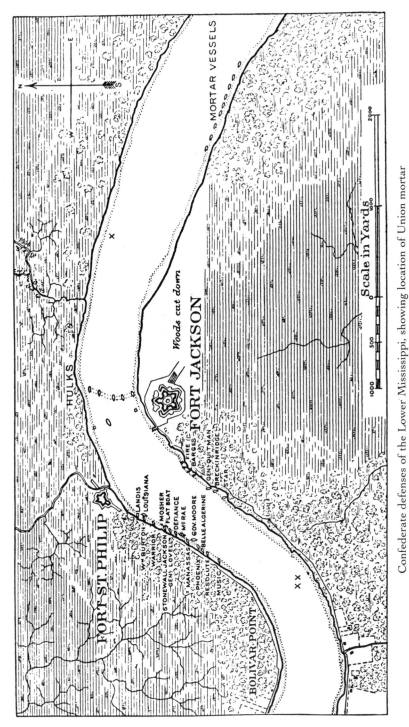

Confederate defenses of the Lower Mississippi, showing location of Union mortar
vessels at the opening of the bombardment.

From *Battles and Leaders of the Civil War*

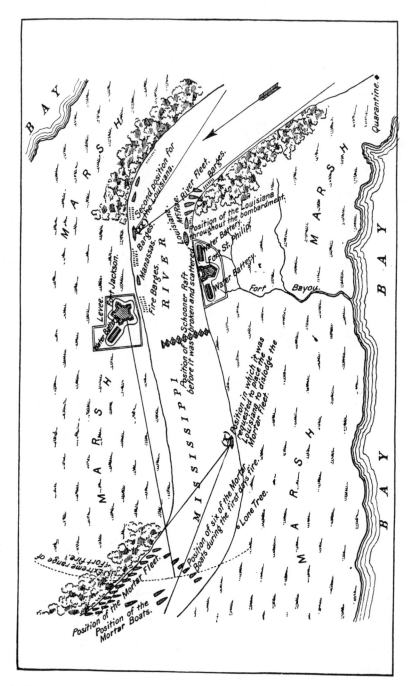

The bombardment of Forts Jackson and St. Philip, from April 16–24, 1862. Union mortar fleet is downriver at extreme left.
From *Official Records of the Navy*, Ser. I, Vol. 18

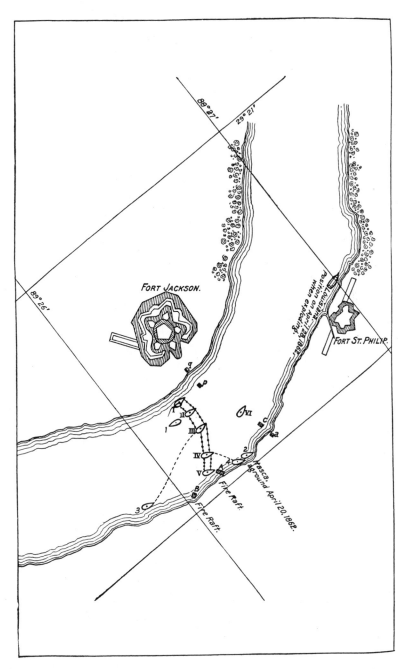

Arrangement of the Confederate barrier below Forts Jackson and St. Philip.
From *Official Records of the Navy*, Ser. I, Vol. 18

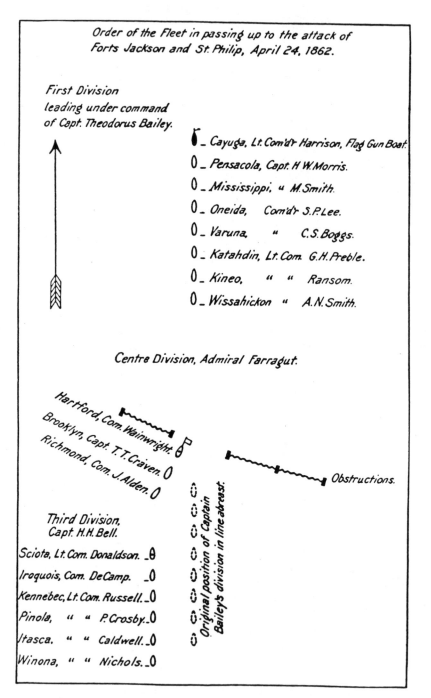

Organization of the Union fleet approaching the attack on Forts Jackson and
St. Philip on April 24, 1862.
From *Official Records of the Navy*, Ser. I, Vol. 18

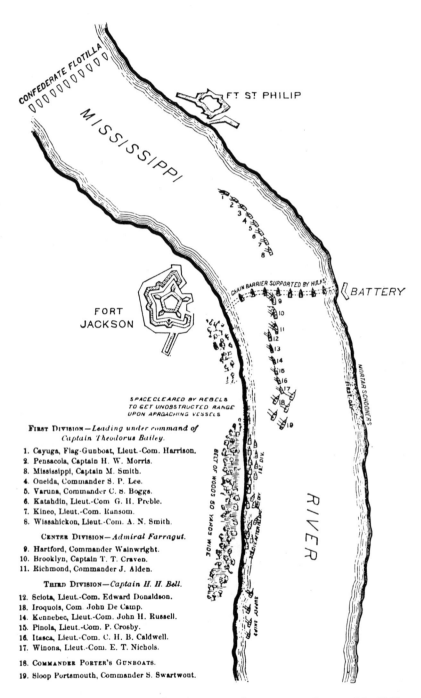

FIRST DIVISION—*Leading under command of Captain Theodorus Bailey.*

1. Cayuga, Flag-Gunboat, Lieut.-Com. Harrison.
2. Pensacola, Captain H. W. Morris.
3. Mississippi, Captain M. Smith.
4. Oneida, Commander S. P. Lee.
5. Varuna, Commander C. S. Boggs.
6. Katahdin, Lieut.-Com G. H. Preble.
7. Kineo, Lieut.-Com. Ransom.
8. Wissahickon, Lieut.-Com. A. N. Smith.

CENTER DIVISION—*Admiral Farragut.*

9. Hartford, Commander Wainwright.
10. Brooklyn, Captain T. T. Craven.
11. Richmond, Commander J. Alden.

THIRD DIVISION—*Captain H. H. Bell.*

12. Sciota, Lieut.-Com. Edward Donaldson.
13. Iroquois, Com. John De Camp.
14. Kennebec, Lieut.-Com. John H. Russell.
15. Pinola, Lieut.-Com. P. Crosby.
16. Itasca, Lieut.-Com. C. H. B. Caldwell.
17. Winona, Lieut.-Com. E. T. Nichols.

18. COMMANDER PORTER'S GUNBOATS.

19. Sloop Portsmouth, Commander S. Swartwout.

Order of attack of Farragut's fleet during attack on Forts Jackson and St. Philip, April 24, 1862.

From *Official Records of the Navy*, Ser. I, Vol. 18

believe there was ever a grander spectacle witnessed before the world than that displayed during the great artillery duel which then followed."[4]

The first vessel to engage the water battery was *Cayuga*, which crossed the barrier at exactly 3:30 A.M.. Young Lieutenant George Hamilton Perkins, executive officer of *Cayuga*, piloted his ship through the break in the barrier as both Fort Jackson and Fort St. Philip opened fire on him. *Cayuga* steamed ahead, directly under the guns of St. Philip, replying with broadsides of grape and canister.

"*Cayuga* received the first fire," Perkins wrote,

> and the air was filled with shells and explosions which almost blinded me as I stood on the forecastle trying to see my way, for I had never been up the river before. I soon saw that the guns of the forts were all aimed for the mid-stream, so I steered close to the walls of Fort St. Philip, and although our masts and rigging got badly shot through, our hull was but little damaged.
>
> After passing the last battery and thinking we were clear, I looked back for some of our vessels, and my heart jumped into my mouth, when I found I could not see a *single one*. I thought they all must have been sunk by the forts. Then looking ahead I saw eleven of the enemy's gunboats coming down upon us, and it seemed as if we were "*gone*" sure. Three of these made a dash to board us, but a heavy charge from our eleven-inch gun settled the *Gov. Moore*. . . . A ram, the *Manassas*, in attempting to butt us, just missed our stern, and we soon settled the third fellows "hash." Just then some of our gunboats, which had passed the forts, came up, and then all sorts of things happened.[5]

Perkins might well have wondered what had happened to *Pensacola*, because she wasn't where she was supposed to be.

Pensacola, under Captain Henry W. Morris, had followed *Cayuga* in close formation. Shot and shell rattled through the rigging, and Morris ordered his men to lie down until the ship could bring her broadsides to bear. Lieutenant Francis A. Roe steered the vessel close up to Fort St.

4. *Be3L*, II, 99–100.

5. George E. Belknap (ed.), *Letters of Captain Geo. Hamilton Perkins, U.S.N.* (Concord, N.H., 1886), 67–68. *Governor Moore*, referred to by Lt. Perkins as "settled," was hit but not out of the action.

Philip and "engaged in almost a yardarm conflict. The firing," he observed, "was truly terrible." Smoke lay heavily on the river, and Roe, who could barely see, crept ahead slowly. "The only bells I rang," he said, "were 'slow' and 'stop her.' I lost all trace of land, and sheered over to the Jackson side . . . [where I] at last got a glimpse of the shore line, put the helm aport, and worked along."

In the smoke, *Pensacola* had edged to port, shifting toward midstream and into a position approximately in front of Farragut's Second Division. Morris could not fire the port broadsides without fear of hitting *Hartford*, but he began to absorb fire from both forts and from several Confederate gunboats maneuvering ahead.

Lieutenant Roe, still conducting the steerage, observed the "iron ram dead ahead, coming down upon us." He evaded the *Manassas*, swung *Pensacola* into position to fire her broadsides, attacking the ram "first with a charge from the XI-inch, then the 80-pounder rifle, then the broadside guns in rotation, from forward aft, clean through the whole battery." He watched the ram go downriver, lost in gunfire from *Mississippi*. Ahead lay nothing but open river.[6]

Mississippi, under Captain Melancton Smith, followed *Pensacola* into the smoke and gunfire from the forts. Smith could not see at night and turned the piloting of his vessel over to twenty-four-year-old Lieutenant George Dewey. "You have younger eyes," he said, and when the gunfire started, Smith went to the gundeck and took command of the battery.

Artist William Waud, a civilian guest of Smith, had climbed to the foretop to get a better view of the battle. Waud had witnessed the broadside from *Pensacola* and noticed a dark object approaching dead ahead. He hollered down to Dewey, "Here is a queer-looking customer on our port bow." Dewey spotted "what appeared to be the back of an enormous turtle, painted lead color" and knew it was the dreaded *Manassas*. Having no time to confer with Smith, who was engaged somewhere among the guns, Dewey decided to deal with the ram himself. He sheered into the path of *Manassas*, determined to run her down and end her career, "confident that our superior tonnage must sink her if we struck her fairly."

Aboard *Manassas*, Lieutenant Warley, his head still ringing from *Pensacola*'s broadsides, detected *Mississippi*'s sudden manuever. He had served on the side-wheeler in the old navy and knew she was sluggish. When it came to mobility, *Manassas* was no better, but she had the advantage of a four-

6. *ORN*, XVIII, 201, Morris to Farragut, April 28, 1862; *ibid.*, 768–69, Roe's Diary.

knot current. As Dewey swung to run down *Manassas*, Warley sheered to the side and struck *Mississippi* a glancing blow just abaft the port paddle-wheel.

Smith, who felt the impact but did not see the cause, thought Dewey had run aground. Dewey looked over the port quarter and believed he saw a big hole at the waterline. He hollered, "Man the pumps!" The carpenter shouted back, "I have already, sir, and there is no water in the wells." Dewey was surprised, but grateful. He commented later that "the impact of the ram . . . would have sunk any other ship in the fleet." In fact, *Manassas* had torn out a section of solid planking seven feet long, four feet broad, and four inches deep, and nipped off the heads of fifty copper bolts "as clean as if they were hair under a razor's edge."

While contending with *Manassas*, *Mississippi* sustained irregular fire, mostly from Fort St. Philip. The carpenter reported that ten shots had hit the vessel with eight going completely through. Smith reported severe damage to the outer shaft bearing and to the mizzenmast, which had a hole through it twelve feet above the deck. "I regret," wrote Smith, "that my disabled machinery and a burning steamer that was drifting down upon us did not allow me to take *Manassas* in tow after her surrender," which followed about thirty minutes later.[7]

Oneida, Commander S. Phillips Lee, followed *Mississippi* through the barrier but came to a virtual standstill before reaching Fort St. Philip. Because of the smoke, Lee could not see the cause of the delay, so when *Pensacola* faltered, and then steered away from the eastern shore and back to the center of the river, *Mississippi* followed. In defense of the helmsmen on both vessels, the smoke was so dense that at times they were guided only by the vessel in front or the direction of the current, which flowed erratically across rather than down the river and created a strong eddy off Fort St. Philip. A pilot blinded by smoke would be tempted to helm over into the current, which is probably what happened on *Pensacola* and *Mississippi*, because both vessels were back in the center of the river and steaming toward Fort Jackson when the smoke cleared.

Lee, however, remained in line far behind *Cayuga* and steered for Fort St. Philip, coming so close to the fort's big guns "that the sparks from its immense battery seemed to reach us." Lee had shifted his port 32-pounders to the starboard side, and as *Oneida* passed upriver, Union gunners poured round after round of grape, canister, and shrapnel into the fort, most of it

7. *Ibid.*, 206, 207, Smith to Farragut, Green to Smith, April 26, 1862; George Dewey, *Autobiography of George Dewey, Admiral of the Navy* (New York, 1913), 61–67.

hammering harmlessly against the outer wall. "The terrific fire from the batteries of Fort St. Philip passed over us," Lee wrote, "their guns seeming to be too much elevated for our close position."

Above Fort St. Philip, Lee swung toward the center of the river. From a flash of gunfire he spotted the outline of *Manassas* under power and gliding close by on the port side. The ram passed before Lee could bring his guns to bear, but just ahead the helmsman spotted the dim outline of an enemy gunboat steaming to starboard across the bow. We "ran into it," Lee reported, "with a full head of steam and cut it down with a loud crash on its starboard quarter . . . in a moment, it drifted downstream in the darkness."

Lee held *Oneida* in position above the forts and reshifted the port 32-pounders back to their original position, loading them with solid shot and five-second shells. Lee observed a number of gunboats fading into and out of the screen of darkness and smoke lying over the river, but most of the time he could not be certain whether they were friend or foe. At first the Confederate steamers showed lights and made identifiable targets, but when no fire was returned to *Oneida*'s probing shots, Lee eased up, thinking they might be unarmed transports.

Lee became concerned when he could not find *Varuna*, which was supposed to be directly behind him. Earlier in the action he had seen her showing black smoke, a sure sign that she had been hit and was on fire. Since Confederate vessels burned soft coal, which gave off the same sooty black smoke, Lee feared he could be firing into the damaged *Varuna*. He remained above the forts, and at 5:05 came up with *Cayuga* and spoke with Captain Bailey. Bailey had not seen *Varuna* either and thought she may have gone ahead, but lookouts in the masthead reported nothing above them on the river. Lee went ahead to see for himself.[8]

Varuna, under Commander Charles S. Boggs, had followed *Oneida* through the barrier, broken formation, and under full steam sped by the forts like a greyhound with its tail on fire. When the vessel broke out of the smoke, Boggs found himself in the middle of a swarm of Confederate gunboats. His guns had been loaded with grape, so he switched to five-second shells. Lieutenant Charles H. Swasey, *Varuna*'s executive officer, later claimed that four Confederate steamers were hit by the shells, set on fire, and driven to shore.

Boggs continued upriver and sighted one of the enemy's gunboats firing

8. *ORN*, XVIII, 207–209, 778–79, Lee to Farragut, April 26, 1862, Log of the *Oneida*.

at *Oneida* but sheering toward his ship. *Varuna* had engine trouble, her boilers showing only seventeen pounds of pressure, but in passing the forts she had not taken a single casualty. The enemy vessel steaming toward Boggs was the Louisiana gunboat *Governor Moore*, commanded by Captain Beverly Kennon, formerly of the United States navy.

The action between *Governor Moore* and *Varuna* occurred upriver near Quarantine. Kennon had already sustained casualties, his ship riddled with canister and shrapnel from *Cayuga*, *Pensacola*, and *Oneida*, but his engines had not been damaged and both of his rifled 32-pounders were serviceable.

At daybreak, Kennon spotted a steamer spewing clouds of black smoke and running upriver with a red light at the masthead. Since Confederate vessels carried blue lights, he discerned her to be an enemy. After some of the smoke cleared, he recognized the schooner rig, white smokestack, and long grayish hull of a lone Union gunboat, the *Varuna*. Boggs had outrun the Union squadron and was a good half mile above *Cayuga* and looking for action.

Kennon called for full steam and went after Boggs. A lively exchange of fire took place between *Governor Moore*'s forward 32-pounder and *Varuna*'s stern chaser. As Kennon drew closer, Boggs tried to sheer off and engage his full broadside, but Kennon, in the faster vessel, countered to avoid it. At forty yards, both vessels raked each other with grape, shrapnel, case, and canister, each taking heavy casualties.

Kennon's powder and shell passers on the forward gun had all been shot down, and he went forward to assist. Sixteen of the twenty-three men stationed on the forecastle had been killed or wounded. When *Governor Moore* approached *Varuna*'s beam, Kennon could not depress the forward gun enough to rake the shot across the enemy's deck. "The gun carriage was off its slide," Kennon said, "with its rear transom resting against the heel of the foremast, and I had not the time nor the men to mount it properly. I now pointed the gun through our own deck, at a point 6 feet inside the knightheads and a little to the left of the heel of our bowsprit, and fired through our own deck and raked the enemy fore and aft." That shot and the next killed three men on *Varuna* and wounded several others.

The vessels ranged about ten feet apart but could barely see each other because of the smoke. *Varuna* fired a broadside that Kennon later admitted "swept his decks of nearly every living object." But Kennon stood on top of the hurricane deck and could see the enemy's mastheads above the smoke. "As quick as lightning" he ordered the helm hard aport and rammed

Varuna just abaft the mainmast on the starboard side. Kennon backed off and struck *Varuna* again, this time abreast the smokestack. He heard her ribs breaking and backed off again, this time to get away from the constant musket fire rattling down from her tops. "The *Varuna* was sinking rapidly," Kennon said. "Her head was turned for the shore, which she reached just before she sank."

Before *Varuna* struck the bank, *R. J. Breckinridge*, commanded by Captain James B. Smith of the River Defense Fleet, rammed the crippled vessel on the port beam, then sheered off and steamed rapidly across the river. Smith had evidently looked downriver and observed *Cayuga* and other Union gunboats fast approaching, because he grounded *Breckinridge*, set her afire, and skedaddled ashore with all his crew.[9]

The fate of *Governor Moore* was reported differently by two participants, but the final outcome was the same. Boggs claimed that when Kennon struck *Varuna* the second time, *Governor Moore* swung alongside, enabling *Varuna's* gunners to fire a five-gun broadside of 8-inch shells abaft her armor. "This settled her," Boggs said, "and drove her ashore in flames." Kennon claimed that after disabling *Varuna*, he started downstream to ram *Cayuga* but suddenly came upon most of Farragut's fleet. He reversed course to bring "our stern chaser to bear upon the enemy" but suffered such severe damage to his engines and steerage that he lost control of the vessel and grounded. Kennon ordered the vessel set afire and blown up. Of a crew of ninety-three, he estimated sixty-four killed or wounded, twenty-four captured, and the remaining seven either escaped or unaccounted for.[10]

USS *Katahdin*, under Lieutenant George H. Preble, had followed *Varuna* through the barrier earlier in the morning, and like most of the vessels trailing *Cayuga*, got confused in the smoke. When the air cleared, Preble noticed to port that *Katahdin* had caught up to *Mississippi*. When he sighted the vessels out of position, he ceased firing as he passed. Because most of the helmsmen could not see though the heavy smoke, it is difficult to estimate how much damage the fleet inflicted upon itself. Preble was obviously concerned about striking *Mississippi* or he would not have given the order to cease fire.

Preble was the sixth commander to pass the forts but the first to mention *Louisiana*. "Above the forts," he wrote, "we passed along the broadside and within 50 yards of the iron-plated battery *Louisiana*. To our surprise, she

9. *Ibid.*, 212, 305–306, Swasey to Boggs, April 29, and Kennon to Mitchell, May 4, 1862.
10. *Ibid.*, 210, 307, Boggs to Farragut, April 29, and Kennon to Mitchell, May 4, 1862.

did not fire at us, though she could have blown us out of the water." Preble claims that after passing, he gave *Louisiana* a shot "from the XI-inch pivot and Parrott . . . with good effect, tearing a hole the size of the shell through and through the iron plating of her bow."[11]

Commander Mitchell, who spent the night on board *Louisiana*, credits *Hartford* for the damage done to the ironclad. Mitchell states: "One of the enemies heaviest sloops, supposed to be the *Hartford*, delivered her fire while almost, if not in actual contact with the *Louisiana*. Two of his XI-inch shells struck the forward part of the roof, crushing the railroad iron plating about two-thirds their diameter, and then broke into small fragments." As will be seen later, there is no evidence of *Hartford* engaging *Louisiana*, and the damage was probably done by *Katahdin*. If so, Preble contends that *Louisiana* never fired a gun, although Mitchell claims that "while in actual contact with *Louisiana*'s stern, the *Hartford* received the fire of her three bow guns, the projectiles from which must have passed through her." Had this happened to either *Hartford* or *Katahdin*, it would surely have appeared in a Union report. Preble reported no casualties, for which Mitchell may have deserved a word of thanks.[12]

Lieutenant George M. Ransom's *Kineo* followed *Katahdin* through the barrier, but some vessels of the First Division were beginning to stack up. Ransom must have veered to port, because his vessel collided with *Brooklyn*, which had just sheered to starboard to fire a broadside at Fort Jackson. The collision started *Kineo*'s deck beams, "carrying away the bowsprit and head, giving the topgallant forecastle a slant to starboard, destroying the port waist boat, and wrenching the frame of the vessel . . . much out of line." In passing the forts, *Kineo* took ten shots, but Ransom later discovered that the enemy did less damage to his vessel than *Brooklyn*.

Part of *Kineo*'s damage occurred after she had passed the forts. While working with *Mississippi* to take the grounded *Manassas* in tow, Ransom was hailed by Commander Smith and ordered to take possession of two Confederate gunboats that appeared to have struck their colors. Ransom started downriver and came under fire from CSS *McRae* and the two gunboats. He found himself uncomfortably in range of both forts, and when the pivot gun carriage was disabled by a shot from Fort St. Philip, he headed back upstream quickly but, he claimed, "very reluctantly."[13]

11. *Ibid.*, 215–16, Preble to Farragut, April 30, 1862.

12. *Ibid.*, 215–16, 294–96, Preble to Farragut, April 30, and Mitchell to Mallory, August 19, 1862.

13. *Ibid.*, 217–18, 218–19, 792–93, Ransom to Farragut, April 25, Ransom to Lenthall, April 28, 1862, and Log of *Kineo*.

The last ship in Bailey's First Division, *Wissahickon*, commanded by Lieutenant Albert N. Smith, ran the gauntlet with relative ease. Although ordered to stay close to Fort St. Philip on the eastern shore, Smith somehow managed to ease to port and opened fire on Fort Jackson instead. As day broke and the smoke cleared, he found himself "unavoidably crowded on the west bank of the river." It is a wonder he did not get run over by any of the nine warships behind him. His vessel had been hit only four times in the hull and once in the mainmast, and two men had slight injuries, all of which suggests that Smith lost little time getting above the forts.[14]

Although Farragut had planned to send Bailey's full division of nine vessels through the barrier before he started the Center Division, it did not work that way. The second vessel through, *Pensacola*, faltered in the smoke, stopped and started, causing the third vessel, *Mississippi*, to get out of position to port. After that, the First Division remained out of alignment, some of the vessels meandering all over the river. As a consequence, *Hartford* started early, followed by *Brooklyn* and *Richmond*, thereby causing the collision between *Kineo* and *Brooklyn*. The logs of the last four vessels in Bailey's First Division and the first two vessels in Farragut's Center Division provide evidence that Farragut did not wait for *Wissahickon* to clear the barrier before advancing his own division.

Of the vessels attempting to pass the forts, *Hartford* probably experienced the greatest difficulty. At 3:30 A.M. the flagship got underway and ten minutes later received fire from Fort Jackson and the water battery. As the vessel started through the barrier, nothing could be seen ahead but black, rolling clouds of smoke speckled with flashes of gunfire coming from every conceivable direction. Gun crews lay flat on the decks, listening to the racket of shot and grape screaming and whistling overhead. Farragut held his fire—he needed to know what he was shooting at, and nothing could be seen but smoke.

He climbed into the port mizzen and stood with his feet on the ratlines and his back against the shrouds. With a pair of opera glasses borrowed from Signal Officer Osbon, he peered over dense waves of smoke toward Fort Jackson. The mortars had opened with every gun, and Farragut could follow the descent of the shells as they fell around the fort and exploded. Porter's gunboats had opened on the water battery but had not silenced its six guns. From his perch, Farragut asked Osbon if the gun

14. *Ibid.*, 220, 221, 795–96, Smith to Farragut, April 26, May 2, 1862, and Log of *Wissahickon*.

crews were ready. Osbon answered yes but that *Hartford* was still out of position for her broadsides. Farragut hollered down, "Go forward and see if the bow guns will bear."

At that moment, a shell smacked into the mainmast and sent splinters flying. "We can't afford to lose you," Osbon hollered, halfway up the mizzenmast. "They'll get you up there, sure." Almost as an afterthought, he added, "They'll break my opera glasses if you stay up there."

Farragut reached down, trying to hand off the opera glasses, and grumbled, "Oh, damn the glasses!"

But Osbon shook his head and said, "It's you we want. Come down."

Farragut climbed down just as a shell exploded where he had been standing and cut away some of the rigging.

Hartford made an excellent target, thanks once again to her ubiquitous signal officer. Osbon had hoisted the largest American flag he could find at the peak and then strung smaller flags to the tops of the fore and mainmasts. Farragut reminded Osbon that ships do not fly colors at night. "I thought if we were to go down," Osbon replied, "it would be well to have our colors flying above the water."

Farragut had other matters on his mind and said, "Very well," not realizing that all the gunboats astern had observed the flagship break out her colors and had followed suit. Had they not done so, the huge flag flying from *Hartford*'s peak would have made a choice target for every gunner aiming down the barrel of a Confederate gun.[15]

Hartford opened first with her bow guns, following a few minutes later with a full broadside from the port guns. The smoke rolled back over forecastle, blinding everyone. Once again it was amazing, or perhaps just good luck, that so few Union vessels became entangled. The Center Division, led by *Hartford*, was to stay to port, but nobody realized that the river's current as it approached Fort Jackson pushed vessels navigating upriver toward Fort St. Philip. Some of the ships in the First Division, aware of the bend in the river, had swung sharply to port and actually crossed in front but ahead of the Center Division. To Farragut's surprise, *Hartford* came out of the smoke in close range to but below Fort St. Philip and opened with a starboard broadside. When the smoke cleared, a lookout in the tops reported a fire raft ahead. The helmsman overreacted and grounded the flagship just above the upper water battery, "so close to shore," Lieutenant Albert Kautz wrote, "that from the bowsprit we could

15. Paine, *Sailor of Fortune*, 191, 192.

reach the tops of the bushes . . . we could distinctly hear the gunners in the casemates give their orders . . . as they saw Farragut's flag at the mizzen."

The Confederate tugboat *Mosher,* commanded by Horace Sherman, guided the fire raft alongside *Hartford,* and "in a moment the ship was one blaze all along the port side, halfway up to the main and mizzen tops."[16] In the midst of fighting the fire, some of the men prepared to jump overboard, but Commmander Wainwright, shouting commands through a speaking trumpet, calmly walked the deck: "Take your places at fire quarters," and hoses began to appear everywhere. Between the roar of flames and the shouting and hollering of the men, nobody heard an enemy shell crash through the upper deck and explode in the cabin, setting the interior of the ship on fire. It was not discovered until flames broke through the windows.[17]

With fire engulfing the port side of *Hartford,* the starboard gunners kept pounding away at Fort St. Philip's lower water battery. "For a moment," said Lieutenant Kautz, "it looked as though the flag-ship was indeed doomed." He located Farragut on the port side, clasping his hands high in the air, and heard him exclaim, "My God, is it to end this way!" Flames shot up through the ports, threatening to drive men from their guns, but Farragut steadied himself and paced the deck, shouting, "Don't flinch from that fire, boys. There's a hotter fire than that for those who don't do their duty! Give that rascally little tug a shot."

About that time young Master's Mate Edwin J. Allen, with a hose in his hand, jumped into the mizzen rigging and began dousing the flames. Farragut got out of the way and noticed a man bending over the deck uncapping shells. At first he did not recognize his signal officer because Osbon had his coat thrown over his head to keep his hair from singeing. Farragut walked over to the hunched-over figure and said, "Come, Mr. Osbon, this is no time fore praying." Osbon removed the cap from a third shell, looked up, and replied, "Flag-Officer, if you'll wait a second, you'll get the quickest answer to prayer you ever heard of." He rolled the 20-pound shells over the side, letting them fall into the burning raft below. They exploded with "a terrific noise," and when Farragut peered over the rail, the fire raft had "a big hole in her." As the flames died away, *Hartford* backed her engines. Slowly the bow slipped off the bank, and the ship continued up-

16. *ORN,* XVIII, 154, 295, Farragut to Fox, April 25, and Mitchell to Mallory, August 19, 1862. Comdr. Mitchell claims *Mosher* was sunk by a broadside from *Hartford,* but there is no mention of the sinking in *Hartford*'s records (*B&L,* II, 64, 90).

17. Diggins, "Recollections," 88–90.

river, firing broadsides into Fort St. Philip as she passed. Despite having been grounded under the guns of the fort, *Hartford* sustained only twelve casualties, two killed and ten wounded.[18]

Brooklyn, under Captain Thomas T. Craven, followed *Hartford* into the smoke, and when Fort Jackson's water battery opened, Craven replied with a broadside of grape. In the resulting smoke, *Brooklyn* missed the opening in the barrier and swung alongside one of the hulks. This detour probably occurred about the time *Brooklyn* collided with *Kineo.* Craven suspected he had gotten too far to starboard, steered to port, and struck the hulk to the left of the opening. The steam anchor, hanging from the starboard quarter, tore along the hulk and became entangled in the barrier chain. For several minutes, *Brooklyn* lay motionless under the guns of both forts until somebody rambled up with an axe and cut the hawser.

Brooklyn eased forward, steamed a short distance, and collided with the raft of logs anchored on the far end of the barrier. Believing that the propeller had been damaged, Craven shut down the engines. Once again *Brooklyn* came under heavy fire. "Stand by the starboard anchor," Craven trumpeted, but the engine room reported no damage and the captain ordered full ahead. By then *Brooklyn* had taken a beating, and she was still below the forts. Midshipman John R. Bartlett wrote:

> There were many fire-rafts, and these and the flashing of guns and bursting shells made it almost as light as day, but the smoke of the passing fleet was so thick that at times one could see nothing ten feet from the ship. While entangled with the rafts, the *Brooklyn* was hulled a number of times; one shot from Fort Jackson struck the rail just at the break of the poop and went nearly across, plowing out the deck in its course. Another struck Barney Sands, the signal quartermaster, and cut his body almost in two.
>
> The ship was now clear of the hulks and steamed up the river, throwing shells and shrapnel into Fort Jackson as fast as the guns could be loaded and fired. When just abreast of the fort a shot struck the side of the port of No. 9 gun on the port side, and at the same time, a shell burst directly over the gun. The first captain's head was cut off and nine of the gun's crew were wounded. I was standing amidships between two No. 10 guns, and was struck on the back by the splinters and thrown to the deck. I was on my feet in a moment

18. *Be³L,* II, 64, 90; Paine, *Sailor of Fortune,* 196, 197; *ORN,* XVIII, 722, Log of *Hartford.*

and turned to my port gun. There were only two men standing at it . . . the others were all flat on the deck, one of them directly to the rear of the gun. The gun had just been loaded, and I pulled this man to one side, clear of the recoil, and fired. . . . After the discharge of the gun the men on the deck got up and came to their places. None of them were seriously hurt. The captain of the gun found a piece of shell inside his cap, which did not even scratch his head; another piece went through my coat sleeve.[19]

At this point, *Brooklyn* came opposite Fort Jackson, and moving slowly, got swept by the same cross-current that grounded *Hartford* on the eastern bank. Craven was probably surprised to find himself scraping the bottom of the river a scant sixty yards from the guns of Fort St. Philip. The eleven XI-inch starboard guns delivered three broadsides in passing, which Craven claimed "completely drove the rebels from their guns, silencing their fire."

Craven worked upriver and observed *Hartford* with a fire raft alongside and burning against the bank. Once again he slowed engines until the flagship was out of trouble. Turning upstream, he passed Fort St. Philip and engaged *Louisiana*, but failed to damage the ironclad. A 9-inch shell from the ironclad struck *Brooklyn*'s bow a foot above the waterline, and had it exploded, the vessel would have gone to the bottom. This fact was uncovered later, after the shell had been cut from the forward timbers. *Louisiana*'s gunners had forgotten to remove the lead patch from the fuse, thereby preventing the shell from exploding.[20]

Brooklyn's wayward course continued because Craven did not know where he was. "I had nothing else to do," he said, "but to push on, according to orders, and get above the forts, and supposing from the direction of the noise and flashes of light that I was steering in the right direction, we went on at full speed."

Instead of going upriver, he recrossed and found himself staring into the batteries of Fort Jackson, which raked *Brooklyn* with a "terribly scorching fire." Once again *Brooklyn* "grazed the shore," this time on the western side, then sheered off and headed back upstream.

"As we swung out into the current," Midshipman Bartlett said, "we began to see the vessels ahead fighting with the Confederate gun-boats, and a few moments later the cry came aft, 'A steamer coming down on our port

19. *ORN*, XVIII, 196–97, Craven to Mrs. Craven, May 16, 1862; *B&L*, II, 62–63.
20. *ORN*, XVIII, 197; *B&L*, II, 65.

bow.' We could see two smoke-stacks and the black smoke from them." Bartlett climbed the poop ladder and saw a "good-sized river steamer coming down on us, crowded with men on her forward deck, as if ready to board."

Craven ordered his crew to stand by to repel boarders, and the gunners loaded shrapnel with fuses cut to one second. "As she approached," Bartlett wrote, "Craven gave the vessel a sheer to starboard, and we began with No. 1 gun, the guns aft following in quick succession, the shells bursting almost immediately as they left the guns. There was a rush of steam, shrieks from the people on board the steamer, and when it came time for my No. 10 gun to fire, the steamer was lost in the smoke." Thus ended the career of the River Defense gunboat *Warrior*, which Captain Stevenson ran ashore on the eastern bank and set afire. Poor Captain Stevenson, who had tried so hard to profit from the war. What an ignominious way to end his career.[21]

The misadventures of *Brooklyn* did not end with *Warrior*. When the smoke cleared, the starboard gunners, peering through the ports, shouted, "The ram! The ram!" Craven, who had never left the forward edge of the poop since *Brooklyn* had gotten underway, called out, "Give her four bells! Put your helm hard-a-starboard!" As the vessel came about, *Manassas*, a few yards away, fired her lone gun, striking *Brooklyn* about five feet above the waterline amidships and knocking several men off their feet. A moment later the ram, which had lost much of her motive power, crashed into *Brooklyn*, jarring her fore and aft. From below, reports indicated that the blow had failed to penetrate *Brooklyn*'s chain armor.

Midshipman Bartlett looked out of No. 10 gun port and saw the ram lying low in the water alongside *Brooklyn*. "A man came out of her little hatch left," he said, "and ran forward along the port side of the deck, as far as the smoke-stacks, placed his hands against one, and looked to see what damage the ram had done. I saw him turn, fall over, and tumble into the water." Bartlett did not know why the man fell until he asked the leadsman in the chains.

"Why, yes, sir," the leadsman replied. "I saw him fall overboard, —in fact, I helped him; for I hit him alongside of the head with my hand-lead."[22]

21. *B&L*, II, 65–66; *ORN*, XVIII, 195, 197, 270, Lowry to Craven, April 25, Craven to Mrs. Craven, May 16, Duncan to Pickett, April 30, 1862. Lt. Lowry claimed the vessel was *Warrior*, which may have been the result of subsequent deduction.

22. *B&L*, II, 67.

Craven called for full steam and ordered *Brooklyn* upriver. A few moments later another large vessel appeared off the starboard side running downriver. Bartlett had the lock string in his hand, the gun depressed and loaded with a 9-inch shell when somebody hollered, "Don't fire! It is the *Iroquois!*" Seeing black smoke pouring from her stack, and noticing her location, Bartlett shouted up to Craven, "It can't be the *Iroquois!* It is not one of our vessels, for her smoke-stack is abaft her mainmast!" Craven repeated the order, "Don't fire!" and Bartlett watched CSS *McRae* slip by unharmed.[23]

Craven steamed up the river and joined the fleet reassembling above the forts. A few days later, when men examined *Brooklyn's* coal bunkers to determine why the ship kept filling with water, they found that *Manassas* had driven the chain armor deep into the starboard hull below the waterline; inside, they patched five feet of planking that had splintered and crushed inward. "The only thing that prevented the prow of the *Manassas* from sinking us," Bartlett said, "was the fact that the bunker was full of coal." Despite all the difficulty Craven encountered in running the forts, the officers inspecting the damage could count only seventeen hits by enemy gunfire. But of all Farragut's vessels, *Brooklyn* reported the highest number of men killed—nine—with another twenty-five wounded.[24]

Richmond, under Commander James Alden, followed behind *Brooklyn* but cleared the barrier without becoming entangled. Her crew lay on the deck, their guns loaded, until coming "so close to Fort Jackson," Alden wrote in his log, "that we could throw a stone into the fort; we were so close that all their shots passed over us." *Richmond* steamed by, firing her broadsides directly into the parapets. A shot tore off a gun captain's head, and as his body fell, still holding the lock string, the gun discharged once more. Acting Master's Mate John B. Bradley ascended the ladder to the topgallant forecastle with a message for the captain. In the act of saluting, a fragment struck him in the forehead and he fell dead. Four men received wounds, and the vessel was hit seventeen times above the waterline. Compared to other vessels in the fleet, *Richmond* got off easy.[25]

Bell's Third Division, led by *Sciota*, under Lieutenant Edward Donaldson, followed in *Richmond's* wake, cleared the barrier, and steamed up-

23. *Ibid.*, 67.

24. *Ibid.*, 69; *ORN*, XVIII, 177–79, 186–87, List of Killed and Wounded, and Dewhurst, Pickering, and Toy to Craven, April 28, 1862.

25. *ORN*, XVIII, 178–79, 739–40, Log of *Richmond*, and List of Killed and Wounded.

river, taking only two casualties and light damage. *Iroquois*, under Commander John De Camp, eased in astern of *Sciota* and ran into all kinds of trouble with CSS *McRae*.

Lieutenant Thomas B. Huger's *McRae* had entered the action early, exchanging shots with *Cayuga* and other vessels in Bailey's First Division as they passed the forts. *McRae*, a converted packet ship, carried six light 32-pounders and one 9-inch shellgun pivoted amidships, and of all the vessels in Mitchell's small squadron, excluding *Louisiana*, she was the most heavily armed. Huger moved *McRae* into midstream and began to exchange broadsides with every Union vessel that came into range. Twice the ship narrowly escaped being run down by Union gunboats emerging from the smoke. Most of them passed without firing a shot, thinking the *McRae* was one of their own.

In the confusion of darkness, smoke, and intermittent flashes of light, Huger observed *Iroquois* coming up on the right. Huger, who had served in the United States navy since March 5, 1835, was a lieutenant on the USS *Iroquois* in the Mediterranean when he tendered his resignation. From the forecastle of *McRae*, he may have recognized the dim outline of *Iroquois* as she steamed toward him. "We sheered to port, and delivered our starboard broadside," said Lieutenant Charles W. Read, "and sheering quickly the other way, gave him our port broadside." Grape and langrage (slugs once used for damaging sail) swept the decks of *Iroquois*, wounding several men. As *McRae* passed, *Iroquois* replied with one 11-inch shell and one round of canister. A shell that exploded in *McRae*'s sail room and set the ship on fire probably came from *Iroquois'* gun. Huger started the pumps, but the fire burned fiercely, threatening to penetrate the thin bulkhead separating the sail room from the shell lockers, and he nosed the vessel against the bank to extinguish the fire.

Three hundred yards away, several Union gunboats passed, firing shells and shrapnel into *McRae*. As Huger backed off the bank, he was struck by a fragment and mortally wounded. "Savez" Read took over, moved the vessel into midstream, and started upriver after the Union fleet, only to find his vessel alone among eleven of the enemy. He changed course and started downriver, but the tiller ropes parted and an eddy carried him into the bank. While trying to back off, he spotted the River Defense boat *Defiance* lying a short distance above and flying a white flag. He sent Lieutenant Thomas Arnold to the boat with instructions to tear down the flag and force the crew to fight their guns, since the vessel did not appear to be damaged. At dawn, Read moved *McRae* off the bank and returned to Fort St. Philip.

After the fight with *McRae*, *Iroquois* steamed upriver with eight men killed and twenty-four wounded. Four miles above the forts, *Iroquois* captured Steam Launch No. 3 with forty Confederate soldiers, many of whom had been wounded during the bombardment of the forts. De Camp reported the *Iroquois* "badly injured in her hull . . . all our boats are smashed, and most of them are not worth repairs."[26]

Kennebec, commanded by Lieutenant John H. Russell, followed *Iroquois* as far as the barrier chain. There, Russell became entangled in the log raft, got clear, tried again, and ran into one of the hulks, "cutting her down to the water's edge." In a second effort he cleared the barrier but took a shot at the waterline. By then it was daylight. Russell gave up the effort and steamed back downstream, coming to anchor beside *Harriet Lane*.[27]

Lieutenant Crosby's *Pinola* started toward the barrier behind *Kennebec*, lost sight of her, and came upon *Iroquois*. A shell that damaged *McRae* could also have come from *Pinola*. Crosby believed he had twice hit a vessel to starboard that he first mistook for *Iroquois*, but *McRae* would have been in that position at the time Crosby passed the forts. *Pinola*, besides being shot up badly, reported three killed and seven wounded, mostly from its engagement with the forts. By the time the vessel joined Farragut's fleet upriver, most of the Confederate gunboats had been destroyed or captured.[28]

Itasca, under Lieutenant Charles H. B. Caldwell, and *Winona*, under Lieutenant Edward T. Nichols, evidently formed on *Kennebec*, because both ships ran afoul of "a mass of logs and drift stuff held by chains and moorings of the hulks." *Itasca* and *Winona* then became entangled with each other, and by the time they separated dawn broke. Caldwell tried to make a run past the forts, but Fort Jackson's gunners lowered their sights and ripped up *Itasca*'s bulkheads and smashed a boiler. Steam poured through the engine room, driving the engineers and firemen to the deck. With what little power remained, Caldwell swung the vessel into the current and under fire from the enemy, headed back downriver.

Winona stood out even sharper in the morning light. As Nichols moved above the barrier fire, Fort Jackson's guns hulled the vessel and killed or

26. *Ibid.*, 221–22, 332, De Camp to Farragut, May 3, and Read to Whittle, May 1, 1862; Scharf, *Confederate Navy*, 286–87.

27. *ORN*, XVIII, 224, 225, 808–809, Russell to Farragut, April 29, 1862, and Log of *Kennebec*.

28. *Ibid.*, 222–23, 804–805, Crosby to Farragut, April 26, 1862, and Log of *Pinola*.

wounded the crew manning the rifled gun. Nichols sheered, got swept into the cross-current, and unexpectedly found himself directly under the guns of Fort St. Philip. "Sheering off," Nichols wrote, "I shot across to the Fort Jackson side, but owing to the obscurity of the smoke, got so close to shore that I had no room to turn upstream, and was forced to head down. At this time both forts were firing nearly their entire batteries at me." Nichols recrossed the barrier and reported his vessel to Porter.[29]

Running the forts at night proved to be the right decision, despite the opportunity for error. Throughout the hours of darkness, both forts had their guns elevated too high and could not see the effect of their firing. Some of Farragut's vessels ran the gauntlet with no damage to their hulls and little to their tops. But when daylight came, four of the last vessels through the barrier were shot up badly, and three of them were forced to retreat.

Of the Confederate vessels involved in the fight, only three of them took an active part in defending the forts—*Governor Moore, McRae,* and *Manassas.* Not much has been said about *Manassas,* but the turtle was very much in the fight, and at times, seemingly everywhere.

Before the action opened, the *Official Records* placed *Manassas* above Fort Jackson, but Lieutenant Warley, her captain, stated that she was moored above Fort St. Philip. This is very possibly true, because when Warley moved to engage *Cayuga,* the River Defense boat *Defiance* ran into him, and these vessels were all gathered along the east bank of the river above Fort St. Philip. Warley cleared from *Defiance,* spotted a large ship (*Pensacola*) standing across the river, and made for her. The vessel sheered out of the way and *Manassas* passed "grazingly" under her counter. "The muzzle of our guns," Lieutenant Roe observed from the deck of *Pensacola,* "almost touched it."

Warley then came up on "a large side-wheel steamer (*Mississippi*), and tried to strike her on the wheel, but struck her on the quarter." The collision buckled a few of *Mississippi's* planks below the waterline, and for his insolence, Warley listened to a broadside roar directly over his pilothouse.

Warley then headed for the barrier chain, moving rapidly with the current. He considered going down farther and attacking Porter's mortars but came under friendly fire from Fort Jackson. He turned upriver, finding temporary shelter in the smoke, and several minutes later observed *Brooklyn* lying across the stream. "Ordered resin thrown into the furnaces

29. *Ibid.,* 225–26, 226–27, Caldwell to Farragut and Nichols to Farragut, April 30, 1862.

to make steam rapidly," Warley stated, "drew the valves all open, and ran into her, firing my gun loaded with a 5-second shell when within a few feet." (This was the shell that entered *Brooklyn's* bow and failed to explode.) Thinking the ram had become disabled, Warley reversed engines, hoping he could make his way back to the forts, but found he still had power enough to stem the current. As dawn broke, he spotted *Iroquois* steaming rapidly upriver. At twenty yards astern of the Union ship, he ordered the gun fired, but ramming *Brooklyn* had knocked it off its carriage. "The *Iroquois* put on steam," Warley said, "and ran away from me as though I had been at anchor."

Ahead he observed *McRae* engaging *Iroquois* and three other gunboats. He worked the ram upriver, but it was slow going. By the time he got there, *McRae's* fire bell was ringing and most of the Union vessels had passed upstream. To give *McRae* time to extinguish her fires, Warley continued after *Iroquois* and *Pinola*, but when he came around the bend below Quarantine and counted "ten or twelve" enemy vessels, he knew he had come too far.

Mississippi and *Kineo* pulled out of the squadron and steamed after the ram, one on either side of the river. With the exception of her plating, *Manassas* had nothing left with which to fight and no speed to enable her to escape, so Warley ran the ironclad onto the east bank, ordered her delivery pipes cut, and sent the crew through the forward gunport and into the swamp. *Mississippi* followed, but because of damaged machinery, she could not tow off the ram. Men from *Mississippi* boarded, set the ironclad afire, and returned to the side-wheeler. Gunners fired a few rounds at the ram's plating, enough to jar *Manassas* loose from the bank. She floated downriver and was next seen working her way past the forts. Captain M. T. Squires at Fort St. Philip admitted mistaking the ram for a disabled Union vessel and firing seventy-five times without striking her once. The ironclad passed the barrier and was next seen by Porter's gunboats.[30]

The approach of the dreaded *Manassas* created quite a stir among the bummers. Porter was among the observers and told the story as follows:

> It was reported to me that the celebrated *Manassas* was coming out to attack us, and sure enough, there she was apparently steaming alongshore and ready to pounce upon the . . . defenseless mortar vessels. Two of our steamers and some of the mortar vessels opened

30. *Ibid.*, 205–206, 336–37, 769, Smith to Farragut, April 26, Warley to Mallory, August 13, 1862, Roe's Diary; *B&L*, II, 89–91.

fire upon her, but I soon discovered that the *Manassas* could harm no one again, and I ordered the vessels to save their shot. She was just beginning to emit smoke from her ports . . . and was discovered to be on fire and sinking. Her pipes were all twisted and riddled with shot, and her hull was also cut up. . . . I tried to save her as a curiosity, by getting a hawser around her and securing her to the bank, but just before doing so, she faintly exploded. Her only gun went off, and, emitting flames through her bow port, like some huge animal, she gave a plunge and disappeared under the water.[31]

Louisiana played no useful role in the defense of the river or the city of New Orleans. This cannot be blamed upon its commander, Charles F. McIntosh, who was by reputation a fighter. Only six of the ironclad's sixteen guns could be fired, and those sparingly. Every Union vessel passing *Louisiana* sprayed her with shot, shell, grape, and canister without causing any damage to her heavy casemate. No one was injured inside, but McIntosh, her commander, was mortally wounded by splinters flying off a wooden barricade erected for sharpshooters on the outside deck. Two large shells dented some of the plating on the forward deck and left a hole about nine inches wide. During the battle, *Louisiana* never moved from her mooring above Fort St. Philip.[32]

At daylight, April 24, 1862, fourteen of Farragut's seventeen vessels lay at anchor near Quarantine. One of them, *Varuna*, lay against the bank disabled. Three vessels failed to get above the forts and returned to Porter's squadron below the barrier. New Orleans lay lightly defended upriver. Barely a vessel was left in the river to contest Farragut's fleet. As Commander Alden wrote in his log: "Mississippi River. Victory! Victory! The American flag floats over everything on the Mississippi River this morning."[33]

But not quite. No, not yet.

31. *ORN,* XVIII, 357–58, Porter to Welles, April 25, 1862.
32. *Ibid.,* 294–95, Mitchell to Mallory, August 19, 1862.
33. *Ibid.,* 739, Log of *Richmond.*

FIFTEEN   *High Noon at City Hall*

Major General Lovell was among the spectators witnessing the early stages of the Union fleet passing the forts. On April 23 he had gone down the river in a small steamboat to induce Commander Mitchell to move *Louisiana* below the barrier, and he was still there when USS *Cayuga* came under the guns of the forts. Lovell stayed only long enough to convince himself that the forts would not stop Farragut's vessels. "I returned at once to the city," he stated, "narrowly escaping capture, and giving orders to General [Martin L.] Smith, in command of the interior lines, to . . . make all possible resistance to the enemy's fleet at the earthwork batteries below the town." The guns at Chalmette, however, pointed mostly inland, emplaced there to enfilade an infantry attack. Worse, the high stage of the river made the guns untenable because passing gunboats could fire directly into the rear of the earthworks. Lovell had been confident he could repulse an attack from ground forces, but this was different.

Before the general reached New Orleans, he had already decided that if Farragut got his fleet above the forts the city could not be defended. He woke Mayor John T. Monroe, along with members of the city council, and told them so. A member of the council suggested that a thousand "desperately bold men" could easily be recruited to board the enemy's vessels and carry them by assault; and Lovell ordered Major Samuel L. James to seize the necessary steamers and attempt it. When James could find no more than a hundred volunteers, Lovell returned to his original plan — evacuation.

In the city of New Orleans, Lovell had no heavy guns and no forces trained to contend with Farragut's firepower. Most of the Confederate infantry had been sent to the forts, along with all of the best guns. Moreover, much of the powder for the guns at Chalmette had been transferred to *Louisiana*, leaving General Smith with only about twenty rounds per gun. The troops in the city consisted of about three thousand militia armed with shotguns, some ninety-day volunteers who were disbanding to go home, and three regiments of new recruits who were still without arms.

If the city were subjected to a siege, the civilian population of 170,000 citizens and slaves would be starved into submission within three weeks, because there would be no way to bring in supplies. Because of high water, the swamps around the city were full, and the only outlet passable by land was west through Kenner and then north along the Jackson Railroad. Lake Pontchartrain had not yet been occupied, and Lovell ordered all available steamers assembled at Metairie. Once Farragut came in force, Lovell realized that both outlets would be sealed off. He had little time left, and he could not waste it.

Over initial objections from civilian officials, Lovell loaded his three thousand troops with their baggage and supplies on the Jackson Railroad and sent them to Camp Moore, seventy-eight miles to the north. He also recalled troops from nearby outposts, ordering them to spike their guns and bring their small arms. As they filed into the city, he marched them to Metairie, where waiting steamers shuttled them across the lake to Madisonville. From there they were to find their way to Camp Moore. Finally, he rounded up all the loose guns, loaded them on freight cars or steamers, and sent them upriver to Vicksburg.

Later in the morning Lovell convinced most of the public officials that evacuation would transform New Orleans from a "military position into that of an ungarrisoned city." He believed that Farragut would be unable to occupy the city immediately or demand a surrender until Butler entered the city, thereby giving the Confederate army quartermaster ample time for the "undisturbed removal of the vast amount of public property . . . on hand at the time."[1]

While Lovell had spent part of the night of the attack at Fort St. Philip, Commander Whittle had spent it asleep in his room at the St. Charles Hotel. An aide brought a message to his room at 5:40 A.M. advising him that the Union fleet had passed the forts and was now at Quarantine. It was the last message Colonel Ignatius Szymanski of the Chalmette Regiment would send. USS *Cayuga* steamed over to the bank, and Captain Bailey ordered

1. *ORN*, XVIII, 255–56, Lovell to Cooper, May 22, 1862; ORA, VI, 565–66, Lovell's Testimony.

the colonel to pile up his arms and come aboard. He then sent a detail ashore to cut the telegraph wires.[2]

Whittle dispatched Szymanski's telegram to Governor Moore, who was also sleeping soundly at the St. Charles Hotel, and Moore dressed hurriedly and telegraphed Jefferson Davis. There is no indication that Whittle ever notified Mallory, and the wire to Davis erroneously implied that Farragut's fleet had been divided, which was precisely what Davis hoped to hear. Lovell was less vague. Upon reaching the city he sent a wire to the War Department: "The enemy has passed the forts. It is too late to send any guns here; they had better go to Vicksburg." Neither Moore nor Whittle understood the seriousness of the situation until Lovell joined them for breakfast at the hotel.[3]

Since his arrival in New Orleans, Whittle had assumed no responsibility for the completion of *Mississippi*, but now he could no longer avoid it. The Naval Office instructed him to send the hulk upriver where it could be completed. Whittle may not have received the wire, because it never appeared among his papers, but after breakfast he sent for Commander Arthur Sinclair, who was to take command of the vessel whenever the Tifts finished her, and instructed him to "use every exertion in his power to get her upriver, and failing to do so, to destroy her." Having given Sinclair an order, Whittle dropped the matter and turned his attention to transferring the public treasure to a steamer waiting at the wharf.[4]

Sinclair went directly to the Tifts and asked how much longer it would take to finish the vessel. Nelson Tift replied, "In my opinion, two weeks." Sinclair had only been on site for three weeks, but he did not believe the vessel would be operational before July. Two of her three propellers still lay on the dock, the armoring had just been started, she had no rudder, her ports were not installed, and she had no guns.

In a futile effort to tow the vessel to safety, Sinclair attempted to secure two steamers, *St. Charles* and *Peytona*, but found they had been commandeered by Lovell. The general rescinded the order, but Sinclair was unable to take possession of the boats until the evening of April 24, because the crews had a "great indisposition" to help him.

At dark the two steamers pulled *Mississippi* into the river but could not stem the current. With great difficulty the crews worked the unfinished

2. *ORN*, Ser. 2, I, 437, and *ORN*, XVIII, 349, Whittle testimony; *ORN*, XVIII, 172, Bailey to Welles, May 7, 1862.
3. *ORA*, VI, 883, Davis to Moore, Lovell to Jones, April 24, 1862.
4. *ORN*, XVIII, 350, Whittle testimony.

ironclad out of the main current and brought her back to Jefferson City. "We tugged at her the whole of that night . . . instead of making headway we lost ground," Sinclair reported. Whittle came on board, listened to the problems, and left, stating flatly, "Save her if you can, but do not let her fall into the hands of the enemy." Whittle thought it best to destroy the vessel.

At 4 A.M. on April 25, Colonel James Beggs of the Vigilance Commit-tee came on board and promised to provide additional steamers within twelve hours. Sinclair figured if Beggs could deliver steamers by 4 P.M., he ought to be able to get them sooner himself. He left orders with Lieutenant James I. Waddell, CSN, that if the enemy hove in sight during his absence to set fire to the vessel immediately. He then went on board *Peytona* with Asa Tift and steamed down to the city, where they found numerous tugs and steamboats tied to the levee or rocking at anchor but no crews to man them. Their owners looked equally distressed, claiming the crews had de-serted to "look after their own private concerns."

Sinclair glanced downriver and noticed smoke from the approaching Union vessels. With Asa Tift in tow, Sinclair started back to *Peytona,* and as he rounded the point, he saw flames curling through the ports of *Mis-sissippi.* Asa Tift looked shocked and asked Sinclair, "What is the cause of this?" As Sinclair explained his orders, Asa Tift shook in despair. They stopped briefly at Jefferson City to pick up Asa's brother and found Nel-son Tift shedding tears as he watched the hulk burn. Union vessels "would have followed her up the river," Sinclair said softly, "and before we could have cast the hawsers they would have captured her."

Despite the loss, the Tifts were probably grateful to Sinclair for getting them out of New Orleans. While Sinclair and Asa Tift were downriver, a group of disgruntled citizens appeared at the yard swinging a rope. They had come to hang the Tifts. Waddell stood them off until *Peytona* arrived and deposited both brothers safely on board.

Sinclair explained to the crowd that the vessel had been torched by his order. Together they watched her burn, a huge fiery creature—ugly, im-posing, and useless. The hulk finally broke away from her moorings and drifted slowly downriver. "She was a formidable ship," Sinclair said later, "the finest of the sort I ever saw in my life. She would, in my opinion, not only have cleared the river of the enemy's vessels, but have raised the blockade of every port in the South." Sinclair may have exaggerated, but no one would ever know.

Sinclair started back to the city to offer his services to General Lovell.

On the way he met Lieutenant David P. McCorkle, CSN, who told him the enemy had reached Canal Street and that General Lovell had evacuated the city. Sinclair returned to the Jefferson City shipyard, climbed on board *Peytona*, and with the remaining naval personnel, escaped to Vicksburg.[5]

Before Farragut moved upriver to New Orleans, he paused briefly at Quarantine, resting his men, attending to the wounded, and making repairs. Details swabbed splotches of blood and the mangled remains of the dead from the decks, then settled down to a quick breakfast. A squad of marines went ashore and took possession of a group of buildings displaying white flags. Three vessels were missing, and nobody at Quarantine knew their fate. A short distance downriver the sunken *Varuna* rested stern on against the bank, her colors still flying from the masthead. As the fleet passed, each vessel "dipped [its] colors and gave her three cheers." *Varuna*'s crew had all been saved, sixty of them going to *Pensacola*.

Farragut, anxious to be on his way, ordered the fleet to form in a double column, and at 10 A.M. eleven vessels started upriver, led once again by Captain Bailey in *Cayuga*. *Kineo* and *Wissahickon* remained behind to bury the dead, collect the weapons of the prisoners captured at Quarantine, and support the landing of General Butler's troops.[6]

Farragut's fleet had taken casualties, but aside from the sunken *Varuna*, most of his vessels had not been damaged seriously. *Kineo* absorbed nine shots, but her worst injury occurred when she collided with *Brooklyn*. *Cayuga*, first across the barrier, was hit forty-two times, mostly in the tops. Because of her extended time under the guns, *Hartford* sustained eighteen damaging shots (Farragut reported a total of 32) and had two guns disabled. *Brooklyn* was hit sixteen times and *Mississippi* eleven, but their most serious damage was inflicted by *Manassas*, and both vessels were leaking. *Richmond* absorbed thirteen shots and *Pensacola* nine, none causing serious damage. *Iroquois* was cut up badly, but the other vessels passing the forts were barely damaged at all. Of three vessels failing to get beyond the forts, *Itasca* was put out of action by a shot in her boilers. Farragut's casualties totaled 36 killed and 135 wounded. Another 2 men had been killed and 24 wounded prior to passing. Signal Officer Osbon's prediction of one hundred casualties had been a little conservative, but Farragut must have been pleased that his losses were not greater. When he started the

5. *ORA*, VI, 628, testimony of Nelson Tift; *ORN*, Ser. 2, I, 488–93, 511, Sinclair testimony; *ibid.*, 537–38, Nelson Tift testimony; *ibid.*, 770, Asa Tift testimony.

6. *ORN*, XVIII, 722, 769–70, 789, Roe's Diary, Log of *Hartford*, Log of *Katahdin*, Farragut to Welles, May 6, 1862.

fleet for New Orleans at 11 A.M., he must have felt satisfied with the morning's work.[7]

As the fleet steamed ahead, evidence of panic floated downriver. Hundreds of half-submerged cotton bales drifted down like so much flotsam, interspersed with burning ships carrying more of the South's white gold. "As far behind us as we could see," Alden wrote, "there were clouds of black smoke ascending from the rebel's burning fleet; two or three blew up and the river was covered with fragments. Every house we passed, men, women, and children came running down to the bank of the river, waving handkerchiefs and white flags." At 8 P.M. the fleet came to anchor eight miles below the Confederate batteries at English Turn, which Farragut wanted reconnoitered to determine their strength before he tried to pass them.[8]

At 4 A.M. on April 25 the fleet continued upriver, threading its way past three large fire rafts and through tons of floating implements thrown into the river at New Orleans. People on riverside plantations gathered along the bank, some waving American flags and shouting words of welcome, some sullen and staring. At 11 A.M. *Cayuga*, well ahead of the fleet, came under fire from two mud fortifications at Slaughter House Point, the 5-gun battery at Chalmette on the east bank and the 9-gun Magee Line opposite. Lieutenant Napoleon B. Harrison replied with his 11-inch broadsides. Hearing the sound of gunfire, *Hartford*, *Pensacola*, and *Brooklyn* steamed ahead, each receiving a raking fire from the enemy until they could bring their broadsides to bear. Thirty minutes later the batteries were in shambles and all the Confederate gunners fled to the woods. By then, General Smith's guns had exhausted their twenty rounds of ammunition.[9]

"We now passed up to the city," Farragut said, "and anchored in front of it." Lieutenant Roe was amazed at the devastation. "Everywhere," he wrote, "on both banks, was a long blaze of burning cotton, and sheds, ships, docks, and wharves." In a sudden downpour, the unfinished *Mississippi* drifted by, spewing clouds of dense black smoke as she floated with the current. "Everything seems to have gone to destruction," Alden wrote in his journal. "The wharves were broken in . . . dry docks destroyed and vessels sunk all along the river. We thought that the rebels had set fire to the city before we got to it . . . but there was not one house on fire in the city."

7. See various damage reports in *ORN*, XVIII, 168 and *passim*; also Surgeon Foltz Report, *ibid.*, 176–80.

8. *Ibid.*, 740–41, Alden's Journal.

9. *Ibid.*, 158, 740, 756, Farragut to Welles, May 6, 1862, Log of *Cayuga*, and Alden's Journal.

At 2 P.M. thousands of soldiers and citizens stood on the levees and watched the fleet come to anchor. USS *Mississippi* stood in close to the wharf, her band striking up "The Star-Spangled Banner." The crowd thickened, and "when the people heard the glorious old aire," Alden wrote, "they cheered and waved their hats and handkerchiefs. At the same moment a troop of horsemen came riding up one of the streets and fired a volley into the men, women, and children. If it had not been for the innocent people . . . we would have fired a whole broadside of grape into them." [10]

Rain was still falling hard when Farragut sent Captain Bailey ashore to demand the peaceful surrender of the city. Accompanied by young Lieutenant Perkins, Bailey rowed to the wharf at the foot of Laurel Street in a small boat carrying a flag of truce. "When we reached the wharf," Perkins wrote, "there were no officials to be seen; no one received us, although the whole city was watching our movements, and the levee was crowded in spite of a heavy rain-storm. Among the crowd were many women and children, and the women were shaking rebel flags, and being rude and noisy."

Bailey asked where he might find the mayor, and a "German" stepped forward and offered to lead them to the council room. "As we advanced," Perkins said, "the mob followed us in a very excited state. They gave three cheers for Jeff Davis and Beauregard, and three groans for Lincoln. Then they began to throw things at us, and shout, 'Hang them!' 'Hang them!' We both thought we were in a *bad fix*, but there was nothing for us to do, but just go on."

Young George W. Cable, later of the 4th Mississippi Cavalry, stood in the crowd and hooted "Hurrah for Jeff Davis!" About every third man, he said, had a weapon out. Cable observed Bailey and Perkins "walking abreast, unguarded and alone, looking not to right or to left, never frowning, never flinching, while the mob screamed in their ears, shook cocked pistols in their faces, cursed and crowded, and gnashed upon them. So through the gates of death those two men walked to the City Hall to demand the town's surrender. It was one of the bravest deeds I ever saw done." [11]

At City Hall, Mayor John T. Monroe, backed by members of the council and the Committee of Public Safety, received the Union officers solemnly. Captain Bailey explained that he came on behalf of Flag Officer Farragut to demand the surrender of the city, the hoisting of the United States flag over certain public buildings, and the lowering of the state flag flying above City Hall. The mayor replied that New Orleans was under martial law

10. *Ibid.*, 158, 740–41, 770, Farragut to Welles, May 6, 1862, Roe's Diary, Alden's Journal.
11. *B&L,* II, 21.

and that Captain Bailey must refer his demands to General Lovell. As to the flag of Louisiana, Monroe flatly refused to lower it. Bailey asked the mayor to send for General Lovell, who arrived at City Hall about thirty minutes later and said he would "never surrender," claiming he had fifteen thousand troops under his command. Lieutenant Perkins thought the general "very pompous in his manner and silly and airy in his remarks." After further consideration, Lovell stated he would leave the city with his troops and defer the matter of surrender to the mayor and his council.

During this discussion, Perkins recalled, "the mob outside had by this time become perfectly infuriated. They kicked at the doors and swore they would have us out and hang us!" Members of the council went outside and made speeches, keeping the crowd to one side of the building. Inside, Mayor Monroe agreed to consult with the council and send a formal reply to Farragut in the morning. On the opposite side of City Hall, Lovell arranged for an escort and a closed carriage to convey Bailey and Perkins back to the levee. "Finally," Perkins wrote, "we got on board ship all right; but of all the black-guarding I ever heard in my life that mob gave us the worst."[12]

At 6:30 that evening, Mayor Monroe met with his advisers to tell them that with the withdrawal of Lovell and the troops, the city no longer had any means of defense. We must "yield to physical force alone," he said, but continue to maintain allegiance to the Confederate government. Before taking further action, the council wanted to meet again in the morning. Monroe worried that the delay might try Farragut's patience, and at 6 A.M. the following morning he sent his private secretary, Marion A. Baker, and the chief of police to *Hartford* with an explanation.

Both men were conducted on board and taken to Farragut's cabin, where Baker found the flag officer assembled with Bailey and Bell, as if he had been expected. Farragut agreed to give the council time to finish its deliberations, but to make certain no time was wasted, he sent Lieutenant Albert Kautz and Midshipman John H. Read ashore, accompanied by twenty marines under the command of Second Lieutenant George Heisler. Kautz carried a second demand for the surrender of the city, to be manifested by hoisting the Stars and Stripes over all public buildings.

The moment the emissaries reached the levee they were met by another snarling mob. The marines formed a line while Kautz warned the crowd

---

12. Belknap (ed.), *Letters of Perkins*, 70–71; *B&L*, II, 95.

that if a single shot were fired, Farragut would open fire from every ship and level the town. A few fist-shakers replied by shoving women and children to the front, shouting, "Shoot, you— Yankees, shoot!"

Kautz located an officer of the City Guards and waved him over. After he explained the importance of getting to City Hall, the officer suggested that the marines return to the ship lest their presence provoke trouble. Kautz, Read, and a single marine with a white flag attached to his raised bayonet made their way to City Hall, "cursed and jostled" every step of the way. "The mayor," Kautz wrote, "declined to surrender the city formally, but said as we had the force we could take possession."[13]

While Kautz negotiated with the mayor, another mob arrived from a different section of the city and threw the shredded remnants of a Union flag through an open window at City Hall. At the time, Kautz did not know Farragut had sent Captain Morris with two squads of marines from *Pensacola* to the United States Mint to raise the Stars and Stripes. A citizen, William B. Mumford, took exception to the act and promptly hauled it down. The mob seized the flag, paraded it through the streets with fife and drum until they reached City Hall, where they ripped it apart in front of Lieutenant Kautz. Kautz happened to be present a few days later when Farragut explained the incident to General Butler. Referring to Mumford, Butler said, "I will make an example of that fellow by hanging him." Farragut replied amusedly, "You know, General, you will have to catch him before you can hang him." Poor Mumford—Butler caught him and kept his word.

Once again, the mob outside threatened to break down the doors of City Hall and invited "the—Yankees" to "come out and be run up to lampposts." Provost Marshal Pierre Soulé stepped outside and quieted the crowd long enough for Kautz and the others to slip into a waiting carriage at the rear exit and make their escape. However, the rabble in the streets was not to be fooled again. Some men in the crowd observed the carriage pulling away from City Hall, and they started running up St. Charles Street in an attempt to cut it off. Many were armed, but Kautz and the others beat them back to the levee and reported to Farragut. "Few people ever knew," Kautz said, "what an important service Mr. Soulé thus rendered to New Orleans."

Kautz delivered the mayor's reply to Farragut, which said simply, "Come and take the city; we are powerless." Monroe added courageously, "As to

13. *Ibid.*, 91–92, 95–96.

the hoisting of any flag than the flag of our own adoption and allegiance, let me say to you, sir, that the man lives not in our midst whose hand and heart would not be palsied at the mere thought of such an act."[14]

Farragut had time on his side and wisely waited for the city to exhaust its anger. With *Richmond, Brooklyn, Pensacola,* and *Oneida* following, Farragut weighed anchor and journeyed upriver about twenty miles, destroying batteries at Carrollton and capturing several vessels. The flotilla headed back to New Orleans the following day, its prizes in tow. It was Sunday morning, and thousands of people stood on the levee and watched the vessels pass. Some waved handkerchiefs and cheered for Jefferson Davis, and a few gave three timid cheers for the Union.

CSS *McRae* came up the river from the forts, flying the Confederate flag at her gaff and a white flag at the fore. The ship was filled with wounded, and Lieutenant Read asked permission to take them ashore. Farragut consented on the condition that Read depart the next day and return to the forts, "taking with him neither men nor materials." Read agreed, but on the morning of April 28 *McRae* was found sunk and abandoned at Algiers with all her pipes cut. This action annoyed Farragut, who felt Read should have surrendered the vessel. Read later claimed that his ship was too battered to save. Since Farragut had no time to argue protocol, he let the matter drop.[15]

On April 28 Farragut reopened negotiations with Mayor Monroe, reminding him of the possibility that "fire from this fleet may be drawn upon the city at any moment, and . . . the levee would, in all probability, be cut by the shells." If the mayor and the City Council persisted in resisting the terms of surrender, Farragut advised them to remove the women and children within forty-eight hours. Captain Bell carried the message, and when Monroe asked when the forty-eight-hour ultimatum began, Bell said, "It begins from the time you receive this notice." The mayor glanced at his watch and said, "You see, it is fifteen minutes past 12 o'clock." Bell nodded and a few minutes later left in a carriage with a promise from Monroe to give Farragut a reply the following day.

On the morning of April 29, Soulé, accompanied by Baker, delivered two letters from Mayor Monroe. The mayor again reminded Farragut that the city had no power to resist whatever forcible acts the "United States naval forces may choose to exercise." On the matter of the state flag, Mon-

14. *Ibid.,* 92–93, 97; *ORN,* XVIII, 231–32, 771, Monroe to Farragut, April 26, 1862, and Roe's Diary.
15. *ORN,* XVIII, 697, 742, Bell's Diary, Alden's Diary.

roe told Farragut that if the flag officer had the power to destroy the city, then his forces had the power to remove the flag. Moving to the subject of the threatened bombardment, the mayor reminded Farragut there was no possible exit from the city for its 170,000 inhabitants. "Our women and children can not escape from your shells if it be your pleasure to murder them on a question of mere etiquette. . . . We will stand your bombardment, unarmed and undefended as we are."[16]

Soulé then delivered a long diatribe on the vicissitudes of international law, which Farragut finally interrupted by saying, "I am a plain sailor, and it is not expected that I should understand the nice points of international usage. I am simply here as commander of the fleet, and I aim only to do my duty in this capacity." Through ignorance, Farragut had raised a puzzling international problem by advising foreign consuls of the possible need for them to remove their families from the city. They all signed their names to a protest suggesting that Farragut simply haul down the offending flag instead of destroying a defenseless town by firing upon it.[17]

While Farragut contemplated his next action, Soulé returned to City Hall to find General Lovell still in town. Lovell had visited the mayor the previous evening, promising to return with his force. He believed Farragut was running out of ammunition and proposed a combined night attack supported by ferryboats. Soulé, along with several others, supported the plan, but Mayor Monroe opposed it, convinced that any aggressive action would result in the bombardment of the city. In the midst of the discussion, Captain Bell arrived at City Hall with Lieutenant Kautz and Boatswain's Mate George Russell. The forts had surrendered, Bell reported, and Farragut was sending a force of marines to raise the Stars and Stripes on the Customhouse and the Mint. He reminded the mayor that "the lowering of the flag over City Hall should be the work of those who had raised it." Farragut had yielded on that point, and Bell was there to see it done.

"Very well, sir, you can do it," the mayor replied, "but I wish to say that there is not in my entire constituency so wretched a renegade as would be willing to change places with you."

Bell asked to be shown the way to the roof. "All seemed to be afraid to do it except one excited red-bearded individual, who," Bell wrote, "accompanying me to the third flight of stairs, said in a very excited manner . . . 'There, sir; up through those narrow stairs, it is more than a man's life is worth to go to the top or to haul down the flag.'"

16. *Ibid.*, 233–34, Monroe to Farragut, April 26, 1862.
17. *Ibid.*, 238–40, Correspondence of foreign consuls; *B&L*, II, 98.

From the roof of City Hall, Lieutenant Kautz looked down upon the street. With bayonets fixed and glinting in the sunlight, two hundred and fifty marines held the approaches to the building. A pair of howitzers manned by sailors from *Hartford* pointed up and down the streets. Around the grounds swarmed the mob, pressing closer. At that moment Mayor Monroe came down the steps of City Hall, walked over to a howitzer, folded his arms, stood before the muzzle, and eyed the gunner. On the roof, Lieutenant Kautz fumbled with the knotted halyards, drew his sword, and cut them. Down came the flag. Kautz and Russell folded it and gave it to Bell. Moments later the three officers walked out of City Hall, gathered up the marines and their howitzers, and marched away with the flag. "Then cheer after cheer rang out for Monroe," George Cable wrote, because everyone was "well pleased that, after all, New Orleans never lowered her colors with her own hands."[18]

No Stars and Stripes fluttered from the bare flagstaff atop City Hall. The property, after all, did not belong to the United States government.

At the end of his report to Welles covering the capture of New Orleans, Farragut added, "I sent on shore . . . and hauled down the Louisiana State flag from the city hall, as the mayor had avowed that there was no man in New Orleans who dared to haul it down, and my convictions are, that if such an individual could be found, he would have been assassinated."[19]

On April 29, with New Orleans occupied by only 250 marines and two howitzers, General Butler steamed back down the river to bring up his troops. The capture of the city had been a great opportunity, and he had missed it. Farragut, always generous, attempted to share the credit, but Butler confided his feelings to his wife by writing, "This I deem wholly an unmilitary proceeding on his [Farragut's] part to run off and leave forts behind him unredeemed, but such is the race for the glory of capturing New Orleans between him and Commodore Foote that thus we go."[20]

Butler would find Commander Porter not so generous as Farragut.

18. *Bell*, II, 21, 93, 99; *ORA*, VI, 569, James Testimony; *ORN*, XVIII, 698, Bell's Diary.

19. *ORN*, XVIII, 159, Farragut to Welles, May 6, 1862.

20. *Ibid.*, 159, 697, Farragut to Welles, May 6, 1862, Bell's Diary; Farragut, *Life of Farragut*, 250; Butler, *Private and Official Correspondence*, I, 422 (April 26, 1862). Foote commanded the Union naval squadron upriver.

Two hours after the last of Farragut's fleet passed Forts Jackson and St. Philip on the morning of April 24, an uncommon stillness pervaded the lower Mississippi. The bummers lay on the floor of the bomb boats and slept, the morning sun warm upon their stiff backs. Those on watch dipped water from the river and washed the powder and grime from their faces. Others heated a pot of coffee and nibbled on hardtack, glancing from time to time at the smoke rising above the forts, and waited for orders. Ammunition was running low, but they were almost too tired to care.

At Fort Jackson, General Duncan assessed his situation with bloodshot eyes. *Louisiana* still lay against the bank, a formidable-looking hulk with minor damage, but useless. She had fired but twelve shots during the engagement, Duncan reported caustically. *McRae*, anchored beside the ironclad, was badly damaged topside by shrapnel and grape, but her machinery was still functional. By some miracle, the River Defense boat *Defiance*, whose captain was drunk, survived the battle, but the other vessels were gone, shoved against the bank and burning or floating downriver like so much flotsam. The number of dead and wounded may never be known, but the New Orleans *Daily Crescent* pegged the number at seventy-four killed and seventy-two wounded.

The forts had taken six days of constant bombardment and a hail of shot, shell, and shrapnel, but they still had most of their men and almost all their guns. Fort Jackson was filled with craters and debris, but despite the havoc inside, only four guns had been destroyed, and eleven carriages damaged, along with thirty beds and traverses. In and around the fort, all the buildings had burned. Levees had been cut, and water flooded the casemates. The drawbridge over the moat was smashed, and all the causeways leading from the fort blown up by bombshells. In places, the walls were cracked and broken. Of six guns in the water battery, one was still serviceable. Between the fort and the landing, only one small boat had survived to ferry men back and forth. But in the wreck and ruin of Fort Jackson, after being battered by 7,500 13-inch mortar shells, only fourteen men lay dead in wet, shallow graves, with another thirty-nine wounded.

Across the river, Fort St. Philip had escaped most of Porter's bombardment and was still in good fighting condition, reporting two dead and four wounded, caused mostly by the passing of Farragut's fleet.[1]

Porter waited through the morning silence, watching the Confederate flags still floating above the forts. General Butler left his transports and came up from Head of Passes for a conference. Should he attack head on, or should he wait? Porter asked him to wait and at 9:30 A.M. dispatched *Owasco*, with its commander, Lieutenant John Guest, under a flag of truce to demand the surrender of the forts. Fort Jackson opened with two guns, and Guest sheered across the stream, only to be greeted by a shot from Fort St. Philip. *Owasco* steamed for the opening in the barrier and returned undamaged, and Butler got his answer.

Before the war, Porter had worked with a survey team along the Delta and knew the topography of the area better than Butler. He put the general on board *Miami* and advised him to land troops on the seaward side of Fort St. Philip and to approach it from the rear. *Sachem* joined *Miami* to help move Butler's transports and then take a position in the bay where her guns would discourage the Confederates from trying to escape through the swamps behind Fort St. Philip.

An hour later, a boat from Fort Jackson flying a flag of truce hailed *Owasco*. Guest received the officer in charge, who apologized for the firing upon the flag. He returned to the fort with Porter's terms but replied an hour later that Colonel Higgins considered the Union demand "inadmissible."[2]

Higgins' refusal to surrender caused a resumption of the bombardment, which Porter had hoped to avoid. At noon the bummers opened, spacing their rounds to conserve powder, and stopped at sundown. Porter worried about *Louisiana* and erroneously reported to Welles that "Farragut had unknowingly left a troublesome force in his rear, consisting of four

1. New Orleans *Daily Crescent*, April 29, 1862; *ORN*, XVIII, 372–73, Survey Map, Porter to Welles, April 30, Duncan to Pickett, April 30, 1862.

2. *ORN*, XVIII, 358, 368–69, 379, Guest to Porter, April 28, and Porter to Welles, April 25, 1862.

steamers and a powerful steam battery of 4,000 tons and 16 heavy guns." He feared Mitchell might bring on an engagement and send the lightly armed bomb boats to the bottom. As a precaution, he sent most of the schooners downriver to "refit," leaving six in position to bombard the rear of Fort Jackson if Duncan attempted to evacuate. Porter placed five gunboats below the forts to guard against attack and to harass the enemy. There was no reply from the forts.[3]

On the same morning, Duncan discovered most of the mortar fleet gone and concluded that Farragut would return to enfilade the forts from upriver or else use the river to bring down Butler's troops from Quarantine. The guns of both forts faced downriver. Duncan discussed the situation with Higgins and Mitchell and decided the best location for *Louisiana* was above Fort Jackson, where her guns could bear on enemy vessels rounding the upriver bend. Once again Mitchell refused his help, claiming that no steamers were available to transfer the ironclad to the opposite side of the river. Duncan reminded him that *Defiance* was available, but Mitchell replied that he could not locate her captain. Since Mitchell remained unpersuaded, Duncan's men spent the remainder of the day, and most of the next, adjusting traverses on the few guns that could be pivoted to fire either upstream or down.

The expected attack did not come, but on April 26 observers on the parapets of Fort Jackson could see a steady stream of enemy transports working their way up the bay to the landing at Quarantine. Duncan, shut off from all communication, could only guess at the situation upriver, but Mitchell, acting independently, contacted the enemy under a flag of truce and was told that New Orleans had surrendered. The information was premature, but Mitchell believed it. He hurried the news over to Duncan, advising him that *Mississippi* had been destroyed. If Duncan chose not to believe Mitchell, evidence appeared at 4 P.M. when the smoldering wreck of the hulk drifted by Fort Jackson.

By daylight on April 27 the enemy had moved even closer. Fort St. Philip reported six Union vessels in the back bays, and a dozen or more launches had been observed landing troops at Quarantine. One gunboat had worked her way into the mouth of Fort Bayou and lay in the immediate rear of the fort.[4]

At noon Porter again demanded the surrender of the forts. Colonel Higgins replied that since he had received no offical notification of the sur-

3. *Ibid.*, 369.
4. *Ibid.*, 270–72, 443, Duncan to Pickett, April 30, Mitchell to Duncan, April 24, 1862.

render of New Orleans, "no proposition for a surrender can be . . . entertained here." But both Duncan and Higgins sensed the fight had gone out of the men, especially after Mitchell let it leak that New Orleans had surrendered. Duncan gave the men a "pep talk," praising their courage and patriotism, although many of them were foreign enlistments who sulked after the fighting stopped. "Be vigilant," he said, "and stand by your guns . . . all will be well."[5]

But all was not well. At midnight the garrison at Fort Jackson mutinied in mass, seizing the guard and posterns, reversing the field pieces commanding the gates, and spiking the guns. Some gathered up their weapons, drifted out of the gates, and deserted. Those who remained behind formed in front of their officers and refused to fight any longer, claiming that the city had surrendered and that the enemy was poised to attack by land and by water from all four sides. While these discussions were taking place near the skeletal remains of the citadel, officers who had gone to the parapets to stop the men from spiking guns were met by scattered musket fire. Pressed by force of arms, Duncan let those men leave who no longer wished to defend the fort in order to count the number remaining. One half of the garrison departed immediately, many the very men who had stood most loyally beside their guns during the height of the fighting. After sizing up the few remaining stalwarts, mostly officers and regulars, Duncan concluded that "they were completely demoralized, and that no faith or reliance could be placed in the broken detachments . . . left in the forts."[6]

With the departure of the mutineers, Duncan discovered that every small boat at the fort had vanished with them. He had no knowledge of conditions at Fort St. Philip and no means to communicate with the fort until morning. Butler's troops had already landed on the eastern side of the river, so Fort St. Philip was the point most threatened, but after the mutiny Duncan could not afford to reinforce it from Fort Jackson. Even had men been available, he now lacked the means to transport them across the river. "With the enemy above and below us," Duncan wrote, "there was no chance of destroying the public property, blowing up the forts, and escaping with the remaining troops."

At daylight on April 28, Lieutenant Charles N. Morse obtained a small boat and crossed to Fort St. Philip, returning with Commander Mitchell and Lieutenant Shryock. Mitchell suggested taking *Louisiana* up to Quarantine, five miles away, to attack Butler. Duncan considered this offer in-

5. *ORA*, VI, 543–44, Higgins to Porter, and Duncan to soldiers, April 27, 1862.
6. *ORN*, XVIII, 272, Duncan to Pickett, April 30, 1862.

credible, because Mitchell had just refused to move the ironclad a mere few hundred yards downriver to meet the guns of Farragut's fleet. Mitchell, however, had men working on *Louisiana*'s machinery and hoped to have the propellers operating that day. He returned to Fort St. Philip to evaluate progress on the ironclad, promising to keep Duncan informed. After Mitchell left, Captains M. T. Squires and Richard C. Bond of the Louisiana Artillery and Lieutenant Joseph K. Dixon met with Duncan at Fort Jackson and agreed to surrender. Word of the mutiny at Fort Jackson had spread to the garrison at Fort St. Philip, and morale began to tumble. Duncan believed further resistance was impossible and sent a boat under a flag of truce to Porter accepting the terms of surrender proposed on April 26.

Months later, Mitchell claimed that Duncan failed to inform him of the surrender, although white flags streamed from the fore of *Harriet Lane* as Porter steamed up to Fort Jackson, and from every other masthead within sight, including *Kennebec*, *Westfield*, and *Winona*, which followed behind Porter's flagship. As Duncan and his staff stepped on board *Harriet Lane* to sign the surrender, *Louisiana* was sighted coming downstream toward Porter's gunboats. Black smoke curled upward from open ports, and the ironclad's big guns bristled at the openings. From time to time, as the fire reached the powder, one of the guns discharged and sent a shell whistling aimlessly across the river.[7]

The ink had not dried on Lieutenant Colonel Higgins' acceptance of the surrender when Lieutenant Wainwright rushed into Porter's cabin to report *Louisiana* on fire.

"This is sharp practice," Porter howled, "and some of us will perhaps be blown up. . . . If you can stand what is coming, we can, but I will make it lively for those people if any one in the flotilla is injured."

"We do not consider ourselves responsible for anything the naval officers may do," Duncan replied. "Their course had been a remarkable one throughout the bombardment. They have acknowledged no authority except their own, and although I am commanding officer here, I have no power to coerce them."

As Duncan spoke, "there was stir on the deck, a kind of swaying of the vessel to and fro, a rumbling in the air, and then," Porter wrote, "an explosion which seemed to shake the heavens. The *Harriet Lane* was thrown two streaks over, and everything in the cabin was jostled from side to side."[8]

7. *ORN*, XVIII, 274.
8. Porter, *Incidents and Anecdotes*, 53.

With more than ten thousand pounds of powder in her magazine, *Louisiana* exploded close to shore near the water battery at Fort St. Philip. The casemate blew off the ironclad, sending a shower of iron plates into the water battery, killing one man and wounding another. The explosion occurred about one hundred yards above *Owasco*, but no one aboard the gunboat was injured.

The destruction of the ironclad initiated a controversy upon which nobody agreed. Mitchell claimed the ironclad was destroyed before he heard a surrender was in process, but he had informed General Duncan that "in no event would the enemy be allowed to obtain possession of the *Louisiana*."[9] Both Porter and Duncan reported *Louisiana* destroyed under the flag of truce while the surrender was taking place. Mitchell's credibility as a naval commander, or for simply reporting facts, is best summarized in the report of the sinking by Lieutenant Warley, who had fought and lost *Manassas* and then joined Mitchell as senior officer. According to Warley, Duncan advised Mitchell that he intended to surrender the forts but that the capitulation did not include *Louisiana*. Mitchell immediately called a council of war, attended by Warley, during which time Porter's gunboats were working upriver with white flags fluttering at their fores. "I then proposed that we should at once destroy the vessel before a summons to surrender could be made," Warley wrote. "My suggestion was adopted. Arms were thrown overboard, the magazine partially drowned . . . , the vessel set on fire, and officers and men put upon two steamers, in which they crossed the river. . . . [Lieutenant William C. Whittle, Jr.] was sent to inform Captain Porter that the magazine was only partially drowned, and that the explosion would be heavy. His answer was if we could stand it, he could."

After the explosion, Commander Mitchell, bearing a white flag on a transport, came on board *Harriet Lane* and surrendered the navy to Lieutenant Wainwright. Warley wrote that Wainwright raged over the destruction of *Louisiana* under a flag of truce and said that "if he had not supposed [Mitchell's] transport to contain wounded men he would not have come alongside but stood off and poured broadsides into her until she sank."[10] If any report is to be believed, it is probably Warley's. Duncan had informed Porter that the surrender did not encompass Mitchell's command, and Porter made the mistake of not demanding that the navy be included.

9. *ORN*, XVIII, 298–99, Mitchell to Mallory, August 19, 1862.
10. *Ibid.*, 342, Warley's report, July —, 1865.

Porter, who still sought vindication for failing to destroy the forts in forty-eight hours, demanded that General Duncan and Colonel Higgins sign their surrender "to the mortar flotilla." Porter, Wainwright, and Commander William B. Renshaw signed for the Union. General Butler, whose force never penetrated the swamps in time to participate in the surrender, missed another opportunity to share in the glory because he had gone to New Orleans to secure transports for the troops. Porter's exclusion of Butler, more than Farragut's capture of New Orleans, festered over the years and later escalated into open hostility between career admiral Porter and retired general Butler.[11]

At 4 P.M. on April 28, the officers and men of Fort Jackson marched on board *Kennebec* and started for the city. As they steamed upriver, the Confederate flag still flew above the forts, a token of respect granted by Commander Porter, but as the vessels rounded the bend and drew out of sight, Captain Charles H. Manning's 4th Massachusetts Battery marched into the fort and raised the Stars and Stripes. Major Horace O. Whittemore's 30th Massachusetts took possession of Fort St. Philip. Their tenure lasted one day, whereupon Butler transferred them to New Orleans to occupy the city and replaced them with the 26th Massachusetts. On the evening of May 1, the 30th Massachusetts landed at New Orleans and marched up the streets with the regimental band blaring "Yankee Doodle."[12]

The dust had hardly settled over Fort Jackson when the seeds of the Porter-Butler controversy began to sprout by way of conflicting reports published in the national news. Farragut, who had captured the real prize with his sailors and marines, was momentarily upstaged when Butler took possession of the forts and announced that they were "quite uninjured" and "as defensible as before the bombardment." Porter's ego sustained another shock when First Lieutenant Godfrey Weitzel, Butler's chief engineer, reported on May 5, 1862, that "Fort St. Philip stands, with one or two slight exceptions, to-day without a scratch. Fort Jackson was subjected to a torrent of 13-inch and 11-inch shells during a hundred and forty-four hours. To an inexperienced eye it seems as if this work were badly cut up. It is as strong today as when the first shell was fired at it." Brigadier General John W. Phelps, commanding Butler's First Brigade, made a quick assessment of the damage to Fort St. Philip and generally

---

11. Butler to Stanton, April 29, 1862, in Butler, *Private and Official Correspondence*, I, 428.
12. *ORA*, VI, 508–509, Phelps to Strong, April 30, 1862.

agreed with Weitzel's appraisal, but he found Fort Jackson "very much injured by the bombardment." Butler never referred to Phelps's report, discarding it as written by a man with an "inexperienced eye."[13]

Porter, whose skin was no thicker than Butler's and whose thirst for recognition as great, found himself in a cross-fire coming from both Farragut and Butler. Because Duncan had surrendered the forts "to the mortar fleet" a day before Farragut officially occupied New Orleans, several northern newspapers reported that the city had "been captured by the mortar fleet under the command of Commodore Porter." Captain Craven, whose *Brooklyn* was battered passing the forts, reacted to a quotation in the New York *Herald* by writing his wife, "This is all I suspected it would be, and as I ventured to say more than six weeks ago to Captain Farragut, that it would be. 'Porter's mortar boats and Butler's expedition' have been all the talk ever since last November, and one of my remarks when in consultation one night upon the proper mode of attack was, 'Should we be so fortunate as to succeed, it will appear in all of our journals as Commander Porter's victory; but should we unfortunately fail, it will be published as the defeat of the Gulf Squadron, under Flag-Officer Farragut.'"[14]

Farragut mostly ignored the squabble. The first official report of the Union victory did not arrive in Washington until May 8, when Captain Bailey reached Fort Monroe and wired Welles. Even then, recognition of Farragut's accomplishments came slowly. The newspapers had already showered praises on Porter and Butler and were hesitant to publish the facts. For a few weeks, only the Naval Office and Lincoln's cabinet knew the real story. By then, Farragut was too busy planning his next move, and he let Porter and Butler bicker over the scraps of recognition — and they did.[15]

Butler respected Farragut and praised him appropriately, and because Farragut did or said nothing to embarrass or discredit the general, no vituperations or petty verbal skirmishes marred their relationship. Butler even admitted that Farragut was "far too busy fighting the war" to go around meddling in incidental matters. Unlike Farragut, Porter could not leave "incidental" matters alone, but neither could Butler.[16]

Butler, although he was with Farragut in New Orleans at the time,

13. Weitzel's report in Farragut, *Life of Farragut*, 219; Butler, *Private and Official Correspondence*, I, 428.

14. *ORN*, XVIII, 195–96, Craven to wife, May 16, 1862.

15. *Ibid.*, 149–50, Bailey to Welles, May 8, 1862.

16. *Butler's Book*, 807.

claimed credit for the surrender of the forts on the premise that he was the senior officer present, or at least the senior "military" officer, the one to whom enemy "military forces" should surrender. To support his view, his troops captured roughly 250 of the mutineers who had fled the forts through the swamps and given themselves up to the first Union private they encountered. His failure to obtain the appropriate surrender, Butler claimed, resulted from not having any ships. Furthermore, valuable time had been lost by "that superbly useless bombardment" which wasted, Butler said, eight days. While Porter rocked contentedly at anchor downriver, unaware of Butler's mischief, the general had the ear of every news correspondent covering the occupation of New Orleans. [17]

When Butler's antics began to infiltrate Porter's euphoria, he responded with characteristic effusions of anger. "*Butler* did it all!!!" he complained bitterly to Fox. "So I see it stated by that blackguard reporter of the *Herald* who acted as Farragut's Secretary and Signal officer [Osbon], and who had his nose everywhere. If you could have seen the trouble I had getting old Butler and his soldiers up to the Forts, to take charge of them (after we took possession) you would laugh at the old fool's pretensions. . . . Let Uncle Sam try to rebuild Jackson and he will see what it costs, and let him fire a few casemate guns, he will soon have it tumbling about his ears."[18]

The battle for New Orleans was over, but the battle between Porter and Butler had just begun. Regarding the damage to Fort Jackson, a map on page 372 of the *Official Records of the Union and Confederate Navies*, volume 18, is a more accurate representation of fact than all the words wasted by two ambitious adversaries during the balance of their productive lives.

17. *Ibid.*, 348, 368; West, *Second Admiral*, 139, 142; Parton, *Butler*, 250.
18. Thompson and Wainwright (eds.), *Fox Correspondence*, II, 113.

Epilogue

The Confederacy's loss of New Orleans was fraught with consequences. Napoleon III, with imperialistic intentions toward Mexico, had sought an opportunity to recognize the Confederacy, and he hoped this might be accomplished jointly with Great Britain. In exchange for French favor, the Confederate government had already agreed not to interfere if Napoleon sent troops into Mexico. In England, the scandalous *Trent* affair had recently shifted from the boiling point of intervention to a grudging simmer. If Farragut had failed—followed a month later by General Thomas "Stonewall" Jackson's devastating Valley Campaign and another month later by Major General George B. McClellan's embarassing defeats in Virginia—intervention may have looked much more attractive to the European powers, especially with a good portion of the United States navy lying at the bottom of the Mississippi River. If, during the spring of 1862, any battle of the war kept Europe neutral, it was Farragut's victory on the lower Mississippi.

This supposition is supported by James M. Callahan, perhaps the earliest and one of the more capable authorities on Confederate diplomacy, who claimed that Napoleon was held back by England and the people of France. Through his ministers, Napoleon had discussed intervention on several occasions with John Slidell, Confederate commissioner to France, who argued for recognition and with it the dismantling of the blockade. Earlier in the war Napoleon had contemplated intervention without Great Britain, but the capture of New Orleans changed his mind. After that, he would not consider the matter without Great Britain taking the initiative. Slidell continued to hope, but Napoleon remained noncommittal.[1]

---

1. James Morton Callahan, *The Diplomatic History of the Southern Confederacy* (Baltimore, 1901), 101.

The celebrated *Louisiana* and *Mississippi*, two powerful rams upon which the South depended to defend New Orleans and sweep the Union fleet from the Mississippi, were products of wishful thinking and experimental technology. Despite their fearful appearance and heavy guns, the ironclads were sloths in the water, poorly designed and underpowered. Considering the South's limited resources, they probably should not have been built, at least not together at the same time and in the same place. Unfortunately, the brief moments of glory for CSS *Virginia* (*Merrimack*) and the ram *Arkansas* still lived in the minds of the Confederate Naval Office, and for four years Mallory spent almost every inflated dollar he could raise to replicate those solitary moments. Historian James Russell Soley said, "Had the *Louisiana*, with her armament and armor, been properly manned, equipped, and propelled so as to equal or exceed in speed Farragut's ships, nothing but a miracle would have saved him from a serious loss." Another historian, Charles B. Boynton, added nearly the same words about *Mississippi*.

Unfortunately for the Confederate defenders of New Orleans, neither vessel, as designed, would have equaled the speed of Farragut's slowest vessel. Had their engines been installed in time, there is some doubt whether the bulky behemoths could have stemmed the swift current. The Tift brothers, although well-intentioned and patriotic entrepreneurs, knew nothing of boat building, and the results confirmed it. In the final weeks of her life, *Louisiana* received full attention as the builders rushed it to completion, but all the time in the world may not have made any difference.[2]

More than the loss of the ironclads, even had they met the expectations of the Naval Office, was the loss of the lower Mississippi to the Confederacy. The port of New Orleans was closed as a center of southern trade, finance, manufacturing, and shipbuilding, and supplies and beef flowing from Texas into the eastern Confederate states had to find alternative and more exposed routes. Any possibility for trade with Europe and the West Indies ended when Farragut's fleet passed the forts and anchored off the levee at New Orleans. Important river towns like Natchez, Vicksburg, and Memphis were suddenly vulnerable to attack from north and south. The Union could now invade Mississippi, Arkansas, and northern Louisiana by marshaling its troops at New Orleans and transporting them upriver, thereby forcing the Confederacy to thin its scant resources to protect its flanks. Even Mobile, a hundred miles by water to the east, could now be

2. James R. Soley, *Admiral Porter*, 96; Charles B. Boynton, *The History of the Navy During the Rebellion* (2 vols.; New York, 1867), II, 213.

reached by land or by sea. The loss of New Orleans forced a change in Confederate military strategy at a time when what in June was to become the Army of Northern Virginia repulsed the Army of the Potomac and forced every blue-coated volunteer into a fortified camp at Harrison's Landing.

The capture of New Orleans boosted Union morale at a time when good news was crucial to the North. The loss of the city had the opposite effect upon the Confederacy, and for the first time southerners began to question the competence of their government. Many people considered the loss of New Orleans outrageous and inexcusable.

Two investigations took place, one concerning the navy with Secretary Mallory at its center, and the other a court of inquiry "upon the fall of New Orleans" at the request of Major General Lovell. The investigation of the Navy Department took place in Richmond and began on September 2, 1862, when testimony was given before five members of the House and five members of the Senate. The scope of the investigation extended beyond the causes leading to the loss of *Louisiana* and *Mississippi*, entailing Mallory's overall shipbuilding program, including other ironclads such as *Arkansas* and *Tennessee*, and the numerous commerce destroyers and corvettes being built in Europe. The European vessels, although outside the scope of this text, provide important insight into Mallory's multiple methods of attempting to build a navy.

Mallory was a man anxious to get results. He was also like a semiskilled engineer trying to operate a complicated apparatus equipped with ten puzzling drive gears but no manual of operation. He kept shifting gears, hoping to find the right one. In Europe, he involved too many people in contractual matters without establishing a method for coordinating their activities, so that naval officers and agents often found themselves at cross-purposes with no one in charge. In New Orleans, Mallory tried to build two ironclads, leaving matters in the hands of inexperienced contractors. When his contractors hollered for parts, Mallory put on his hat, walked over to the Tredegar Works on the James River and old Kanawha Canal, and expedited them himself. Then he removed Flag Officer George Hollins, who knew the river, from the Mississippi squadron at a critical moment and replaced him with Commander Mitchell, who soon demonstrated his inability to work with either General Duncan or the River Defense Fleet. A few weeks before Farragut's attack, Mallory sent William C. Whittle to New Orleans to command the naval station there. Whittle limited the scope of his own activities regarding the ironclads because Mallory, whatever his intentions, failed to order him to take charge of the vessels until the last moment.

While the forts below New Orleans braced for the Union attack, Mallory spread his meager financial resources all over the South and Europe on a grandiose building plan that could never be implemented. He failed to concentrate his limited funds on the resources available to him. This failure, manifested by the loss of New Orleans, had no effect on changing his administrative habits. In the end, Mallory survived the investigation and received a vote of confidence.

The committee investigating the Naval Department contained a majority of Mallory supporters. Regardless of pages of damaging testimony, skillful pro-Mallory examiners like Thomas J. Semmes, with intermittent help from committee chairman Clement C. Clay, neutralized anti-Mallory witnesses by careful cross-examination and tactical interruptions aimed at striking out offensive statements. Charles M. Conrad, who had been a member of Mallory's original Naval Affairs Board, said, referring to Mallory, that "from a very early period I was impressed with the conviction that there was a want of intelligence, and especially of energy, promptitude, and forethought in the administration of the Department." But when Conrad was pressed hard for details, he had difficulty providing specifics.[3]

When Hollins testified, the commodore stated that if Mallory had not prevented him from bringing his mosquito fleet downriver, Farragut may have been stopped at the forts. "I felt confident," Hollins said, "that I could whip the enemy." Both General Lovell and Beverly Kennon agreed that if Hollins had taken charge of all the vessels afloat, the outcome would have been different. They referred to the transfer of Commander Whittle to the department a few days before the attack as a crucial mistake. Lovell criticized the "divided command" in New Orleans and the latitude given the steamboat captains to do as they pleased. The more questions Semmes asked, the more culpable Mallory became. Since this was not the type of testimony Semmes wanted, he concluded the questioning of Hollins and moved to another matter.[4]

While the investigation of the navy progressed in Richmond, a court of inquiry was held for Commander Mitchell in the Naval Office. After hearing the testimony, Flag Officer Samuel Barron wrote, "from all the evidence adduced . . . Commander Mitchell did all in his power to sustain the honor of the flag and to prevent the enemy from ascending the Mis-

3. *ORN,* XVIII, 723–24, Conrad testimony.
4. *Ibid.,* 474–76, 480, 525–26, 624, 659–60.

sissippi River; and that his conduct and bearing throughout the period of his service . . . was all that could be expected by the country and the naval service of a capable and gallant officer." Barron's conclusions were correct to a degree. Mitchell could not be blamed for having no ships with which to fight, since Mallory had sent all available vessels upriver. Nor could he build more because the two unfinished ironclads had soaked up most of the money, material, skilled workmen, and ship-building capacity in New Orleans.

The proceedings and findings of the court were approved by Secretary Mallory on March 17, 1862, while his own investigation was still in process. Mitchell's exoneration certainly worked wonders for his own case.[5]

The investigation of the navy, which started on September 4, 1862, finally concluded on March 24, 1863, and the committee asked to print the testimony. The official ruling was delayed until December, 1863, the next scheduled meeting of Congress. By then, Vicksburg had fallen and the entire Mississippi fell under Union control. The official verdict on Mallory's administration read as follows:[6]

> Taking into consideration the poverty of our means and the formidable power and boundless resources of our enemy at the beginning of this war, our people have no sufficient cause for shame or discouragement in the operations of our Navy. What has been and is being done to resist the enemy on the waters of our rivers and on the sea, should inspire confidence, and excite strong hope that our Navy will yet prove an efficient and worthy ally of our noble armies in achieving our independence. It has already won the admiration and applause of neutral nations, for its gallant and glorious achievements; and, if we should succeed in getting into service the war vessels completed and in progress of construction, the Committee believes that our naval triumphs will yet rival the brilliant and heroic achievements of our land forces.[7]

For the very same reasons that *Louisiana* and *Mississippi* never made an iota's difference in preventing Farragut from passing the forts, the com-

5. *Ibid.*, 319–20, Barron to Brent, December 5, 1863, Mallory to Barron, March 17, 1862.

6. For the complete testimony of the investigation, the most available source is *ORN*, Ser. 2, I, 431–809.

7. *Proceedings of the Confederate Congress*, 1st Congress, 4th Session, Feb. 17, 1864.

mittee's belief that Confederate naval triumphs might rival the "brilliant and heroic achievements" of the army never materialized. Thus the investigation of the navy ended. But what about the military? Were they to be vindicated also?

On May 2, 1862, General Lovell asked for a court of inquiry. If he had failed to do so, the people of New Orleans, who felt betrayed, would have screamed for one even through General Butler's cordon of Union occupation. From the beginning, some of the city's citizens had been skeptical of Lovell because of his northern antecedents. Now they shouted treason and not only wanted Lovell tried for surrendering the city without firing a shot, but wanted him removed from command in Louisiana. For his own private reasons, President Davis ignored Lovell's request for months, although military protocol demanded that a general officer's request for an inquiry into his professional capabilities be given prompt action.[8]

Lovell learned later from former senator William McKendree Gwin the reasons for the delay. Davis had confided to several of his Richmond colleagues that New Orleans had fallen because Lovell had failed to keep the government in Richmond informed. Had Lovell warned the War Department, Davis claimed he would have taken prompt action to provide the required reinforcements. Lovell showed Gwin copies of his correspondence to Richmond, and the former senator left convinced that a court of inquiry would exonerate Lovell but condemn Davis, who had been practicing a little face-saving at Lovell's expense. Lovell understood the president's embarrassing position and wrote to Davis magnanimously suggesting that the War Department had failed to keep the president informed and offering to withdraw his request for a court of inquiry rather than make public "the weakness . . . of the Government." Once again Davis, who would never admit to a "weakness of the Government," failed to reply.[9]

In December the War Department relieved Lovell from command and did not reassign him. Lovell went to Richmond and wrote Davis a reminder asking that his case not be "permitted to escape" the president's attention. An unprecedented nine months had elapsed since Lovell had requested the court of inquiry. When Davis failed to respond, Lovell used his influence in Congress and asked for a review of the official correspondence between himself and the War Department. Within a few days

8. Jones, *Rebel War Clerk's Diary*, I, 135.

9. *ORA*, VI, 570, Lovell to Cooper, May 2, 1862; Gustavus W. Smith, *Confederate War Papers* (New York, 1884), 96.

the House of Representatives took the matter out of Davis' hands and ordered the court held.[10]

Finally, on April 4, 1863, a court composed of Generals Thomas C. Hindman, Thomas F. Drayton, and William M. Gardner, along with Major L. R. Page, judge-advocate, met in Jackson, Mississippi, to hear testimony. They might have selected a different location for their meetings had they known General Grant's forces would be passing through the town about five weeks later on their way to Vicksburg. Subsequent meetings took place in Charleston, South Carolina, and finally Richmond.[11]

Three months later, on July 9, General Hindman released the opinion of the court, vindicating Lovell and placing much of the responsibility back on the War Department for stripping New Orleans of troops. Hindman cited the failure of the navy to have the ironclads serviceable and to "cooperate efficiently with General Lovell." In two small matters Hindman found Lovell slightly at fault in failing to advise the War Department of the insecurity of the chain and cable barrier, and in failing to give proper orders for the evacuation of troops at Chalmette. Otherwise, they wrote, "General Lovell displayed great energy and an untiring industry in performing his duties. His conduct was marked by all the coolness and self-possession due to the circumstances and his position, and he evinced a high capacity for command and the clearest foresight in many of his measures for the defense of New Orleans."[12]

Lovell waited for reassignment, but orders did not come. As for the court of inquiry, President Davis and the War Department ignored it. Months passed, and still Lovell's appeals to the War Department went unanswered. In 1864 General Joseph E. Johnston, whose relationship with President Davis was not much better than Lovell's, asked repeatedly that Lovell be assigned to his command but never received a reply. Finally, Lovell joined Johnston during the Atlanta campaign as a volunteer staff officer.[13]

On July 17, after Major General William T. Sherman's army had crossed the Chattahoochie and was closing in on Atlanta, Davis shelved Johnston and replaced him with General John B. Hood. Hood lost at Nashville and

10. Smith, *Confederate War Papers*, 98–99; *ORA*, VI, 655, Harrison to Seddon, February 4, and Seddon to Davis, February 27, 1863.

11. For the most available source of Lovell's Court of Inquiry, *ORA*, VI, 556–655.

12. *Ibid.*, 641–42.

13. Smith, *Confederate War Papers*, 114–15.

resigned. On February 22, 1865, General Robert E. Lee, now command-ing all Confederate armies, called Johnston back to duty. Once again Johnston asked for Lovell, and this time he got him, but not because Davis made the decision. Lee disagreed with Davis' opinion of Lovell. Three years earlier he had praised Lovell's defense of New Orleans and fully agreed with Lovell's evacuation and the manner in which he conducted it. Even Union General William S. Rosecrans, who fought Lovell's corps at Corinth, Mississippi, on October 3–4, 1862, and again at Coffeeville on December 5, gave him high praise for his military skills.[14]

Either way, General Lovell's career was over. He had lost New Or-leans. For that President Davis could not forgive him, and neither could the people of the South. They called him a "third-rate general," and per-haps, like so many others both North and South, he was, but no one would ever really know. Lovell never had another chance to demonstrate his mil-itary skill.

Davis attempted to explain his reasons for sacking Lovell when he wrote *The Rise and Fall of the Confederate Government,* but his bias was manifested by statements that conflicted with official records as well as testimony given during Lovell's court of inquiry. In the aftermath of the war, while Davis worked on his reflections, he missed an opportunity to offer Lovell a forgiving if not well-deserved apology. He could have looked back upon the country that had once elected him to a position of power nearly equal to that of a dictator, a country where so many cities had been turned into rubble, the great, rich farmland laid to waste, and a once wealthy agrar-ian economy destroyed in nearly every town and village across the Con-federacy. All was gone. All but New Orleans.

General Lovell could not have fought for New Orleans without de-stroying it, and he knew it. New Orleans and the surrounding towns were spared, along with countless lives and millions of dollars worth of prop-erty, thanks to General Lovell, a northerner who fought for the South, and David Glasgow Farragut, a southerner who fought for the North.

While Lovell's military career ended with the capture of New Orleans, Farragut's naval career, which had begun fifty-two years earlier, sky-rocketed. By the end of the Civil War, no naval officer had seen more ma-jor battles than Farragut—although his foster brother, Davey Porter, came the closest.

14. *ORA,* VI, 652–53, Lee to Lovell, May 24, 1864; Mark M. Boatner, III, *The Civil War Dictionary* (New York, 1959), 494.

Farragut's original orders from Welles designated two objectives: first, New Orleans, and then Mobile.[15] General Butler had barely set up administrative shop in the Crescent City when Farragut began planning his attack on Forts Morgan and Gaines, the guardians of Mobile Bay. But Welles postponed this campaign and sent Farragut upriver to cooperate with Flag Officer Charles H. Davis. Farragut hated the river, but he was now a rear admiral, and he still followed orders. The river was no place for his sloops of war, but there he stayed until Vicksburg and Port Hudson surrendered in July, 1863.

In August, Farragut returned home to begin preparations for the assault on Mobile Bay. A year later he fought his way through another gauntlet of fire, and took possession of the bay. On December 23, 1864, Welles rewarded him with promotion to vice admiral, a new grade created the previous day. By then, the war had begun to wear down. The only significant naval action remaining was the reduction of Fort Fisher, which brought two old adversaries together again—General Butler and Davey Porter.

The general had spent the balance of 1862 incurring the enmity of Orleanians by his questionable administrative practices, which earned him the sobriquet of "Spoons" Butler for allegedly stealing silverware from local citizens. His "confiscation" practices raised concern in Washington, and War Secretary Stanton recalled him in the late autumn of 1862. The winter of 1863–64 found Butler in command of the Army of the James. When his command became bottled up at the Bermuda Hundred and then later failed in a joint mission with the Army of the Potomac near Petersburg, Grant looked for a safe place to deposit Butler until the war was over. Unfortunately, Grant needed somebody to take charge of the landing force at Fort Fisher and with some reluctance gave the command to Butler.

Unlike Butler, Porter distinguished himself. After the capture of New Orleans he was promoted to acting rear admiral over dozens of senior officers. For two years he commanded the Mississippi Squadron with distinction, earning the official thanks of Congress on three separate occasions. But between himself and Butler, the bickering never stopped over who deserved the credit for capturing Forts Jackson and St. Philip.

Near the end of the war, and perhaps with a little irony in mind, Secretary Welles and General Grant gave Butler and Porter an opportunity to

15. *ORN*, XVIII, 7–8, Welles to Farragut, Jan. 20, 1862.

work together as comrades in arms for the good of the Union in the joint attack on Fort Fisher. Once again Butler demonstrated his lack of generalship and Porter his capability as a naval officer. Butler's first and only try at Fort Fisher resulted in a military debacle of the first order. By this time Lincoln had been reelected and Grant no longer had misgivings about cashiering the powerful political general. Three weeks later Porter teamed up with Major General Alfred H. Terry and captured Fort Fisher.

On July 25, 1866, Congress promoted Farragut to full admiral, the first in the history of the United States navy. In 1870, his foster brother, Porter, who had spent so many lantern-lit hours on the lower Mississippi writing his carping reports to Assistant Secretary Fox, became the second admiral of the navy.

Ben Butler returned to his former profession, law and politics. He was elected to Congress in 1866, this time as a Republican, and pulled together a strong coalition to impeach President Andrew Johnson. He failed in his attempt to have the Senate convict and remove Johnson, and later he failed again as a candidate for president. But Ben Butler was not a failure. He died an extremely wealthy man, but how he became so rich is still a mystery. Some people believe Butler's rise to wealth started down in New Orleans, but that is another story.

After the war ended, Mallory, now a prisoner in Fort Lafayette, New York, wrote an appeal to President Andrew Johnson asking for a pardon and restoration of his citizenship. The letter substantiates claims made by Mallory's opponents to his nomination as naval secretary on the grounds that he opposed secession. "I was never a member," Mallory wrote, "of a convention or a legislature of any state that advised or counselled Secession." He reminded Johnson that he had served in the Senate from 1851 to 1861, and over a span of ten years "no word or sentiment of disloyalty to the Union ever escaped me." After Florida seceded on January 21, 1861, he withdrew from the Senate at the command of the governor, an "act which," Mallory claimed, "in view of its causes and attendent [*sic*] circumstances, was the most painful of my career." Mallory dreaded the perils of secession and believed the differences in political philosophies between North and South could be resolved by means other than war. "I could never regard it [secession] as but another name for revolution, and to be justified only as a last resort from intolerable oppression." Mallory concluded his appeal to President Johnson by claiming that his position in Davis' cabinet had been forced upon him. He had not desired the post but felt coerced to accept it. "In February, 1862," Mallory wrote, "I requested and requested the acceptance of my resignation, which President Davis declined."[16]

Mallory's disclaimer may have been written from the head rather than from the heart, because there were few men in the Confederate cabinet who had supported the Confederate cause with more energy. But by February, 1862, when Davis refused Mallory's attempts to resign, the naval secretary had lost confidence in himself and in his ability to support the war effort. Unfortunately, this wavering occurred at a critical moment for New Orleans. Mallory, perhaps facing the probability that he would be blamed for the failure of the Confederate navy in the Mississippi River, wanted critics to look for another scapegoat.

In the end, Mallory got his wish. Paroled on March 10, 1866, he eventually returned to his home in Pensacola, but he never forgot what once he called the most stunning blow of his lifetime. When word reached Richmond that New Orleans had fallen, he wrote in his diary, "The destruction of the Navy at New Orleans was a sad, sad blow, and has affected me bitterly, bitterly bitterly."[17] Two weeks later, in a letter to his wife, Mallory confided, "I do not know how you discovered that the naval losses on the Mississippi affected me; but the fact is . . . that they almost killed me, and I am ashamed to say that I have lain awake at night with my heart depressed and sore, and my eyes filled with tears, in thinking over them. Our men fought splendidly, and merited by their gallantry the victory they had not the force to achieve. This has made me very weak, and neutralized the effect of all the medicine I have taken: but I am getting over it."[18]

But he, like thousands of others, never did.

16. Stephen B. Mallory Letter Book, Manuscript Division, Library of Congress, Mallory to President Andrew Johnson, June 21, 1865, also September 27, 1865, for follow-up letter.

17. Mallory Journal, Part 1, p. 19.

18. Mallory to Mrs. Mallory, May 11, 1862, quoted in Durkin, *Mallory*, 208.

Appendix

Union Vessels and Commanders in the Passage of the Forts:[1]

First Division: Capt. Theodorus Bailey
USS *Cayuga:* Lt. Napoleon B. Harrison
USS *Pensacola:* Capt. Henry W. Morris
USS *Mississippi:* Cmdr. Melancton Smith
USS *Oneida:* Cmdr. Samuel Phillips Lee
USS *Varuna:* Cmdr. Charles S. Boggs
USS *Katahdin:* Lt. George H. Preble
USS *Kineo:* Lt. George M. Ransom
USS *Wissahickon:* Lt. Albert N. Smith

Center Division: Flag Officer David G. Farragut
USS *Hartford:* Cmdr. Richard Wainwright
USS *Brooklyn:* Capt. Thomas T. Craven
USS *Richmond:* Cmdr. James Alden

Third Division: Cmdr. Henry H. Bell
USS *Sciota:* Lt. Edward Donaldson
USS *Iroquois:* Cmdr. John DeCamp
USS *Kennebec:* Lt. John H. Russell
USS *Pinola:* Lt. Peirce Crosby
USS *Itasca:* Lt. Charles H. B. Caldwell
USS *Winona:* Lt. Edward T. Nichols

1. *ORN*, XVIII, 166.

CONFEDERATE VESSELS AND COMMANDERS IN THE PASSAGE OF THE FORTS:[2]

Confederate Navy: Commander John K. Mitchell
  CSS *Manassas:* Lt. Alexander F. Warley
  CSS *McRae:* Lt. Thomas B. Huger
  CSS *Louisiana:* Cmdr. Charles F. McIntosh
  CSS *Jackson:* Lt. Francis B. Renshaw
  Louisiana Gunboat *General Quitman:* Lt. Alexander Grant
  Louisiana Gunboat *Governor Moore:* Capt. Beverly Kennon

River Defense Fleet: Capt. John A. Stevenson
  Gunboat *Warrior:* Capt. John A. Stevenson
  Gunboat *Stonewall Jackson:* Capt. George M. Phillips
  Gunboat *Resolute:* Capt. Isaac Hooper
  Gunboat *R. J. Breckinridge:* Capt. James B. Smith
  Gunboat *Defiance:* Capt. Joseph D. McCoy
  Gunboat *General Lovell:* Capt. Burdett Paris

The other vessels were either steam launches or unarmed tugs and utility vessels.

ARMAMENT: UNION VESSELS[3]

USS *Brooklyn:* twenty-two 9-inch Dahlgrens; one rifled 80-pounder; one rifled 30-pounder; two 12-pounder howitzers. *Total:* 26 guns.
USS *Cayuga:* one 11-inch Dahlgren; two 24-pounder howitzers; one rifled 30-pounder Parrott. *Total:* 4 guns.
USS *Hartford:* twenty-four 9-inch Dahlgren; two rifled 20-pounder Parrotts; two 12-pounder howitzers. *Total:* 28 guns.
USS *Iroquois:* two 11-inch Dahlgrens; two 9-inch Dahlgrens; one 50-pounder; four 32-pounders; one rifled 6-inch Sawyer; one 12-pounder howitzer. *Total:* 11 guns.
USS *Itasca:* one 10-inch Dahlgren; two 32-pounders; one rifled 20-pounder. *Total:* 4 guns.
USS *Katahdin:* one 11-inch Dahlgren; one rifled 20-pounder Parrott;

    2. *Ibid.*, 249.
    3. *ORN*, Ser. 2, I, 48–242 *passim*, *B&L*, II, 74–75. The *Official Records* do not show the guns temporarily transferred from USS *Colorado*.

two 24-pounder howitzers. *Total:* 4 guns.

USS *Kennebec*: one 11-inch Dahlgren; one 20-pounder Parrott; two 24-pounder howitzers. *Total:* 4 guns.

USS *Kineo*: one 11-inch Dahlgren; one rifled 20-pounder Parrott; two 24-pounder howitzers. *Total:* 4 guns.

USS *Mississippi*: one 10-inch Dahlgren, nineteen 8-inch Dahlgrens; one 20-pounder; one 12-pounder. *Total:* 22 guns.

USS *Oneida*: two 11-inch Dahlgrens; four 32-pounders; three 30-pounders; one 12-pounder howitzer. *Total:* 10 guns.

USS *Pensacola*: one 11-inch Dahlgren; twenty 9-inch Dahlgrens; one rifled 100-pounder; one rifled 80-pounder; two 12-pounder howitzers. *Total:* 25 guns.

USS *Pinola*: one 11-inch Dahlgren; two rifled 20-pounder Parrotts; two 24-pounder howitzers. *Total:* 5 guns.

USS *Richmond*: twenty 9-inch Dahlgrens; one rifled 80-pounder Dahlgren; one rifled 30-pounder Parrott. *Total:* 22 guns.

USS *Sciota*: one 11-inch Dahlgren; one rifled 20-pounder Parrott; three 24-pounder howitzers. *Total:* 5 guns.

USS *Varuna*: eight 8-inch Dahlgrens; two rifled 30-pounders. *Total:* 10 guns.

USS *Winona*: one 11-inch Dahlgren; one rifled 20-pounder Parrott; two 24-pounder howitzers. *Total:* 4 guns.

USS *Wissahickon*: one 11-inch Dahlgren; one 20-pounder Parrott, two 24-pounder howitzers. *Total:* 4 guns.

ARMAMENT: CONFEDERATE VESSELS[4]

CSS *General Quitman*: two 32-pounders.

CSS *Governor Moore*: two rifled 32-pounders.

CSS *Jackson*: two 32-pounders.

CSS *Louisiana*: two 7-inch rifled; three 9-inch shell guns; four 8-inch shell guns; seven rifled 32-pounders. *Total:* 16 guns.

CSS *Manassas*: one 32-pounder carronade.

CSS *McRae*: one 9-inch pivot shell gun; six 32-pounders; one 9-pounder. Total: 8 guns.

4. *ORN*, XVIII, 249–50; *ORN*, Ser. 2, I, 254–72 *passim*.

Gunboat *Defiance*: one 32-pounder.
Gunboat *General Lovell*: one 32-pounder.
Gunboat *R. J. Breckinridge*: one 24-pounder.
Gunboat *Resolute*: two 32-pounders.
Gunboat *Stonewall Jackson*: one 24-pounder.
Gunboat *Warrior*: one 32-pounder.

PORTER'S MORTAR FLOTILLA: COMMANDERS AND ARMAMENT[5]

Steamers:

USS *Clifton,* Acting Lt. Charles H. Baldwin: two 9-inch Dahlgrens; four 32-pounders; one 30-pounder. *Total:* 7 guns.

USS *Harriet Lane,* Lt. Cmdr. Jonathan M. Wainwright: three 9-inch Dahlgrens; two 24-pounder howitzers. *Total:* 5 guns.

USS *John P. Jackson,* Acting Lt. Selim E. Woodworth: one 9-inch Dahlgren; four 32-pounders; one rifled 6-inch Sawyer. *Total:* 6 guns.

USS *Miami,* Lt. Cmdr. Abram D. Harrell: two 9-inch Dahlgrens; one rifled 80-pounder; four 24-pounder howitzers. *Total:* 7 guns.

USS *Owasco,* Lt. Cmdr. John Guest: one 11-inch Dahlgren; one rifled 20-pounder; two 24-pounder howitzers. *Total:* 4 guns.

USS *Portsmouth,* Cmdr. Samuel Swartwout: sixteen 8-inch Dahlgrens; one rifled 20-pounder; one 12-pounder howitzer. *Total:* 18 guns.

USS *R. B. Forbes,* Acting Vol. Lt. William Frye: two 32-pounders, one rifled 30-pounder Parrott. *Total:* 3 guns.

USS *Westfield,* Cmdr. William B. Renshaw: one 9-inch Dahlgren; four 8-inch Dahlgrens; one rifled 100-pounder. *Total:* 6 guns.

Mortar Schooners:

USS *Adolph Hugel,* Acting Master Hollis B. Jencks
USS *Arletta,* Acting Master Thomas E. Smith
USS *C. P. Williams,* Acting Master Amos R. Langthorne
USS *Dan Smith,* Acting Master George W. Brown
USS *Geo. Mangham,* Acting Master John Collins, Jr.
USS *Henry Janes,* Acting Master Lewis W. Pennington
USS *John Griffith,* Acting Master Henry Brown

5. *ORN,* XVIII, 25; *B&L,* II, 74.

USS *Maria J. Carlton,* Acting Master Charles E. Jack
USS *Matthew Vassar,* Acting Master Hugh H. Savage
USS *Norfolk Packet,* Lt. Watson Smith
USS *Oliver H. Lee,* Acting Master Washington Godfrey
USS *Orvetta,* Acting Master Francis E. Blanchard
USS *Para,* Acting Master George N. Hood
USS *Racer,* Acting Master Alvin Phinney
USS *Sarah Bruen,* Acting Master Abraham Christian
USS *Sidney C. Jones,* Acting Master Robert Adams
USS *Sophronia,* Acting Master John A. Darling
USS *T. A. Ward,* Lt. Walter W. Queen
USS *William Bacon,* Acting Master William P. Rogers

Barks:
USS *A. Houghton,* Acting Master Newell Graham
USS *Horace Beals,* Lt. K. Randolph Breese

Brig:
USS *Sea Foam,* Acting Master Henry E. Williams

All the mortar schooners carried one 13-inch mortar and two 32-pounders, with the following exceptions: *Horace Beals* did not carry a mortar but was armed with two 32-pounders and one 30-pounder Parrott; *Maria J. Carlton* and *Dan Smith* each carried a mortar but two rifled 12-pounders in lieu of two 32-pounders. In addition to one mortar and two 32-pounders, *Norfolk Packet* and *John Griffith* each carried two 12-pounder howitzers. The bark *A. Houghton,* which remained below the forts, carried two 32-pounders.[6]

BATTERIES OF THE FORTS[7]

Fort Jackson:
Barbette:	2 10-inch columbiads
	3 8-inch columbiads
	1 7-inch rifled gun

6. *Ibid.,* 26.
7. *Ibid.,* 75; *ORN,* XVIII, 390, Harris to Gerdes, May 4, 1862. Harris counted 75 guns at Fort Jackson.

	2 8-inch mortars
	6 42-pounders
	15 32-pounders
	11 24-pounders
	1 8-inch howitzer
	1 7 3/8-inch howitzer
Casemates:	10 24-pounder howitzers (flank)
	14 24-pounders
Parade:	1 6-pounder
	1 12-pounder howitzer
Water Battery:	1 10-inch columbiad
	2 8-inch columbiads
	1 10-inch sea-coast mortar
	2 rifled 32-pounders
	Total: 74 guns

Fort St. Philip:

On Face:	4 8-inch columbiads
On Salient:	1 24-pounder
Covered Way:	1 8-inch mortar
	1 10-inch siege mortar
	1 13-inch seacoast mortar
Upper Battery:	16 24-pounders
Lower Battery:	9 32-pounders
	6 42-pounders
	1 7-inch rifled gun
	1 8-inch columbiad
	4 24-pounders
NE Battery:	4 10-inch seacoast mortars
Parade:	1 6-pounder
	1 12-pounder
	1 24-pounder field howitzer
Total:	52 guns
Total guns in the forts:	126 guns

CASUALTIES:[8]

	Killed	Wounded	Total
Fort Jackson	9	33	42
Fort St. Philip	2	4	6
Total Forts:	11	37	48

Union Fleet (April 24, 1862)

	Killed	Wounded	Total
Hartford	3	10	13
Brooklyn	9	26	35
Richmond	2	4	6
Pensacola	4	33	37
Mississippi	2	6	8
Oneida		3	3
Varuna	3	9	12
Iroquois	6	22	28
Cayuga		6	6
Itasca		4	4
Kineo	1	8	9
Pinola	3	7	10
Sciota		2	2
Winona	3	5	8
Portsmouth		1	1
Harriet Lane	1	1	2
Total Fleet	37	147	184

8. *ORN*, XVIII, 283, 284, Morse to Lewis, April 26, 1862, and Burke to Higgins; *ibid.*, 177–80, 180–81, Foltz to Farragut, May 1, 18, 1862; *B&L*, II, 73.

BIBLIOGRAPHY

PRIMARY SOURCES

Manuscripts

Henry E. Huntington Library and Art Gallery, San Marino, California
 Fox, Gustavus Vasa. Papers.
 Porter, David Dixon. Papers.
 Welles, Gideon. Papers.
Howard-Tilton Library, Tulane University, New Orleans, Louisiana
 Roy, John. Memorandum Book.
Library of Congress, Washington, D.C., Manuscript Division
 Fox, Mrs. Gustavus Vasa. Diary. Blair Papers.
 Lincoln, Abraham. Papers.
 Mallory, Stephen R. Letter Book.
 Porter, David Dixon. Papers. 1842–1864.
 ———. "Private Journal of Occurrences During the Great War of the
  Rebellion, 1860–1865." 2 vols.
 Wells, Gideon. Papers.
Louisiana State University, Baton Rouge, Louisiana, Louisiana and Lower
Mississippi Valley Collection
 Moore, Thomas O. Papers.
 Roy, John. Diary.
 Solomon, Clara E. Diary.
New York Public Library, Manuscript Division
 Diggins, Bartholomew. "Recollections of the Cruise of the U.S.S. Hartford,
  Admiral Farragut's Flagship in Operations on the Mississippi River."
 Wharton, Thomas Kelah. Diary.
University of North Carolina, Chapel Hill, Southern Historical Collection.
 Mallory, Stephen R. Journal.
University of Texas, Austin, Archives.
 Bragg, Braxton and Mrs. Papers.

Newspapers
Baton Rouge *Daily Advocate*
New Orleans *Bee*
New Orleans *Commercial Bulletin*
New Orleans *Daily Crescent*
New Orleans *Daily Delta*
New Orleans *Daily Picayune*
New Orleans *True Delta*
New York *Herald*
New York *Times*
Richmond *Dispatch*

Published Documents
Documents of the Second Session of the Fifth Legislature of the State of Louisiana, 1861. Baton Rouge, 1861.
Executive Documents Printed by Order of the 36th Congress, 1859–1860, Series 49. Washington, D.C., 1860.
Journal of the Congress of the Confederate States, 1861–1865. Reprinted in Washington, D.C., 1904, as *Senate Document No. 234, 58th Congress, 2nd Session.*
Official Guide of the Confederate Government from 1861 to 1865 at Richmond. Richmond, n.d.
Official Journal of the Proceedings of the Convention of the State of Louisiana, 1861. New Orleans, 1861.
Official Records of the Union and Confederate Navies in the War of the Rebellion. 30 vols. Washington, D.C., 1894–1927.
Proceedings of the Confederate Congress, 1st Congress, 4th Session, February 17, 1864. Richmond, 1864.
Proceedings of the Court of Inquiry Relative to the Fall of New Orleans, Published by Order of the Confederate Congress. Washington, D.C., 1862.
Reports of the Naval Engagements on the Mississippi River Resulting in the Capture of Forts Jackson and St.Philip and the City of New Orleans, and the Destruction of the Rebel Naval Flotilla. Washington, D.C., 1862.
U.S. House of Representatives, *Report on the Internal Commerce of the United States, by William P. Switzler, Chief of the Bureau of Statistics, Treasury Department. House Executive Document No. 6, Part II, 50th Congress, 1st Session.* Washington, D.C., 1888.
The War of the Rebellion: A Compilation of the Official Records of the Union and Confederate Armies. 130 vols. Washington, D.C., 1880–1901.

Published Primary Sources
Bacon, George B. "One Night's Work, April 20, 1862: Breaking the Chain for Farragut's Fleet at the Forts Below New Orleans." *Magazine of American History,* XV (1886), 305–307.
Bartlett, Napier. *A Soldier's Story of the War: Including the Marches and Battles of the Washington Artillery and Other Louisiana Troops.* New Orleans, 1874.
Belknap, George E., ed. *Letters of Capt. Geo. Hamilton Perkins, U.S.N.* Concord, N.H., 1886.

Biographical and Historical Memoirs of Louisiana. 2 vols. Chicago, 1892.

Blair, Montgomery. "Opening the Mississippi." *United States Service Magazine: A Monthly Review of Military and Naval Affairs,* IV (January, 1881), 36–42.

Booth, Andrew B., comp. *Records of Louisiana Confederate Soldiers and Louisiana Confederate Commands.* 3 vols. New Orleans, 1920.

Boynton, Charles B. *The History of the Navy During the Rebellion.* 2 vols. New York, 1867.

Brown, George W. "The Mortar Flotilla." *Personal Recollections of the War of the Rebellion.* New York, 1891.

Bulloch, James Dunwoody. *The Secret Service of the Confederate States in Europe, or, How the Cruisers Were Equipped.* 2 vols. New York, 1884.

Butler, Benjamin F. *Autobiography and Personal Reminiscences of Major-General Benj. F. Butler: Butler's Book.* Boston, 1892.

———. *Private and Official Correspondence of General Benjamin F. Butler During the Period of the Civil War.* 5 vols. Norwood, Mass. 1917.

Corsan, W. C. *Two Months in the Confederate States, Including a Visit to New Orleans Under the Domination of General Butler.* London, 1863.

Craven, John J. *Prison Life of Jefferson Davis.* New York, 1866.

Dawson, Sarah Morgan. *A Confederate Girl's Diary.* Boston, 1913.

Davis, Jefferson. *The Rise and Fall of the Confederate Government.* 2 vols. New York, 1881.

DeLeon, T. C. *Four Years in Rebel Capitals.* Mobile, 1892.

Dewey, George. *Autobiography of George Dewey, Admiral of the Navy.* New York, 1913.

Dorsey, Sarah A. *Recollections of Henry Watkins Allen, Brigadier-General Confederate States Army, Ex-Governor of Louisiana.* New Orleans, 1866.

Driggs, George W. *Opening the Mississippi.* Madison, 1864.

Farragut, Loyall. *The Life of David Glasgow Farragut: First Admiral of the U.S. Navy.* New York, 1879.

Foltz, Jonathan M. *Surgeon of the Seas: The Adventurous Life of Surgeon General Jonathan M. Foltz in the Days of Wooden Ships.* Indianapolis, 1931.

Greeley, Horace. *The American Conflict.* 2 vols. Hartford, 1866.

Hill, Frederic S. *Twenty Years at Sea, or Leaves From My Old Log Books.* Boston and New York, 1893.

Howe, M. A. DeWolfe, ed. *Home Letters of General Sherman.* New York, 1909.

Johnson, Robert Underwood, and Clarence Clough Buel, eds. *Battles and Leaders of the Civil War.* 4 vols. New York, 1887–1888.

Jones, J. B. *A Rebel War Clerk's Diary.* 2 vols. Philadelphia, 1866.

Mahan, Alfred Thayer. *The Gulf and Inland Waters.* New York, 1883.

———. *Admiral Farragut.* New York, 1892.

McHatton-Ripley, Eliza. *From Flag to Flag.* New York, 1889.

Merrick, Caroline E. *Old Times in Dixie Land: A Southern Matron's Memories.* New York, 1901.

Morgan, James Morris. *Recollections of a Rebel Reefer.* Boston, 1917.

O'Conner, Thomas. *History of the Fire Department of New Orleans from the Earliest Days to the Present Time.* New Orleans, 1895.

Owen, William Miller. *In Camp and Battle with the Washington Artillery of New Orleans.* Boston, 1885.

Paine, Albert Bigelow, ed. *A Sailor of Fortune: Personal Memories of Captain B. S. Osbon.*

New York, 1906.

Parton, James. *General Butler in New Orleans*. New York, 1864.

Porter, David Dixon. *The Naval History of the Civil War*. New York, 1886.

——. *Incidents and Anecdotes of the Civil War*. New York, 1885.

Preble, George H. *History of the Flag of the United States*. Boston, 1882.

"Reminiscent of War Times, Eventful Days in New Orleans in the Year 1862." *Southern Historical Society Papers*, XXIII (May, 1895), 182–86.

Rowland, Kate M., and Mrs. Morris L. Croxall, eds. *The Journal of Julia LeGrand, New Orleans 1862–1863*. Richmond, 1911.

Russell, William Howard. *My Diary North and South*. Boston, 1863.

Scharf, J. Thomas. *History of the Confederate Navy from Its Organization to the Surrender of Its Last Vessel*. New York, 1887.

Semmes, Raphael. *Memoirs of Service Afloat During the War Between the States*. Baltimore, 1869.

Smith, Gustavus W. *Confederate War Papers*. New York, 1884.

——. "Mansfield Lovell." *Fifteenth Annual Reunion of the Association of the Graduates of the U.S. Military Academy, 1884*. East Saginaw, Mich., 1884.

Soley, James R. *The Blockade and the Cruisers*. New York, 1883.

——. *Admiral Porter*. New York, 1903.

Thompson, Robert M., and Richard Wainwright, eds. *Confidential Correspondence of Gustavus Vasa Fox, Assistant Secretary of the Navy, 1861–1865*. 2 vols. New York, 1920.

Vandiver, Frank E., ed. *The Civil War Diary of General Josiah Gorgas*. Tuscaloosa, 1947.

Walker, Jennie Mort. *Life of Captain Joseph Fry: The Cuban Martyr*. Hartford, 1875.

Watson, William. *Life in the Confederate Army: Being the Observations and Experiences of an Alien in the South During the American Civil War*. New York, 1888.

Welles, Gideon. *The Diary of Gideon Welles, Secretary of the Navy Under Lincoln and Johnson*. 3 vols. Boston and New York, 1909–1911.

——. "Admiral Farragut and New Orleans," *The Galaxy: An Illustrated Magazine of Entertaining Reading*, XII (November, 1871), 817–32.

Younger, Edward, ed. *Inside the Confederate Government: The Diary of Robert Garlick Hill Kean*. New York, 1957.

Secondary Sources

Bernath, Stuart L. *Squall Across the Atlantic: American Civil War Prize Cases and Diplomacy*. Berkeley and Los Angeles, 1970.

Black, Robert C., III. *The Railroads of the Confederacy*. Chapel Hill, 1952.

Bland, T. A. *Life of Benjamin F. Butler*. Boston, 1879.

Boatner, Mark M., III. *The Civil War Dictionary*. New York, 1959.

Bonham, Milledge L., Jr. "Louisiana's Seizure of the Federal Arsenal at Baton Rouge, January, 1861." *The Historical Society of East and West Baton Rouge Proceedings*, II (1917–1918), 47–55.

Bragg, Jefferson Davis. *Louisiana in the Confederacy*. Baton Rouge, 1941.

Bruce, Robery V. *Lincoln and the Tools of War*. New York, 1956.

Callahan, James Morton. *The Diplomatic History of the Southern Confederacy.* Baltimore, 1901.

Carter, Hodding. *The Lower Mississippi.* New York, 1947.

Caskey, Willie M. *Secession and Restoration of Louisiana.* Baton Rouge, 1938.

Dufour, Charles L. *The Night the War Was Lost.* New York, 1960.

Durkin, Joseph T. *Stephen R. Mallory: Confederate Navy Chief.* Chapel Hill, 1954.

Eliot, Ellsworth, Jr. *West Point in the Confederacy.* New York, 1941.

Faust, Patricia L., ed. *Historical Times Illustrated: Encyclopedia of the Civil War.* New York, 1986.

Geer, James K. *Louisiana Politics, 1845–1861.* Baton Rouge, 1930.

Gosnell, H. Allen. *Guns on the Western Waters: The Story of River Gunboats in the Civil War.* Baton Rouge, 1949.

Hesseltine, William B. *Lincoln and the War Governors.* New York, 1948.

Hill, Jim Dan. *Sea Dogs of the Sixties.* Minneapolis, 1935.

Holtzman, Robert S. *Stormy Ben Butler.* New York, 1954.

Jones, Virgil Carrington. *The Civil War at Sea.* 3 vols. New York, 1960–62.

Kendall, John S. *History of New Orleans.* 3 vols. Chicago, 1922.

Kendall, Lane Carter. "The Interregnum in Louisiana in 1861." *Louisiana Historical Quarterly,* XVI (1933), 175–208, 374–408, 639–69; XVII (1934), 124–38, 339–48, 524–36.

Lewis, Charles Lee. *David Glasgow Farragut: Our First Admiral.* Annapolis, 1943.

Lewis, Paul. *Yankee Admiral.* New York, 1968.

Lonn, Ella. *Foreigners in the Confederacy.* Chapel Hill, 1940.

McLure, Lilla, and J. Howe, eds. *History of Shreveport and Shreveport Builders.* 2 vols. Shreveport, Louisiana, 1937, 1951.

Merrill, James M. *The Rebel Shore: The Story of Union Sea Power in the Civil War.* Boston, 1957.

Nevins, Allan. *The War for the Union.* 2 vols. New York, 1960.

Niven, John. *Gideon Welles: Lincoln's Secretary of the Navy.* New York, 1973.

Odom, Van D. "The Political Career of Thomas Overton Moore, Secession Governor of Louisiana." *Louisiana Historical Quarterly,* XXVI (October, 1943), 975–1054.

Owsley, Frank Lawrence. *King Cotton Diplomacy.* Chicago, 1931.

Perry, Milton F. *Infernal Machines: The Story of Confederate Submarine Warfare.* Baton Rouge, 1965.

Pomeroy, M. M. *Life and Public Services of Benjamin F. Butler.* New York, 1868.

Pratt, Fletcher. *Civil War on the Western Waters.* New York, 1956.

Rightor, Henry, ed. *Standard History of New Orleans, Louisiana.* Chicago, 1890.

Roberts, W. Adolphe. *Lake Pontchartrain.* Indianapolis, 1946.

Robinson, William Morrison, Jr. *The Confederate Privateers.* New Haven, 1928.

Roman, Alfred. *The Military Operations of General Beauregard in the War Between the States 1861 to 1865: Including a Brief Personal Sketch and a Narrative of His Services in the War with Mexico 1846-8.* 2 vols. New York, 1884.

Rooney, William H. "The First 'Incident' of Secession: Seizure of the New Orleans Marine Hospital." *Louisiana Historical Quarterly,* XXXIV, No. 2 (April, 1951), 135–42.

Shugg, Roger Wallace. *Origins of Class Struggle in Louisiana.* Baton Rouge, 1939.

————. "A Suppressed Cooperationist Protest Against Secession." *Louisiana Historical Quarterly*, XIX, No. 1 (January, 1936), 197–209

Sinclair, Harold. *The Port of New Orleans*. Garden City, 1942.

Spencer, Warren F. *The Confederate Navy in Europe*. University, Alabama, 1983.

Strode, Hudson. *Jefferson Davis, Confederate President*. New York, 1959.

Warner, Ezra J. *Generals in Gray: Lives of the Confederate Commanders*. Baton Rouge, 1959.

West, Richard S., Jr. *Mr. Lincoln's Navy*. New York and London, 1957.

————. *The Second Admiral: A Life of David Dixon Porter, 1813–1891*. New York, 1937.

Williams, T. Harry. *P. G. T. Beauregard: Napoleon in Gray*. Baton Rouge, 1954.

Winters, John D. *The Civil War in Louisiana*. Baton Rouge, 1963.

INDEX